HO
GRAIL

THE TRUE STORY
OF
BRITISH WRESTLING'S REVIVAL

GREG LAMBERT

authorHOUSE®

Dedicated to my good Wacker, Nina Neely (1908-1988).

Special thanks to Mark Kay, Alex Shane, Dann Read and Dino Scarlo, without whom none of this would have been possible.

Thanks also to Bill Apter, for such a glowing foreword.

But don't think this means our feud is over, old man. It will *never* be over.

AuthorHouse™
1663 Liberty Drive
Bloomington, IN 47403
www.authorhouse.com
Phone: 1-800-839-8640

Published by AuthorHouse   11/16/2012

ISBN: 978-1-4772-4315-2 (sc)
ISBN: 978-1-4772-4316-9 (e)

Contents

FOREWORD

by Bill Apter

British Wrestling has a phenomenally rich history.

The televised wrestling show on ITV's World of Sport, a mainstay of the airwaves since the 1950s, fed the appetite of the fanatical devotee as well as the casual viewer. Fans would fill arenas to capacity to witness classic battles between legends such as Jackie Pallo, Giant Haystacks and Big Daddy, just to name a few.

But in 1988 a severe blow was dealt to the UK wrestling public. British Wrestling was taken off the country's television screens and the live arena shows took a hard hit.

With this came the invasion of the American 'Hulkamania' era and UK fans joined that bandwagon. When the World Wrestling Federation (WWF) came to town, that's where the crowds' ticket buying gravitated. The UK stars had taken a back seat to all the new cartoonish ways of the WWF. Tradition as the UK fans were used to was getting a beating.

Greg Lambert was a huge wrestling fan. He knew the tradition but also welcomed the fever that the WWF was bringing the world over. His deep passion drove him to seek out a role in the business and in the early part of 2002, he was able to work his way in as a commentator for New Era Wrestling. That led to a meeting with the editor of the UK wrestling magazine Power Slam and he became part of the brand with his hard-hitting editorials and interview style. Readers felt through Greg Lambert they were getting the best of both worlds—the old school tradition and the new, dazzling style of wrestling coming from the US.

In the mid-2000s, I was booked to appear as a special guest at several wrestling shows in the UK under the banner of the Frontier Wrestling Alliance (FWA), then run by wrestler-promoter-entrepreneur Alex Shane. Alex's FWA was a combination of the traditional wrestling styles mixed in with the US showbiz element. It proved to be very successful as fans flocked to the FWA's special shows in numbers not seen in many years in the UK.

When I entered an FWA dressing room for the first time I was warmly greeted by everyone. I jokingly slapped the high-flying Jonny Storm around and when he fell, put him in my patented 'six-second-figure-four-leglock'. As he screamed for mercy and I released the grip, standing there was Greg Lambert. He extended a warm handshake and we became instant friends. Through my trips there we talked and wrestling history was always on the talking table.

On March 19 2005 when I was an editor of Total Wrestling magazine, I was booked to appear at the FWA's International Showdown in Coventry to present an award to the legendary Mick Foley (yes, a legend even back then!) In front of 3,500 screaming fans I was stopped short in my verbal tracks when Lambert, who was managing Alex Shane this night, came to the ring to let me know the award should go to Shane. I told him that if he didn't get out of the ring I would "Power Slam his ass through the mat!" This brought out a very hostile Shane who was going to do something equal to my threat to Lambert—but to me. Luckily Foley came to the ring and saved me!

The back-and-forth between Greg and I runs through my brain every few days. I had such a good time with him doing that vignette.

I could go on and on but here is what all this is leading to. The United Kingdom wrestling scene has a small handful of people who are trying to keep it alive and bring it back to the numbers it enjoyed back in the World of Sport days. Greg Lambert is one of those few who devoted his life to that mission.

We all appreciate all you have done for the business Greg—and all you will continue to do as well. I hope you all enjoy his book, because few are better qualified to tell the true story of British Wrestling's revival.

Bill Apter

To Matthew
Hope you enjoy it!

Greg Leary

"Aim for the moon. That way, if you miss you'll still be amongst the stars."

W. Clement Stone

CHAPTER I

REVIVAL

It all started one Saturday night when I turned on the radio.

Quite by accident, whilst twiddling with the dial on my battered old wireless, I stumbled across a programme all about professional wrestling. And life was never the same again.

"talkSPORT, listen to the Wrestletalk, talkSPORT, listen to the Wrestletalk . . ."
The basic but catchy jingle said it all. This was Wrestletalk; Britain's first ever nationwide weekly wrestling radio chat show. I couldn't believe my luck. A radio show, where people talked about nothing but wrestling for two hours? As a massive fan of the World Wrestling Federation (WWF), it was my idea of broadcasting heaven. And it sure beat a night in front of the TV with the missus watching Casualty.

So I began to listen avidly to the talkSPORT channel on Saturday nights, while hunched in the tiny spare room of my house in the North Lancashire seaside town of Morecambe. I soon became hooked on the show mainly thanks to the performances of the two hosts; former children's TV presenter turned radio DJ, Tommy Boyd, and a little-known British wrestler called 'The Showstealer' Alex Shane.

What on earth was Tommy Boyd doing involved in pro wrestling? I was intrigued. This famous figure from my childhood, the presenter of popular ITV programmes like Magpie and The Wide Awake Club, now professed to be a long-time wrestling fan.

As for Alex Shane, I had heard his name before . . . but only from the briefest of mentions given to the minor leagues of British Wrestling in magazines such as Power Slam. These publications were dominated by coverage of the much higher profile WWF and other American promotions. They hardly ever mentioned British Wrestling, and hadn't since the days of Big Daddy and Giant Haystacks. So I didn't know much about what happened to the UK grappling scene afterwards.

I soon became really impressed with how the fast-talking Shane was more than a match for his experienced sidekick Boyd. The odd couple had terrific chemistry as a broadcast duo and I was thoroughly entertained by their banter. Shane clearly knew his stuff and his immense passion for wrestling, and particularly *British* Wrestling, was evident. This was clearly not your stereotypical meathead wrestler. Alex was articulate and witty . . . and he possessed that X Factor quality that drew me in and made me want to find out more about him.

Alex Shane was only 22 years old at the time, but had already led an eye-opening life.

The real-life Alexander Spilling still lived on the Andover estate in Finsbury Park, North London; one of the most crime-ridden areas of the capital. Andover was such a dangerous place to live, it was picked as the location for a 2007 fly-on-the-wall documentary called Ann Widdecombe vs The Hoodies. This followed the eccentric ex-Tory MP as she stayed with a family on the estate while trying to uncover its culture of drugs and violence. Soon after the TV cameras left, the family's house was fire bombed. Andover was that kind of place.

As a teenager growing up, Alex had seen two of his closest friends imprisoned; one for drug dealing and the other for burglary. Then one day Alex was on his computer in his house when he heard a loud bang. His next-door neighbour had been gunned down in cold blood just yards from where he was sitting, another victim of London gangland violence. This was certainly a scary environment for an impressionable young kid who was searching for a place to belong.

But Alex didn't follow his mates into the downward spiral of drugs and crime. Instead, he found escapism through his love of magic. At the age of eight, young Spilling was already showing signs of an entrepreneurial mind. A bright and eager boy, he worked as a magician's assistant and would follow his mentor around the children's birthday party circuit. His job was to feed the white rabbits who took part in the magic tricks. Alex sought no payment other than vital titbits of information about the illusions and how they worked.

At around the same time, Spilling had discovered what would become the true love of his life—professional wrestling. After catching his first glimpse of the WWF on ITV in the mid-80s, Alex was bowled over by its over-the-top noise, colour and glamour. He immersed himself in his new pastime with a fanatical zeal, buying all the WWF action figures, using them to simulate his own wrestling matches in his bedroom. He bought all the WWF videos and wrestling magazines too, eagerly poring through each and every one of them to absorb all the knowledge he could.

The teenage Spilling eventually decided he wanted to emulate his TV heroes and become a professional wrestler himself. So Alex began washing cars to raise enough cash to go to the nearest training school. It was hard work scrubbing bonnets, wheels and windows with a chamois leather until his hands were red raw. But for Alex, earning the £20 for a train fare and £10 to cover his training fee was well worth it.

In 1993, the 13-year-old Alex began to make the Saturday and Sunday train journey to Andre Baker's Hammerlock Wrestling training school at the seaside resort of Folkestone, Kent. By his own admission, Spilling was the least physically talented member of the school. The ever-growing adolescent was gangly and clumsy, all arms and legs, and struggled to keep up with his classmates.

But when it came to the art of professional wrestling, Spilling had one major advantage over his fellow students. Alex could talk. Oh boy, could Alex talk . . .

Almost a decade later, the awkward youth who first showed up at the Hammerlock gym was unrecognisable. Alex Spilling was now the super-confident and charismatic 'Showstealer' Alex Shane—not only one of the country's top wrestlers, but a national radio star.

As the weeks went by, I listened as the Boyd/Shane double act evolved into an entertaining on-air rivalry. The odd couple had an on-air argument pretty much on every single episode. These usually kicked off when 'bad guy' Boyd uttered deliberately controversial and ill-informed remarks about wrestling and 'good guy' Shane was forced to set him straight.

Some of their heated rows were radio gold. The best came one night when Boyd scoffed that professional wrestlers don't bleed in the ring for real, but instead use fake stage blood. This simply isn't true. What usually happens is that a wrestler will nick himself during a match with a tiny sawn-off razor blade, hidden in his tights or shorts. With help from an opponent's well-placed blows, these tiny cuts can quickly spread blood all over a wrestler's face and make it look like the 'fight' is more violent than it really is.

After Shane told Tommy this little-known wrestling secret, the aloof outsider refused to believe him. Captivated by the disagreement, the listeners phoned and emailed in their droves, most taking Alex's side. But still Tommy wouldn't have it, instead saying there must be a 'fake blood make-up artist' hidden under the ring! It was great radio.

Shane's honesty about the art of 'blading' was typical of his outlook on the radio show. The Londoner was extremely open about how pro wrestling works—often 'breaking Kayfabe' as this openness is called in the business. In other words, he told the radio audience that wrestling was a form of theatrical and physical entertainment where combatants *did* fight each other for real to some extent, but with a level of co-operation because the winner of the match had been determined beforehand. Like the magic tricks Alex loved so much as a child, professional wrestling is really a clever illusion. And the fact that Wrestletalk was on talkSPORT was a misnomer, because pro wrestling isn't really a competitive sport at all.

Shane said anyone who claimed wrestling was 100% real was insulting the fans' intelligence. His honesty made me sit up and take notice, especially as it was a controversial stand to take. Many of British Wrestling's 'old school' (veterans) would surely not approve. This older generation still wanted to hide wrestling's secrets, clinging to a past era of mystique like magicians refusing to reveal how their tricks are done.

Shane also used the radio show to talk up the virtues of his own company the Frontier Wrestling Alliance (FWA), claiming it was the best of a new breed of British promotions. He said the FWA put on a cutting edge, fast-paced brand of entertainment featuring athletic, hungry and talented youngsters. This youth movement, he said, was the polar opposite of the overweight, middle-aged plodders like Daddy and Haystacks who dominated our TV screens during the '70s and '80s, when British Wrestling was watched by millions of viewers every Saturday afternoon.

Alex claimed that thanks to the FWA, British Wrestling had entered the 21st century. He even went so far as to state on-air that "the era of fat old men in trunks is well and truly over".

As the weeks went by, Boyd and Shane began to talk about a live wrestling show they planned to promote. They called this event Revival—so-named because everybody involved hoped it would bring about the revival of the dormant British Wrestling scene. Revival would take place on Saturday, February 9 2002 at the Crystal Palace National Sports Centre outside London, a venue usually better known for swimming and basketball than the lords and ladies of the wrestling ring.

Tommy Boyd had gone one step further from just being a fan and talking about British Wrestling on the radio. He had actually decided to invest money in it. As the promoter of Revival, Tommy claimed that British Wrestling could enjoy a renaissance with himself at the helm, and enjoy its best days since then-ITV chief Greg Dyke pulled the plug on 33 years of televised British ring wars in 1988.

For weeks prior to the date of Revival, Boyd and Shane took every opportunity to talk up this extravaganza as the biggest British Wrestling event since the days when Daddy, Haystacks and World of Sport pulled in those massive viewing audiences. They said Revival was British Wrestling's comeback after 14 years in the non-televised wilderness of tiny crowds, small halls and holiday camps, after 14 years of being overshadowed by the multi-billion dollar WWF and American Wrestling on Sky TV.

When Alex and Tommy boasted about the exciting new dawn for British Wrestling and also promised that former WWF superstars 'Grandmaster Sexay' Brian Christopher and 'Latino Heat' Eddie Guerrero would be at Revival to add some star power to proceedings, it really

3

grabbed my attention. This just about summed up the state of our country's wrestling scene at the time. Most of the grapplers at Revival would be British. But for me, the Americans were the attraction.

Well, the Americans *and* the promotional skills of Tommy Boyd.

"Remember, if you are at the Crystal Palace Indoor Arena on February 9, in future years you can tell your grandkids that you were there the night that British Wrestling experienced its Revival."

No sooner had those words left Tommy's mouth, I was sold hook, line and sinker. I simply *had* to find a way to go to this magical-sounding event.

My only previous experiences of attending non-WWF wrestling shows were during the 1980s and 1990s when the major British promoters like Max Crabtree or Brian Dixon rolled into my home town for a summer season of family-friendly pantomime in front of a few hundred punters. In fact, travelling the length of the country to watch pro wrestling of any kind was an alien concept for me.

But Boyd and Shane had done such a tremendous job of promoting Revival as something extra-special, groundbreaking, *history-making* even, that I was enticed to convince my wife Sharon that I should venture off for the weekend all on my lonesome. It was almost like a calling. I just felt like I simply *had* to be there. So I spent over £100 on a ticket to the show, a 10-hour return train journey and an overnight stay in a Crystal Palace B&B.

There was one other prime motivation for me going to Revival. The year before, approaching 30 and feeling like I needed a major life change, I'd quit my stressful job as a call centre manager for British Telecom and gone back to university to follow my lifelong dream of becoming a journalist. I was in the midst of a one-year newspaper journalism diploma course at the University of Central Lancashire in Preston. With my childhood best friend Mark Kay, I'd then set up a wrestling news website called WrestlingX.com, just for a bit of fun and writing practice during my spare time.

I hoped that by attending Revival as a budding reporter, I might be able to provide some eye-catching coverage of a watershed event in British Wrestling history. I also set myself a goal of obtaining interviews with my new heroes Tommy Boyd and Alex Shane. This would give our fledgling website some credibility and get us noticed by followers of the cult British scene.

I didn't have any ambitions beyond that at all.

I say 'cult', because the crowd of nearly 2,000 people who bought tickets to see Revival was just a drop in the ocean compared to the glory days of British Wrestling, when Daddy and Haystacks drew 10,000 to Wembley Arena for a televised grudge match in 1981, or the regular crowds of over 10,000 who went to WWF wrestling events both in North America and on their regular tours of Great Britain.

But after 14 years without regular mainstream TV coverage, 2,000 was a sizeable audience for a British Wrestling show, especially as the date of Revival clashed with the infamous Gareth Gates-Will Young Pop Idol final on the telly. This success at the box office proved that Boyd and Shane had done a terrific job of promoting the event. But would Revival itself live up to the hype?

By around 6.15pm, 45 minutes before Revival was due to start, I'd already achieved one of my targets. After arriving at the venue for a pre-show fan gathering, I'd chanced my arm and marched up to a hassled-looking Tommy Boyd, cornering him for a rapid-fire 60-second interview. The main man behind Revival only had time for brief answers, informing me he was excited rather than nervous ahead of the evening's events, and that the reason why he'd got involved in wrestling was because "I do something strange every four or five years".

Boyd also had some words for his Wrestletalk co-host.

"Alex Shane is a pain in the arse. But he's got enormous potential and I hope he fulfils it."

Delighted that my chat with Boyd was safely recorded on my trusty Dictaphone, I then hung around with the steadily increasing and super-lively gaggle of fans gathering in the reception area of the Crystal Palace Sports Centre's Indoor Arena, while trying to ignore the pungent smell of chlorine from the nearby swimming pool.

That's when I first clapped eyes on the man who would change my life.

His towering height was the first thing I noticed. Six foot seven inches tall, broad shouldered, closely cropped dark hair, goatee beard, wearing a skin-tight black T-Shirt over his bulging biceps—Alex Shane definitely looked like a wrestler, like a somebody, like a *star*, the kind of giant figure who would turn heads in an airport lounge, as they say. And when this giant talked, he talked fast in his North London accent, in streams of consciousness and rarely pausing for breath. Shane was also surrounded by a rugby scrum of wide-eyed fans, who hung on his every word. Now here was a guy who commanded attention.

Now bear in mind this was less than an hour before the biggest moment in Alex Shane's wrestling life. Thanks to Tommy Boyd's media connections, TV cameras from satellite channel Bravo were there to tape Revival for a future broadcast. A radio commentary of the event was going out live on talkSPORT to thousands of listeners.

This night was make or break for British Wrestling and Alex Shane, who had a high-profile role both as a wrestling performer and as an organiser behind-the scenes, had to be feeling under immense pressure. Yet when I thrust my tape recorder in his face, he gave a big smile, was charm personified and more than happy to give me five minutes of his time.

In the very first conversation we would ever have, Alex told me how much he hoped Revival being on Bravo was the first step towards a more regular television deal for British Wrestling because "without TV, you can't create superstars". And without superstars, you can't sell out huge arenas and generate big money like the Americans can.

He was absolutely right. The average man in the street would most likely have heard of legendary British grapplers like Daddy and Haystacks because they were on the box every Saturday for years. They were national icons of their time and even today, years after the real-life Shirley Crabtree and Martin Ruane passed away, Big Daddy and Giant Haystacks remain recognisable names to people of a certain age who remember British Wrestling's glory days.

But ask that same average man about Alex Shane and, despite his weekly stint on a national radio programme, you would most likely be met with a blank look.

Although Revival would be screened on satellite television and Bravo's interest was a nice start, the ultimate ambition of Alex, and many other top British wrestlers and promoters, was a return to terrestrial, free-to-air telly, available to 10s of millions of homes. A weekly slot on ITV or maybe Channel 4 was bound to bring British Wrestling back into the mainstream, back into our nation's cultural consciousness and from out of the shadows of the WWF. For British Wrestling in 2002, that was the true Holy Grail.

Then when I asked The Showstealer what to expect from the British wrestlers at Revival, he said: "Go in expecting nothing and come out being surprised. We like to under-promise and over-deliver.

"The Brits may not be as big as the Americans, but when it comes to putting on a quality show, some of these guys are willing to *kill* themselves to entertain. And I'm not talking about them using barbed wire or baseball bats, I'm just talking about going all-out. And that's what's going to happen tonight. I think it will be a really good way of showcasing the talent in Britain."

Alex appeared super-confident that the British wrestlers could rise to the occasion for this, their moment in the national media glare. The Sun was there to cover the event. A documentary crew from Channel 4 was in the house. Executives from Bravo and talkSPORT were keeping a keen eye on what was about to transpire, to see if there was indeed mileage in a British Wrestling resurrection.

As bell time approached, the atmosphere inside the arena was absolutely electric. I was startled by the ear-splitting noise generated by the crowd, which was dominated by 18-30 year-old males, many of them wearing black T-shirts emblazoned with the white building-block style FWA logo. Their primeval chanting, littered with liberal use of bad language, turned the air blue and nearly deafened me in the process. This wasn't the kind of British Wrestling crowd I was used to in Morecambe, with kids running around waving foam fingers while angry old grannies attacked the bad guys with their handbags. It was more like a football crowd.

Anticipation for the show was at fever pitch. And Revival certainly did not disappoint.

A troupe of sexy dancing girls kicked things off with a high-energy routine inside the ring, bringing the kind of glamour to the event more typical of the WWF. Then the matches got under way.

The results of this epic 11-bout card were as follows:

Brian Christopher beat Guy Thunder, Doug Williams beat Flash Barker, Drew McDonald pinned Robbie Brookside, Eddie Guerrero beat Scott Parker, Nikita pinned Lexie Fyfe, Jody Fleisch pinned Jonny Storm, Doug Williams defeated Eddie Guerrero, Jody Fleisch beat Drew McDonald, Ulf Herman upset Brian Christopher, Alex Shane pinned Scott Parker, and Jody Fleisch downed Doug Williams to win the King of England Tournament.

The American superstars definitely earned their money that night. Grandmaster Sexay, the brash and energetic son of Hall of Fame wrestling legend Jerry 'The King' Lawler, revived his popular 'Too Cool' gimmick from the WWF by dancing in the ring with young fans following his quick opening match victory over shaven-skulled English wrestler Guy Thunder. As for Eddie Guerrero, he was desperate to make an impression after recently being fired from the WWF due to drug and alcohol problems. The Latino legend put on a technical wrestling masterclass against an unheralded British wrestler called 'The Anarchist' Doug Williams, who more than held his own and ended up winning the match.

Guerrero was on top form that night and it was a privilege to see his flawless skills in the flesh. Latino Heat would later return to the WWF (after it was forced to change its name to World Wrestling Entertainment or WWE due to legal problems with the World Wildlife Fund) and captured its Heavyweight Title from future UFC World Champion Brock Lesnar. But the Guerrero story was destined to end in tragedy. He was found dead of a heart attack in his hotel room on November 13 2005, aged just 38.

At Revival, though, Guerrero was at the peak of his powers. But although the vast majority of spectators that day had bought their tickets ostensibly to see Eddie and Christopher, they would leave talking about the performances of the European contingent. Like Doug Williams, the homegrown talent lived up to Alex Shane's belief in them and then some.

'The Giant German' Ulf Herman, a 6ft 6in man mountain from Hannover best known for his late '90s tenure with cult American Wrestling promotion ECW, drew gasps from the audience with his spectacular fire-eating entrance. Then this monstrous man battered a hapless young ringside 'security guard', who was thankfully really an aspiring wrestler from the Portsmouth-based FWA training school.

The beautiful female wrestler Nikita, a brunette English rose in electric blue spandex, set all the red-blooded male fans' hearts a-flutter with a win over America's Lexie Fyfe, who six years later would turn up on WWE's flagship weekly TV show Monday Night RAW wrestling while dressed as Hillary Clinton.

Even Tommy Boyd excelled during a short speech on the microphone. Wearing shades indoors like any wrestling heel (baddie) worth his salt, the annoying Boyd reprised his villainous character on Wrestletalk with such a natural arrogance that he was almost booed out of the building.

But taking the honours for match of the night was an astonishing contest between young Essex high-flyers 'The Phoenix' Jody Fleisch and 'The Wonderkid' Jonny Storm. Best mates away from the ring, Fleisch and the long-haired Storm gave the impression they were trying to permanently maim each other during their supercharged ladder match. Their breathtaking series of metal ladder-assisted aerial stunts was the most thrilling live wrestling spectacle I had ever been privileged to witness to that point—and even today it's still in my Top 5 favourite matches of all-time.

Fleisch and Storm may have been smaller than many of their fellow wrestlers, but these young daredevils displayed the kind of gigantic hunger Alex Shane was talking about. This was nothing like Big Daddy bumping Giant Haystacks with his belly. This was British Wrestling, 'new school' style—fresh, youthful and very, very exciting.

Jerome 'Jody' Fleisch was the chosen one that night. The 21-year-old Phoenix was a fearless fan favourite in gold baggy pants, possessing the lithe body of a gymnast and the balance and dexterity of a circus acrobat. Fleisch was blessed with gravity-defying aerial skills, a willingness to take spectacular bumps (falls) and had a knack for absorbing terrible punishment from his opponents, yet still coming back to win.

The likeable underdog from Walthamstow had been selected to become a fully-fledged British star-in-the-making in front of the Bravo TV audience by winning an eight-man tournament to crown wrestling's first 'King of England'. So after Jody pinned Jonny Storm in that amazing ladder match, he upset the veteran 'Highlander from Hell' Drew McDonald in the semi-final and then went on to beat Williams in the final.

7

Then, while most of the wrestlers re-emerged to clap and cheer on the stage, The Phoenix was presented with a gold medal by one of Britain's greatest-ever wrestlers, former WWF Tag Team Champion The Dynamite Kid of The British Bulldogs, whose own desire to push his body to the limits during a critically-acclaimed career had landed him in a wheelchair.

It was a touching end to a fantastic evening's entertainment, a true 'passing of the torch' moment that bridged the gap between British Wrestling's past and what seemed to be a promising future. Most fans certainly went away from Revival waxing lyrical about what they had seen.

But although Jody Fleisch was presented as the star of the show and British Wrestling's new hero, he wasn't the performer who most struck a chord with me. Granted, I was impressed by the efforts of Fleisch, Storm, Williams, Nikita and others, and had been well and truly sold on the new generation of British Wrestling by experiencing this fabulous event in person.

But for me, Alex Shane was the one who stood out from the pack.

Shane's actual match with 'Solid Gold' Scott Parker (no, not the England footballer) was dramatic enough. A crowd-pleasing brawl that spilled out into and amongst the spectators, it included one especially memorable moment when the long-haired Parker threw Shane off the second tier of the Indoor Arena seating area and then jumped off like a stuntman, diving on top of Alex with a flying splash.

Shane's wrestling capabilities were not his biggest strength, though. It was The Showstealer's charisma, his ability to connect with the audience, his presence, his superstar aura, and his confident patter on the microphone that really impressed me. His three catchphrases "Never fear, because The Showstealer is here!", "You must need a check up from the neck up!" and "There are two things you can do about it and that's nothing and like it!" set him apart from the other Brits as someone who had carefully cultivated his own distinctive wrestling persona.

But most of all, I remember the Pavlovian response to Shane's ring entrance. A computerised voice-over generated anticipation in the arena as it counted down to The Showstealer's impending arrival ("Alex Shane will steal the show in five seconds, steal the show in four seconds, steal the show in three seconds, steal the show in two seconds, steal the show . . . ."). Then as the man himself emerged through the curtain, his theme tune kicked in as the singer screamed "SHOW!" repeatedly throughout the chorus.

On the roar of every "SHOW!", Shane thrust his burly arms skyward, and just like fans of American Wrestling superstar Rob Van Dam who mimic RVD's famous double-thumb point, the Arena responded by themselves lifting their arms into the air while yelling "SHOW!" over and over again.

It was quite an eye-opener to see a young British wrestler who had the capability to gain such command and control over nearly 2,000 people, a lot of whom, like myself, had never even seen him before. The Showstealer gripped that crowd in the palm of his hand and he did it, not by hurling himself 10 feet off a ladder onto an opponent or by striking somebody in the head with a metal chair, but by the use of a mere gesture. Such simplicity is the art of the true entertainer.

In February 2002, Dwayne 'The Rock' Johnson, who would later go on to success as a Hollywood action movie hero, was the biggest name in American Wrestling. Having seen Alex Shane perform, and having met him for the first time and experienced his insightful intelligence, verbal prowess and overall larger-than-life personality first-hand, I actually thought The Showstealer had all the attributes to be Britain's answer to The Rock. On that night, I felt he could be the cornerstone of a true resurgence of British Wrestling, the biggest star the UK had seen in years.

As far as I was concerned, Alex Shane really *did* steal the show that night.

On February 9 2002, as British Wrestling experienced its supposed Revival, little did I know that in the ensuing years, I would go from being a fan of Alex Shane and an admirer of his wrestling alter-ego, to being a close friend of Alex Spilling, the complex but fascinating man behind the Showstealer character.

In fact, I would somehow, quite by accident, surpass my wildest dreams by ending up as his right-hand man as he embarked on an all-consuming quest to bring British Wrestling back to prominence, then later actually became the head of the FWA myself . . .

It was one hell of a roller coaster ride. And along the way there were plenty of good times and a fair share of bad times. But—particularly whenever Alex Shane was involved—there were most definitely never, *ever* any dull times.

So this is the story of how a middle-aged wrestling fan from a tiny Lancashire seaside town found himself in charge of the FWA—British Wrestling's most famous company of the past 10 years—as it battled at the forefront of British Wrestling's crusade for mainstream recognition. Along the way, you'll read my opinions on some of the colourful characters I've met, the matches I've witnessed and been involved in, the inside story on the rise and fall of the FWA, and my take on the successes, the failures and the many false dawns experienced by the British Wrestling scene during a tumultuous and extremely significant period in its history.

And I hope you have as much fun reading about it as I've had actually living through it!

CHAPTER 2

DAWN OF A NEW ERA

On Sunday, March 3 2002, Revival aired on the Bravo channel, but not in its entirety. Due to time constraints, the thrilling Jody Fleisch v Jonny Storm ladder match and Alex Shane v Scott Parker brawl were both heavily edited down, doing neither bout any kind of justice. TV ratings were less than had been hoped for. Bravo never broadcast another British Wrestling show again. The digital channel eventually went out of business in 2010.

On Friday, March 22 2002, it was announced that Alex Shane had suffered a serious neck injury at an FWA wrestling show in Walthamstow. According to reports on the internet, there was a chance Shane might never wrestle again.

On Thursday, April 11 2002, it was announced that Tommy Boyd had been sacked from talkSPORT. He was punished for failing to cut off a caller on his radio show who threatened to shoot the entire Royal Family, just hours after the death of the Queen Mother. Boyd disappeared from the public eye for a time. And he never promoted a wrestling show again.

So much for the revival of British Wrestling.

In contrast, my fortunes had taken an upturn since that auspicious day at Crystal Palace. A popular Isle of Man-based fanzine called Pro Wrestling Press had printed my feature-length report on the Revival experience, including those sought-after interviews with Boyd and Shane. I had gained my first teeny-tiny recognition as a wrestling journalist.

Then in May 2002, I graduated from the University of Central Lancashire with a postgraduate diploma in newspaper journalism. This qualification opened doors for me that had previously been closed, as within a matter of months, I'd gained two jobs that I had always wanted.

That July, I began working as a reporter for my local paper The Visitor in Morecambe, recruited by the-then editor Glen Cooper, a gentleman to whom I'll be eternally grateful for giving me the chance to fulfil one of my lifelong ambitions. A couple of weeks earlier, I'd received a phone call from Findlay Martin, editor of Europe's top independent wrestling magazine Power Slam, telling me I'd been successful in my application to become part of his team of freelance writers. Suddenly, I was working for two of my favourite publications, both of which I'd read and enjoyed for years. It was like all my Christmases had come at once. At 30 years of age, all my dreams were suddenly coming true. I honestly couldn't believe it.

With my confidence sky-high, another aim I had, although I thought this one would just be a pipe-dream, was to somehow get involved in the British Wrestling business. And indeed, thanks to my decision to attend Revival, I was about to get the opportunity to do just that, in unusual circumstances to say the least . . . thanks to a chance meeting with a fledgling wrestling promoter named Dann Read.

I bumped into Dann for the very first time outside the Crystal Palace Indoor Arena on the day of Revival. I was going up and down the queue of fans waiting to get in, giving out flyers promoting my website. This strange-looking dude took a flyer, showed an interest in my product, and we got chatting.

Dann was only 19, but he looked and acted a lot older. His appearance was striking; typical of the unusual characters the wrestling business attracts. Bulky, wearing dark clothes, his big toothy grin spreading itself over an untidy goatee beard that sprouted from his chin like wire wool, Dann dressed and acted like a big cheese. He was loud, confident and extremely opinionated. Even his first name, with that unnecessary extra 'n', showed he was someone who knew how to attract attention.

A former trainee wrestler who'd been forced to give up the physical side of the business due to persistent knee injuries, Dann had decided he wanted to involve himself in the management side of wrestling. As we took our seats next to each other in the Arena, he explained he was the host of his own smaller-scale version of Wrestletalk in his home county of Suffolk.

Dann's wrestling chat show aired every week on Ipswich Community Radio (ICR FM) where he worked as a volunteer. As his next project, he was about to promote his first live show and was looking to publicise it on the various wrestling websites and forums that were becoming popular amongst news-hungry British fans during the pre-Facebook and Twitter era when people were still uncovering the full power of the internet.

As we sat in the Arena and talked, Dann talked himself and his promotion New Era Wrestling up as the next big thing. He enthusiastically explained that he had booked exciting independent American wrestler Low Ki as the headline attraction at his event, scheduled for the Ipswich Corn Exchange on Saturday, July 13 2002.

This would be Low Ki's first ever appearance on British soil at a time when fans of WWE RAW and their other weekly programme Smackdown wouldn't have known him from Adam: although eight years afterwards he would become a WWE television superstar under the name of Kaval in a short-lived and unhappy tenure with the world's largest wrestling company. But in 2002 Low Ki was a real darling of the die-hard wrestling fan base who followed the industry microscopically, who were also known as 'smart fans'.

Dann said the show would be built around a one-night, eight-man tournament called the J-Class Cup, based on the annual Super Junior Tournaments in New Japan Pro Wrestling. It would include Low Ki, Jody Fleisch, Jonny Storm and other British wrestlers. He hoped this tournament would become an annual happening. His extravaganza would be called Dawn of a New Era and it would be kind of a sequel to Revival, the next step in British Wrestling's evolution from old-fashioned family slapstick into a cool form of entertainment for young adults.

As I listened to Dann's grand plans, I admit I felt a little sceptical about whether this bombastic teenager could back up his big talk. Still, I agreed to keep in touch with him and see if we could help each other out in future.

You would not believe the amount of times Dann telephoned me over the next five months. It seemed every time he had a new storyline idea for Dawn of a New Era, he would call to ask my opinion. He barely knew me, yet he entrusted me with assisting him in his role as the 'booker'. In wrestling, the booker is the matchmaker, who 'books' all the wrestlers and then decides who will fight each other, and who will win and how.

I was flattered that Dann already trusted me enough to be his confidant although there were times when the frequency of his calls wasn't half irritating. But most of the time, I didn't mind at all. I loved being a teeny-tiny part of the wrestling business.

But my wife Sharon wasn't quite as understanding. She was rapidly turning into a wrestling widow because of the amount of time I spent on the phone to this pest from down south. Now I love my wife dearly. We've known each other most of our lives, having met at secondary school in 1986, started going out in 1989, married in 1996 and now have two children together. But to say that Sharon hates wrestling would be the understatement of the century. "Are you watching that s__t again?" is her usual response whenever RAW comes on.

The constant telephone contact showed that behind the gregarious personality, Dann was feeling the strain. This big-talking teenager had a poorly-paid job in a computer games shop, lived with his mum and stepdad, didn't have a huge support network of friends or family to help him and was staking a lot of money he didn't really have on the success of Dawn of a New Era. Deep down he was terrified of it being a failure, and understandably so. Dann would later tell me that he wouldn't have got through those months if it wasn't for those cathartic late-night chats. I realised right there that life as a wrestling promoter carried a weighty burden of pressure.

During one of these conversations, it came up that I fancied myself as a wrestling announcer. As a teenager, I decided that if I didn't become a writer, I'd be a football commentator. So I would practice in my bedroom while playing Subbuteo, pretending to be John Motson on Match of the Day, adding my own voiceover to the action. Aged 18, I'd even got to the regional finals of a BBC Search for a Sports Commentator competition where I got to add my voiceover to a video of my beloved Liverpool FC in front of the judge, TV sports presenter Steve Rider. I still have a photo on my dining room mantelpiece of the teenage me, full head of centre-parted hair, BBC microphone in hand and headphones on ears, sitting proudly next to the immaculate Mr Rider.

So when I told Dann of my dream, he offered me the chance to commentate on Dawn of a New Era, live on ICR FM. While still at this point a little wary of whether this show was actually going to happen, I jumped at the chance.

In the months leading up to Dawn of a New Era, WrestlingX became the unofficial website for New Era Wrestling. Our site was the first place where the matches for the July 13 show were announced, and we also printed exclusive interviews with some of the wrestlers who would be competing at the Corn Exchange. Thanks to Dann passing on phone numbers, I was able to make my first ever personal contact with Doug Williams, Scott Parker, Jody Fleisch and some other young British wrestlers who had been booked for the tournament like The Zebra Kid, Five Star Flash and Johnny Phere.

I had never heard of Five Star Flash or Johnny Phere before, but Dann rated them both very highly. Apparently they worked for a small promotion in Stoke-on-Trent called Great Britain Hardcore (appropriately shortened to GBH) and Dann said they usually tore the house down whenever they fought each other.

I don't think any British Wrestling show had ever been pushed as hard on the internet as we promoted Dawn of a New Era. By focussing his attention on the online market, Dann was determined to attract smart fans, or 'smarts' for short, who were mainly from the young adult male demographic Alex Shane's FWA had also been courting.

A smart fan can be defined as a wrestling anorak; a die-hard wrestling enthusiast who will travel from anywhere in the country to see a top UK show, pay extra for front row seats, create a rowdy atmosphere, buy wrestling DVDs from the merchandise table and then go home afterwards and create a buzz amongst fellow hardcore fans by discussing the show on an internet forum, often dissecting the performances of the wrestlers to the nth degree. And a smart fan also understands how the wrestling business really works. Or at least, he *thinks* he understands!

"The smart fans were a growing market of people who were prepared to spend money on wrestling," explained Dann in 2012.

"These kind of fans appreciated good wrestling, and this fuelled the wrestlers to work harder in the ring. They were more motivated than when they were working in front of a 'hurray!', 'boooo!' and 'come on children, clap your hands!' type of crowd, which the boys (wrestlers) felt stifled their creativity. It led to a happier locker room and better quality shows."

That's why Dann was trying to tap into that market in 2002. But he also worked his socks off to promote his show in his local area too, despite all manner of obstacles. One night while putting up posters in the town centre, the poor lad was actually beaten up on the street by a gang of thugs, after being mocked for daring to advertise "that fake wrestling crap". Despite being severely shaken up, he refused to allow this setback to stop him from pushing forward.

The anti-wrestling prejudices of mindless yobs weren't Dann's only worry. As a newcomer, he was also struggling to earn the respect of British Wrestling's establishment and was about to discover just how full of egos and politics the business could be. One or two veteran promoters had genuine misgivings about this inexperienced kid thinking he could just waltz in and put on a big blockbuster show first time out . . . and with good reason.

Scott Conway, a 39-year-old businessman from Southampton who had promoted all over England under the banner of The Wrestling Alliance (TWA) since 1986, insisted on being directly involved in Dawn of a New Era so he could keep an eye on how things were run. Conway warned Dann that if he wasn't involved, he would make life difficult by advising certain wrestlers not to appear on the show. So Dann brought Scott in as Master of Ceremonies for the evening and also hired the wrestling ring he used for TWA.

At the time, I thought Conway was out of order by holding Dann over a barrel. Looking back now, I can see Scott was just 'protecting the business', concerned that the inexperienced Read might make British Wrestling look bad and maybe even affect his own reputation and livelihood. Conway might have been influenced by what happened just eight months before, when he had to step in to save a high-profile event called WrestleXpress—the brainchild of a teenage first-time promoter from Barrow-in-Furness called Ryan Hewson, who turned out to be a dreamer and a con-artist.

Hewson had promised the earth, a glittering October 2001 event in the 3,500-seater Coventry Skydome, with an array of all-star international talent like Rob Van Dam, Eric Bischoff and Curt 'Mr Perfect' Hennig, and pay-per-view TV coverage. But he failed to deliver, the show collapsed and Conway had to rescue it by running his own smaller-scale WrestleXpress event in Dagenham.

I never met Hewson myself, but from what I understand, he was full of his own self-importance but well out of his depth. The kid's flirtation with the British Wrestling business would later end in disgrace. In spring 2004 he was convicted of obtaining money by deception and forgery, because he'd used his business partner's credit card to pay for items without permission. I was fascinated by the whole WrestleXpress saga, so I made sure I was present at Lancaster Crown Court that day to report on the court case. "This is a miscarriage of justice!" bellowed

Hewson as the guilty verdict was announced, and he subsequently continued to protest his innocence on various websites for years afterwards.

The WrestleXpress debacle had left a sour taste in a lot of wrestling people's mouths. Maybe Scott thought Dann might be another Hewson. Conway certainly had a major problem with newcomers getting into the wrestling business through 'the back door', as I would find out for myself a few months later.

Anyhow, to give Scott his due, he turned up on the night of Dann's Ipswich event and was completely professional. He came out in a garish double-breasted jacket to his signature tune 'Everybody Needs Somebody To Love' from The Blues Brothers, introduced the wrestlers in his distinctive high-pitched voice, and did a fine job.

But two days before the show, had come what seemed at the time like a major crisis. Dann had a run-in with his 'next-door neighbour' in nearby Norwich, a promoter called Ricky Knight.

Real name Patrick Frary, Ricky had run shows under the banner of World Association of Wrestling (WAW) since 1994 and had been an actual wrestler since 1985. Since then, 'Rowdy' Ricky had seen the best of times and worst of times for British Wrestling.

"I had my first match 27 years ago in Wells, Norfolk, against Jimmy Ocean," Ricky told me in 2012.

"I lasted four rounds and at the end, I was blowing out of my Harris (knackered)!

"Jimmy was a tough character in the ring and a private person in real-life. He had such an aura about him and lots of people didn't know how to take him. If you didn't know him well, you might have thought he was a bit of a 'loop (nutter). But he's certainly not. He just came to do the job, get on with it and go home. I liked him and we became tag team partners."

Ricky and Jimmy became The Notorious Superflys, one of the best tag teams on the British Wrestling scene of the 1990s. These rough and tough bad boys tore up the circuit and had some great matches, especially with a team called The Liverpool Lads—Robbie Brookside and Ian 'Doc' Dean.

"When we won the British Tag Team Championship, it was such an emotional moment," continued Ricky.

"It was what we'd strived for. I feel so sorry for wrestlers today because there are so many promotions and so many belts. I bet if you ask most of the Americans, they wouldn't even know who the British Tag Team Champions are now.

"But back then, there was just Brian Dixon, John Freemantle and Scott Conway as the main promoters. And then in 1994, there was me."

In February 1989, just two months after ITV pulled the plug on British Wrestling, Sky Television had made its debut. One of the new satellite company's crown jewels was regular coverage of World Wrestling Federation events from America. And as the popularity of American Wrestling exploded in the UK, the British scene had gone into a slow and painful decline.

"When I first started wrestling, we never used to peek out of the curtain to see how many fans were out there," continued Ricky.

"We didn't even think about it . . . the houses were always big. Then after British Wrestling came off TV, for the first couple of years it was still OK. But then the crowds started to dwindle and it was a sad time. Even Dixon was struggling and started doing other things for a time.

"When I started to promote, we sold out in Norwich. I began to think this promoting lark was a doddle, but then it went downhill again. We were drawing crowds of 30-40 people and losing money hand over fist. But we carried on.

"It picked up again when Scott Conway brought the former WWF star Earthquake over from North America. He called the rest of us promoters up and suggested we all use Earthquake on our shows, build the British lads around him and give them a shot. Then he brought over (former WWF stars) The Bushwhackers and did the same. Things got better and we eventually didn't need the Americans.

"It got to the point where we ran a show called WAW Fightmare. We got interest from all the TV stations and drew a crowd of 2,000 people."

WAW Fightmare paved the way for Revival, because it proved that with proper promotion, British Wrestling could still attract that size of crowd. The show on April 21 2001 at Norwich Sports Village also had its fair share of exciting action, especially a dazzling ladder match between Jody Fleisch and Ricky's wrestler son, 'The Zebra Kid' Roy Bevis.

Fast forward 15 months, and Ricky and Roy were at the centre of a storm prior to Dann Read's debut show. Days before the event, Ricky decided to withdraw his son from the Dawn of a New Era card. This forced Dann to re-write his script last-minute, because The Zebra Kid—who was something of a local hero in East Anglia—had been originally scheduled to win the J-Class Cup tournament.

Ricky's decision was all due to a misunderstanding. Today, Dann is adamant that other wrestling people were stirring the pot between himself and Ricky at the time, in the game of Chinese whispers that often goes on between wrestlers and promoters on the British scene.

For Ricky's part, he says: "There were a lot of different things going on at the time, a lot of controversy . . . although I can't actually remember why that happened."

It's all water under the bridge now . . . but when Dann phoned me in July 2002 to say Zebra Kid was out, he sounded a broken man. The pressure of promoting his first show was clearly getting to him. By now I felt personally involved in Dawn of a New Era and really wanted it to be a success, especially for Dann. He was trying so hard, bless him, and putting so much time and effort into it.

Dann's fragile emotions just about held up and then finally, the day dawned for the Dawn of a New Era. I remember that Saturday was scorching hot. Mark Kay and I arrived at the Ipswich Community Radio studios, situated near the harbour in Ipswich town centre, and looked out at the boats moored on the shimmering water. It was a rare moment of peace and reflection on what would be an extremely hectic day. For the first time, I was about to discover the sweat and tears, the creative inspiration and the cock-ups, that actually go into producing a live British Wrestling event.

There were 10 hours until the show, and Dann was already panicking. The good news was that Low Ki, the star of the show, had landed safely in England. Dann's concern was that Alex Shane—who since Tommy Boyd's departure had taken over the hosting of the talkSPORT radio show and rechristened it Talk Wrestling—had travelled to Ipswich the day before to record a radio interview with Low Ki. Afterwards, Shane, a notorious ladies' man and party animal, had invited the New Yorker to London to enjoy the city nightlife. Alex had supposedly arranged a lift for the American back to Ipswich that morning, but he still hadn't arrived.

Mark Kay and I have been best mates for 30 years, partly because we share a similar sense of humour. Our ability to poke fun at the often barmy world of British Wrestling has sustained us on many a road trip and got us through some ludicrous and often soul-destroying situations. So we joked that this was clearly an FWA plot to kidnap Low Ki and hold him in a secure location, in an attempt to scupper the most important day of Dann's life. I'm a master of terrible puns, so I christened Alex 'The Low Stealer'. I'm not sure if Dann found it funny though. He didn't trust Alex, was extremely paranoid and wouldn't relax until Low Ki had been safely returned.

Of course Low Ki did eventually turn up safe and sound, with his driver—an FWA trainee called Vicki Solomon. She had agreed to drive the 150 miles from London to Ipswich and back, simply because Alex Shane had asked her to. This was my first experience of Alex's Svengali-like ability to convince the people around him to put themselves out to do him little favours.

At the studios, Mark and I met up with my co-commentator, Dann's ICR colleague and wrestling fan, Nick Kabay. We popped a video of a Low Ki match in the VCR to try out some announcing and were halfway through our practice session when Dann came bursting through the door, almost hyperventilating and making very little sense. "We haven't got a ring bell!" was the gist of his garbled message before he dashed out again. This was a perfect example of how it's almost impossible for a British Wrestling promoter not to forget something vitally important on the day of an event.

Do you remember those Yellow Pages TV ads from years ago? "French polishers? It's just possible you could save my life!" Nick reminded me of that guy as he telephoned every sports and antiques shop in the Ipswich area trying desperately to track down a ring bell. Thankfully a local kick-boxing club had one for hire.

An hour later, Dann returned with Low Ki in tow. Shaven-headed, short but muscular, and with a deep, serious voice that made Darth Vader sound like The Bee Gees, Brandon Silvestry (his real name) was polite, happy to be in England and was up for the challenge of his UK debut.

As Mark, who would be helping out with various errands 'front of house' at the show, gave Low Ki a lift to the venue in his trusty Corsa, I spent the rest of the afternoon at the radio station producing the 'official event programme' . . . or rather, a naff 12 pages of A4 paper hastily stapled together containing all text and no photos. I don't think we ended up selling a single one.

At just after 5pm, I arrived at the Corn Exchange. The ring was set up and most of the wrestlers had arrived. I think it was at that point that I finally realised—we'd talked about it for five months, but this show was actually going to happen!

I noticed Jody Fleisch and Jonny Storm practicing moves in the ring. Slumped in a ringside seat watching them rehearse was a tall, bored-looking scruffy individual with straggly long hair and craggy features. This was Robbie Brookside, The Liverpool Lad who I had seen wrestle at Revival.

A 20-year veteran from Liverpool, Robert Brooks was one of the few to make a full-time living from British Wrestling. Known as 'The Wildcat' and highly respected within UK grapple circles, Brookside had wrestled all over the world, including for two of the globe's biggest companies World Championship Wrestling (WCW) in America and New Japan Pro Wrestling, and was a mainstay of the Birkenhead-based All-Star Promotions.

All-Star has been run since 1970 by Brian Dixon, easily the longest-serving and most successful promoter in the country, with a regular calendar of sell-out events at venues nationwide. Brian is British Wrestling's constant. While other promotions come and go, All-Star keeps on ticking over. Unlike many promoters in Britain, Dixon has actually made a few bob out of the business, by running over 100 low-cost wrestling shows a year and by selling bucketloads of merchandise. Even as recently as October 2012, during a tough economic climate, Dixon ran 15 live events nationwide in a single calendar month.

"I've done about 50 tours for All-Star since I first came over to England in 2001, and it is very much its own animal," said Joe Hitchen, aka the Canadian wrestler Joe Legend, in 2012.

"Most of the other British promotions I've worked for look to be like Ring of Honor or other American indie (independent) promotions. They are catering to 'The Internet'. Brian doesn't even think about The Internet. He promotes 1980s-style wrestling and he'd much rather bring over a Bushwhacker than a Briscoe Brother.

"As long as the crowd is making noise, Brian Dixon is thrilled."

As Dixon's top star, Brookside was hugely respected throughout the world. Dann had brought him in wanting to tap into his wealth of knowledge.

"I can't put into words how highly I think of Robbie Brookside on so many levels," Read told me.

"I've been in the business for two years and I learned more in two minutes being around Robbie Brookside than I had in those two years. I can't say enough good things about him."

The canny Scouser was originally supposed to wrestle Low Ki that night in Ipswich. But after Zebra Kid's withdrawal Robbie would now fight Jonny Storm instead. Before the doors opened, Brookside watched Storm as he rehearsed his acrobatic manoeuvres with Fleisch in front of a near-empty arena.

I noticed there was a bit of real-life friendly tension between the lanky Liverpudlian and the chirpy Essex boy. At one point, Robbie called out mockingly to Jonny: "You do all your 'roly polys', son. I'll still be there for you at the finish of the match."

I found it fascinating to see the contrast between the preparation of Brookside, one of the few remaining survivors from the TV era of British Wrestling, and the carefree new generation of daredevils represented by Fleisch and Storm. The 36-year-old Robbie, with all his experience of the job, certainly didn't feel the need to rehearse. He'd improvise most of his match in the ring as he went along.

17

Also sitting at ringside, huddled together away from where the other wrestlers were greeting each other with handshakes and friendly chat, was the contingent from GBH. This was my first meeting with Five Star Flash, Johnny Phere and another young wrestler who wasn't booked for Dann's show but had travelled with them from up north, Dirk Feelgood.

During our telephone interview a few weeks earlier, Five Star (real name Mark Belton) had struck me as being a likeable lad, if rather belligerent. But on this day, the headstrong Belton was on his best behaviour.

The weekend before, Five Star had attended an FWA show in Telford which was headlined by an appearance from WWF legend Jake 'The Snake' Roberts. Flash got drunk and sat in the front row where he and some other non-FWA wrestlers had amused themselves by taking the mickey out of the Frontier guys. These unprofessional actions had not gone un-noticed, so Five Star went around at Ipswich apologising to all the FWA boys to ensure no more was said about it.

The brooding 18-year-old Johnny Phere (real name Jamie Hutchinson) was very polite if a little nervous. Tonight would be the highest-profile match of this young loner's life. If Phere did well, Dann had big plans for him. The young promoter had even changed Phere's name for the occasion, to Damien Rage. This show was the first and only time this pseudonym would be used.

The sound booth, where Nick and I were to do our commentary, was up on the first floor directly overlooking the ring. We really couldn't have had a better view of the action. Unfortunately, we also couldn't have had a less punctual sound technician. He didn't turn up until an hour after the first bell rang, meaning Nick had to operate the CD player for the wrestlers' entrance music *and* commentate simultaneously.

And due to the venue manager complaining about chairs blocking a fire exit, the show was delayed by 15 minutes. I remember thinking such teething troubles wouldn't happen in the multi-billion dollar WWF. But in the cheapo land of British Wrestling, such mishaps are par for the course.

About 300 people had come to see Dawn of a New Era. A lot of them were smart fans, pulled in by our internet publicity campaign. Even some fans from Germany had made the trip to Ipswich to see Low Ki's European debut including Felix Kohlenberg, who went on to become one of the German scene's most successful promoters with Westside Xtreme Wrestling (WXW).

But 300 meant the building was only a third full.

Dann looked fraught as the show began. He stormed up to the commentary booth to scream at Nick when he accidentally mixed up the theme tunes for one of the early matches. It wasn't Kabay's fault he was having to multi-task because some slack sound guy couldn't turn up on time. But I don't blame Dann for his histrionics. Already, he realised the box office take came nowhere near covering the costs of the show. He would have to pay the difference out of his own wallet.

Now for the good news. The show itself was superb. The results were as follows:

Low Ki beat GBH by submission, Five Star Flash pinned Damien Rage, Jonny Storm and Robbie Brookside wrestled to a double pin, Jody Fleisch pinned Hade Vansen, Doug Williams beat Scott Parker, Scott Parker and Hade Vansen defeated The UK Pitbulls,

Jonny Storm won a five-way elimination match over Robbie Brookside, Low Ki, Five Star Flash and Jody Fleisch to win the J-Class Cup.

Five Star Flash and Johnny Phere did indeed tear the house down, just as Dann had promised. I was particularly taken with Phere's gimmick of a self-absorbed maniac, who threw temper tantrums whenever things didn't go his way. As for the wiry Five Star, that night he lived up to Dann's pledge that he would be as big a risk-taker as Jody Fleisch.

The two unknowns brawled all over the Corn Exchange in extremely aggressive style, throwing in some hard-hitting 21st century-style manoeuvres which had the crowd roaring in approval. The finish was particularly spectacular, as Five Star set a slumped Phere up in a corner with a metal folding chair positioned on his face, climbed to the opposite top turnbuckle and leaped the entire length of the ring with a full somersault flip to drop kick the chair into Johnny's head with a CLANG! The audience counted along in unison as Five Star scored the pinfall.

This match was simply brilliant and I was particularly impressed with the intensity and showmanship of Phere. I realised that night how much potential he had to go further in British Wrestling . . . only as Johnny Phere, not Damien Rage. I *hated* that name.

Robbie Brookside also made a big impact on me at Dawn of a New Era. Although the respected Robbie was usually a firm fan favourite for other British promotions, Dann had cleverly cast him as the evening's biggest villain. And boy, did Robbie relish the role. He expertly riled up the fans, calling them "smart marks" (a derogatory term for smart fans) and "keyboard warriors".

I found Brookside's promo (speech) hilarious and very indicative of his real-life opinions, as all the best promos are. As a proud veteran who knew the job inside out, the Liverpudlian had no time for the nit-picking critics who led wrestling's internet revolution.

I also thought Brookside was magnificent during the five-way elimination main event to decide the J-Class Cup Champion. While his opponents Low Ki, Jody Fleisch, Jonny Storm and Five Star exchanged big moves and aerial assaults, The Wildcat spent most of the bout standing on the ring apron, trying to avoid any physical contact whatsoever.

The story of the match was that Brookside was stalling, hoping his competition would beat each other to a pulp so he could come in at the end and take advantage, like a vulture picking at a carcass. The fans hated him for it, cat-calling him to get in and fight like a man. Similar to how Alex Shane had gained crowd approval with his simple 'SHOW!' gesture at Revival, Brookside's antics demonstrated the art of getting 'heat' (making the fans hate you) by doing next to nothing.

When only Jonny Storm was left, Brookside finally entered the ring with arrogance and twice hit The Wonderkid with his finishing move—a cross-armed slam from the top rope. But he failed to go for the winning pinfall, and his plan backfired when Storm caught him off-guard with a roll-up for the Cup-winning three count to a massive cheer from the Corn Exchange throng.

Doug Williams and Scott Parker also had a dynamic match, brawling right up into the bleachers of the Corn Exchange. I was also impressed with Fleisch's first round opponent Hade Vansen, an Alex Shane trainee from London with male model looks, cat-like movement and a nifty arsenal of martial arts moves.

19

The show ended with Low Ki pounding Williams with his trademark karate chops and kicks until The Anarchist fled, vowing revenge on another day. The original idea was for the American to return to face Williams on the next New Era Wrestling show.

Except, there wouldn't *be* another New Era Wrestling show. Although July 13 2002 was supposed to have been the Dawn of a New Era—it didn't actually turn out that way.

Dann ended up about £1,000 out of pocket. For a teenager with limited income, that was an insane amount of money to lose. So much so, that he abandoned plans for a follow-up show. First Tommy Boyd, and now it seemed Dann Read was to be added to the list of casualties—new British Wrestling promoters who quit this high-risk business after a promising debut.

There were positives though. The show got rave reviews on the most popular and controversial of the British internet forums, the UK Fan Forum (UKFF)—whose members were notoriously hard to impress. Some thought 'Dawn' was even better than Revival. Dann had proven to be a very good booker indeed. This earned him respect from other promoters, which he thoroughly deserved after working so hard.

After the fans had drifted away, and the wrestlers had said their goodbyes and started their journeys either home or to another show in another town, and as Mark Kay and I helped Dann and Scott Conway dismantle the ring and load it back into a van, my new friend Mr Read looked totally shattered—both emotionally and physically. "I can't believe it's over," he kept repeating to himself, in a drained whisper.

When Mark and I were in the car heading back to our Travelodge, we talked about the day's events. We were proud of Dann for pulling off a tremendous show and for achieving his dream, thankful to him for giving us the chance to be involved and sympathetic that he was now virtually broke. We weren't paid for our contribution to the event, but no money had been discussed nor asked for. At the time, we were just happy to be part of it. Dann couldn't have afforded to pay us anyway.

One thing we also said to each other was that we would *never* allow ourselves to get in the same position Dann found himself in. We resolved that if by some twist of fate *we* were ever to become wrestling promoters, we would make sure we learned from his mistakes. We would book a smaller venue, perhaps focus a little more on local advertising to attract kids, families and 'casual fans' rather than relying on the internet, and in general, we'd be a little less ambitious should we ever be in a position to organise a grapple gathering of our very own.

Nine months later, Mark and I were sitting in the box office at the Morecambe Dome. We were emotionally and physically shattered following our first show as promoters. And we were around £1,000 out of pocket.

Welcome to the British Wrestling business!

CHAPTER 3

THE TRUTH ON TALKSPORT

In March 2002, one month before Tommy Boyd was fired from talkSPORT, he'd gone cold on British Wrestling and his double act with Alex Shane had fallen apart.

"The wrestling could have been huge but there aren't really any British wrestlers that would be good enough," explained Tommy, in an interview with the talkSPORT website in 2006.

"Kids would have seen the WWE and then watched the stuff *we* would put on and would think it was rubbish.

"Alex Shane was a very bright guy and best of luck to him. But I don't think you can compare him to some of the guys in the States.

"(talkSPORT boss) Kelvin MacKenzie congratulated me on the way I had put Revival together and executed it. He sent along his head of finance and he was gobsmacked by the whole event and thought there was money to be made out of it. Even ITV showed an interest and there were mentions of it becoming a Saturday night show.

"But then Kelvin wanted a 50% share of the company. As a shrewd guy he saw that there was a market for this kind of an event like I did. I wanted to negotiate as I didn't know who I would be partnered with."

Alex Shane's version of events was slightly different. In December 2002, I interviewed him for WrestlingX. During our 90-minute chat (remember, this guy can *really* talk) he admitted he was grateful to Tommy for getting him onto the radio show in the first place.

But he then went on to say: "Things started working very well when Tommy and I started doing the show. He really did tout me.

"Over the months I spoke to him so much about FWA both on-air and off-air that he took an interest in it . . . from just meeting *me*. He decided that he wanted to run a big British Wrestling show which we all know was Revival.

"He rang me up two days after Revival and said: 'Alex, I want to offer you shares in the new company we're about to form.' I basically was given all these promises.

"Then the tape of Revival went in for editing. My match with Scott Parker had been cut down from 15 minutes to about six minutes. The match that I remember wasn't the one that made it to TV. The 2,000 people standing up doing the 'SHOW!' was taken off.

"I remember when I first saw the footage I nearly cried because Tommy had touted me so much. Then the negatives started coming out. People were saying: 'Aaah, he's not that good'.

"Eventually it got to a point where Tommy, from that video, started to think that maybe he'd put his money on the wrong horse. Jody Fleisch came out looking like a million dollars and I came out looking nothing like that.

"Then Tommy wanted involvement in the FWA. It was looking like this one person, Tommy, would come in and take over at the last minute after we'd laid out the groundwork.

"Look at Revival. Tommy paid for the Crystal Palace Indoor Arena and paid, or over-paid, the Americans. He got the TV cameras there. But everything else was done by the FWA.

"Tommy started to be different towards me in the studio. He would cut me off more and a lot of things went on which were somewhat strange. Then he started pointing out that I was making mistakes.

"I got a phone call from him and he said: 'Alex, after careful consideration I have decided to rest you from the radio show.' So I'd been kicked out of the show after doing all the work that I'd done without a thank you. It was a horrible feeling.

"Things after that really went downhill. I decided I needed a break from wrestling. I needed to take time out. I stopped going to the gym. I stopped looking after myself and stopped training and I just wasn't interested whatsoever.

"And I never once got a phone call from Tommy. Never once—saying: 'How are you?' And I haven't spoken to him since."

Alex went on to explain how he rebounded from being 'rested' from the radio show after Boyd was fired.

"I heard he'd got sacked and I started getting a load of phone calls asking: 'What are you going to do with the radio show? Tommy's gone, are you going to approach them?' I'd always been told by Tommy that talkSPORT didn't like me, (programme director) Bill Ridley didn't like me, they didn't want me there and I was there as a favour to Tommy.

"I spoke to Simon Rothstein (the wrestling reporter from The Sun) and we got a proposal together. I called Bill Ridley and got a meeting with him, and two days after that we were back on air with Talk Wrestling. To my shock it turned out it was actually Tommy who wasn't liked around the station and when he got sacked, many people said they were waiting to get rid of him."

Tommy's response to this, again from March 2006, was as follows:

"That is news to me but (talkSPORT) did owe me some cash. I think Bill Ridley is a good bloke . . ."

My take on all this, is that wrestling turned out to be just a fad for Tommy Boyd and once he was fired from talkSPORT, he had no desire to remain involved in the business. But why did both Boyd and Bravo lose their enthusiasm for British Wrestling almost overnight? Had they realised it wouldn't be as big a money-maker as they'd first imagined? This might partly explain why Tommy suddenly lost faith in Alex and the British Wrestling comeback dream, sending our cult little scene right back to the drawing board.

I think it's a real shame the Boyd-Shane team had to end. I look back on the Wrestletalk and Revival days with fondness and I think the wrestling radio show was much better when Tommy was on it. But his withering assessment of British Wrestling talent was revealing and typical of mainstream radio and TV people.

Boyd's overall opinion, plain and simple, was that the Americans were better. This perception summed up exactly what British Wrestling was battling against, and it was a shame . . . a real shame that Bravo hadn't taken a chance on the FWA and its hungry young British lions of the ring.

But just saying Tommy had kept his talkSPORT job and Alex Shane had continued to be frozen out, things could have been so different. For starters, I might never have taken my next step into the British Wrestling fraternity.

During the summer of 2002, I received a call from Dino Scarlo. I remembered Dino from Revival, when he had accompanied Drew McDonald to the ring as his manager.

Incidentally, the 30-year veteran McDonald, a gargantuan figure from Scotland with a boulder-sized shaven skull and Fu Manchu moustache, was one of the most fearsome characters on the British circuit both when performing and in real life. Ryan Hewson knew this only too well, as longtime wrestling referee Steve Lynskey once told me.

(By the way, please excuse the bad language. It's not my style, but routine where Lynskey is concerned . . .)

"I've met some t__t promoters in 25 years of being involved in British Wrestling, who said they were going to do this and do that . . . but Ryan Hewson was definitely the worst," said Lynskey.

"Hewson first contacted me in 2001, through the UKFF I think it was, and asked me to referee at WrestleXpress, and also find some British wrestlers for him. He told me he wanted big guys, so I got him Drew McDonald, who cancelled two other gigs to do his show. Then I travelled up to London on the train to meet Hewson in this hotel, where he'd hired out the top two floors as offices.

"When I got there, he got really s___ty with me. He said: 'This is a job interview for you, how dare you wear such a cheap suit!' Then he told me he'd decided he didn't want Drew after all, and ordered me to call Drew myself to tell him.

"So I phoned Drew to tell him he was no longer needed, and he went ballistic, saying: 'Put that little f__ker on the phone right noo!'

"Hewson meekly took the phone, and Drew tore him a new arsehole, telling him if he ever got his hands on him, he'd rip him apart and s__t down his throat.

"Even to this day I can still hear Drew screaming at him. The kid was s___ting himself."

Dino Scarlo, with his black waistcoat and shirt, flushed face and slicked-back hair, played the character of a ruthless East End gangster and complemented the Scot perfectly. McDonald and the animated Scarlo were extremely believable as two dangerous villains you wouldn't ever want to meet down a dark alley. Throughout 2001 and 2002, they had caused havoc on the FWA circuit in Portsmouth and London as part of the 'Old School' stable, feuding with Alex Shane's 'New School' in a battle of opposing generations and wrestling philosophies.

In real life, Dino was Alex Shane's mentor, friend and confidant. Dino was a veteran second generation wrestler, whose father Tony Scarlo was also a respected wrestler, trainer and referee, and whose son Tony Discipline is today a famous soap actor, playing Tyler Moon in EastEnders.

Dino was himself an excellent tutor and had become a second father figure to Alex after taking over his training.

"The first time I ever saw Dino was when he and Andre Baker appeared on The Big Breakfast TV show on Channel 4 with Chris Evans," Alex told me recently.

"Andre was always a bit of a 'plastic gangster' and Dino had, let's say, an interesting past. So Andre had gravitated towards Dino.

"I was watching with my mum. They were doing a skit in the wrestling ring and Evans was saying 'Show me some of the fake moves'. Dino put him in his place and I remember my mum laughed. She was impressed that this wrestler was sharp enough to outwit Chris Evans."

Around that time in the mid-90s, the Hammerlock gym boasted a who's who of future wrestling talent. Aside from Alex, there was Jody Fleisch, Doug Williams, Jonny Storm, Paul Travell, Nikita, Dean Ayass, The New Breed and others. All would eventually leave Hammerlock in a mass exodus from the controlling grip of Baker.

"I remember when Jonny Storm left Hammerlock . . . he did something in a match that Andre didn't agree with," Paul Travell told me recently.

"Andre was shouting at him, it was really f___ing hairy. Jonny ended up legging it out of there, because he'd had enough.

"Then after Doug left too, Andre kept threatening to kneecap him. They'd been great mates a couple of months before. I remember thinking that if he could say that about Doug, if I decided to wrestle elsewhere Andre could easily say the same about me. That's why I left, when Jonny Storm introduced me to the FWA."

Alex Shane experienced the darker side of Andre too.

"When I was 19, me and my tag team partner Guy Thunder got an offer to go and wrestle for another company called the UWA," explained Alex.

"I told Andre I wanted to do it and he said yes. But then he tried to sabotage the deal. He was like a father figure to me. I'd been with him for six years, made my pro debut for him at the Leas Cliff Hall in Folkestone (in 1995), and now he was badmouthing me behind my back. I was so pissed off.

"Soon afterwards The Sport newspaper wanted to do an interview with a wrestler who had slept with hundreds of women. I had a reputation as a ladies' man so I agreed to do it, although 'hundreds' was definitely an exaggeration!

"So they sent this reporter to see me and he asked me about the oldest woman I'd ever slept with. I said she was called 'Barbara', which was the name of Andre's mum. It wasn't true, but I knew he was bound to see the article in the press over his bowl of cornflakes one morning.

"At the time, Dino Scarlo was starting to see the manipulative side of Andre too. He found out about what I'd done and he was impressed that this teenager was bright enough to get Andre back, on such an intelligent level. From then on, he took a liking to me.

"Dino said he'd had a dream that I was going to be the next big thing in British Wrestling. Now I didn't have a big relationship with my dad at all. I'd just gone through that emotional turmoil with Andre. And now I had this guy who I'd admired so much when I first saw him on TV, who had a level of faith in me nobody ever had before.

"He instilled such a belief in me that I really was The Showstealer . . . that I really was a *star*."

Andre Baker, meanwhile, would suffer a tragic demise. The man known as 'Sledgehammer' killed himself in 2010, aged just 45. Baker may have been a polarising character, but will be remembered as a significant figure in the revival of British Wrestling. He was a pioneer as one of the first British promoters to copy ECW by doing hardcore matches with wooden tables, chairs and other weapons. Andre was also one of the first to bring over former WWE stars from America like Adam Bomb, Jim 'The Anvil' Neidhart and Jake 'The Snake' Roberts. And he was the first UK promoter to gain any kind of coverage in Power Slam. Baker certainly played his part in dragging British Wrestling into the 21st century.

"Hammerlock was the start of the rebirth of British Wrestling," said Paul Travell.

"It really was the only place to learn back then, and I know, because I'd scoured the country, contacted wrestlers, done everything possible before finding Andre's gym in Kent."

After leaving Hammerlock, Alex Shane had become aware of a new wrestling promotion making a big noise on the south coast. The FWA, run by Mark Sloan, had just run its debut show on February 27 1999. Sloan invited Shane to compete on FWA's second event No Surprises in Portsmouth on July 11 of that year. That day, Alex teamed with Leon Murphy to defeat Kev O'Neil and Excalibur. Now there's an answer to a trivia question if ever there was one. It was Alex Shane's first ever FWA match.

"When I got there, I remember being impressed that they actually had an entranceway," recalled Shane.

"I also remember that night me and Guy Thunder nearly had a fight with 20 doormen, but that's another story!

"That night I met Elisar Cabrera for the first time. Elisar was helping Mark to film the event, and me and Elisar hit it off really well. He was a big and underrated influence in the revival of British Wrestling.

"Elisar and I decided to run shows in London under the name of Capital City Pro Wrestling. The first show I ever ran was in 2000. I was 20 years old, did the worst promoting job ever and we still drew 300 people. But American Wrestling was red-hot on the TV at the time so people wanted to go out and see live wrestling. If I did the same terrible job of promoting today, I'd only draw 40-50 people.

"My concern with the FWA at the time was the way their wrestlers looked. There were a lot of skinny guys. I used to argue with Mark Sloan about it. He'd say to me: 'But look at Eddie Guerrero and Chris Benoit . . . they're smaller guys and they are changing the business'. I said: 'Come on, they are still way bigger than your guys!' When I stood next to Eddie at Revival I couldn't believe how muscular he was."

But Hammerlock's loss of its disillusioned talent turned out to be FWA's gain. Jody Fleisch and Jonny Storm had appeared on the first FWA event. By the time of Sloan's third show in Kidderminster on September 12 1999, he also had Doug Williams on board.

"Jonny, Jody and Doug had all the potential in the world, and when they left Hammerlock and joined the FWA, suddenly FWA had the talent pool," said Travell.

"If Andre hadn't alienated so many people, the FWA would just have been full of people like Sloan. And that's no disrespect to Mark, but he didn't look like a wrestler. Hell, *I* didn't look like a wrestler! But with Jody, Jonny, Doug and Alex, the FWA now had a great mix of people—big guys and talented small guys."

Alex and Mark used to butt heads all the time back then and this continued throughout the FWA years.

"There was a huge gap between my wrestling philosophy and Mark's philosophy," explained Alex.

"I always felt that nothing was impossible. Like Richard Branson, I believed in the mantra of 'screw it, let's do it', even if sometimes it couldn't be done. I would rather try 10 things, fail at eight of them but the two things that work end up being talked about forever, than try nothing out of fear. I wanted to do big, big, *big* shows. But Mark . . ."

In an interview with Fighting Spirit Magazine in 2007, Sloan admitted he was a steady, take-things-slowly, safety-first kind of person who by 2002, recognised he had taken the FWA about as far as he could. Alex wanted to get more involved and take the kind of gambles Sloan himself wasn't willing to take. So Mark stepped aside and allowed Alex and Dino to take control.

"The gap between our wrestling philosophies has narrowed over the years," Alex went on.

"But I felt for years that I stole Mark's baby and I felt bad about it.

"I really respect Mark as a businessman. I hope that when the wrestling history books are written, they recognise him as having made one of the biggest contributions to the British scene."

So by summer 2002, Alex Shane had risen to be the head of the FWA. But his new mentor Dino Scarlo was always there in the background helping him make business decisions about what was best for the company, even regarding the Talk Wrestling radio show. And it was Dino who first approached me with the idea of me making a guest appearance.

I found it extremely flattering to receive a personal call from such a highly-respected man in British Wrestling circles. It kind of came out of nowhere. I'd only been writing for Power Slam for a couple of months and done that lone commentary stint for Dann. My name was barely known inside the wrestling business. But of course, I jumped at the chance. The radio show I listened to every Saturday night, the one where I'd first heard about Revival . . . I was actually going to be part of it! I was overwhelmed with pride.

"Dino had actually come to me and asked me what I thought about Greg after being impressed with some of the articles he'd written on the UKFF," explained Dann, years later.

"I remember the conversation clearly, as I remember all my conversations with Dino. Just after Dawn of a New Era, he'd called me to congratulate me. He said: 'You put on a great show with a far lower budget than we had at Revival. You should be bloody proud of yourself'. That meant the world to me.

"Dino thought Greg talked a lot of sense and wanted to get him more involved."

So in August 2002, I began doing a weekly five-minute phone-in guest slot on Talk Wrestling. My job was to present a 'Worldwide Round-Up' of wrestling news from around the globe. Like I said earlier, my entry into the British Wrestling business was extremely unusual. Most wannabes get their foot in the door either by visiting a training school or by hanging out at shows to pester promoters for a job. But everything I've ever done in the business has happened because I was *invited* to do it.

My guest slots went incredibly well, because I seized the opportunity. While talking about the latest grappling gossip, I tried to copy what I'd heard Tommy Boyd do so effectively on Wrestletalk and what one of my wrestling heroes, Jesse Ventura, used to do as a WWF commentator in the 1980s. I played the bad guy, turned up my natural big-headedness to the max and boasted about my immense knowledge of wrestling facts and figures.

I called myself not plain old Greg Lambert, but Greg 'The Truth' Lambert, the know-all journalist who claimed to be 'the foremost authority on pro wrestling in the world today'. 'The Truth' was the heel persona I would later use when I became a performer with the FWA. I'd actually nabbed the nickname off a boxer called Carl 'The Truth' Williams, one of Mike Tyson's knockout victims during his reign as heavyweight champion of the world. I thought it sounded cool and suitably ironic, because as a wrestling bad guy, 'the truth' was the *last* thing I would tell.

The name also parodied the public's perception of journalists as bare-faced liars. Although the media is supposed to be the eyes and ears of the public, we scribes have a terrible reputation. On TV soaps like Coronation Street, reporters are always portrayed as slimy, unscrupulous sleazebags who would sell their own mother for a scoop. The 2011 'phone hacking' scandal would see the public's opinion of journos slump to an all-time low.

This stereotyping of journalists really gets my goat. In my real life job as a local newspaper reporter in a quiet seaside community, I don't hack anybody's phone, invade people's privacy or write sensationalist stories. But that's the reality of how the public sees us. And for that reason, I'd always felt that a journalist would make a very effective wrestling heel, especially as nobody else had ever played that kind of character before.

I'd read in The Rock's autobiography that his wrestling persona was effective because he was playing his true self, only with the volume turned way up. I'd taken this on board. So The Truth was indeed the real me, a real-life wrestling news reporter, only amplified to a ridiculously exaggerated level.

As the weeks went by, and I continued to give my Saturday night updates on the radio, The Truth really began to rankle with the UKFF, who soon became my unseen enemies. I ripped into the smart marks every single week, pulled them up on their bad spelling and grammar, called them "internet geeks" and "spotty adolescents", and chastised their critical reviews of the British wrestlers and shows they went to see.

The keyboard warriors found my self-absorbed, self-righteous patter extremely irritating. "Who does Lambert think he is? What an idiot!" they wrote. Great, I thought. They're taking notice of me. So too, was Alex Shane. My Worldwide Round-Up went so well that it wasn't long before Alex invited me down to appear on Talk Wrestling live in the studio.

So on September 21 2002, I took the train down to London. There, I was met by Dann Read, who had himself travelled to our nation's capital to hang out with me and share in this auspicious occasion.

For some reason, Dann was dressed all in black. Black shirt, trousers and tie complemented his jet black hair and goatee. When Alex's car arrived at the pre-arranged meeting point of Blackfriars Bridge, The Showstealer took one look at Dann and asked him why on earth he looked like Satan. Dann's over-the-top ways didn't half make me laugh, and I found his vulnerable side rather endearing. It was good to have him around.

We crammed ourselves into the back of the car. Alex was in the front passenger seat, showing off his new Alex Shane Showstealer T-Shirt, cracking one-liners and basically being the life and soul of the journey. The driver was FWA referee, commentator, nightclub DJ and Talk Wrestling co-host Tony Giles. Back then, Tony did a lot of driving for Alex who, like me, has absolutely no inclination to ever learn to drive.

I met some more of British Wrestling's diverse characters that day. Accompanying us to the studio was Greg Burridge, an Essex boy who trained at the Dropkixx school in London and had just started out as a regular with Scott Conway's TWA as the effeminate Baxter Burridge—'Britain's Number One Alternative Lifestyles Wrestler'. A friendly geezer with blonde-haired surfer good looks, Greg was a fellow guest on the radio show that night. He'd later re-invent himself as the Essex chav 'The Pukka One' Darren Burridge and become one of the top stars on the British scene.

When we arrived at the talkSPORT studios I also met Elisar Cabrera. Although Alex was in charge behind-the-scenes, Elisar was the public face of the FWA according to the plotline. At the time, he also dabbled as a director of low-budget horror films and Playboy TV programmes. The bespectacled Cabrera seemed a studious chap, well-spoken but quiet—not at all typical of the wrestling business. His role on the radio show was to filter the phone calls; basically to transfer callers through to Alex and the other presenters in the main studio.

I also met Alex's co-host Simon Rothstein, with whom I hit it off straight away. To me, Simon had the best job in the world. As wrestling reporter for The Sun, he got to meet and interview all the WWE superstars when they came over to Britain. Far from being a hardened, cynical news reporter, he had all the wide-eyed enthusiasm of a kid in a sweet shop and I found him very easy to talk to.

Rather unfairly, Simon *Lilsboy* (his wrestling name) had become the whipping boy for the smart listeners to Talk Wrestling. Simon, a big WWE fan who didn't know quite so much about other promotions, was there to explain wrestling matters in simple layman's terms for any casual listeners or youngsters—who probably made up 99% of the audience.

You see, Alex had turned the show into more of a serious wrestling news and discussion programme. While Tommy Boyd's format was accessible to all listeners and geared towards getting ratings, Alex cared more about the integrity of Talk Wrestling and what the hardcore fans on the internet thought. So Shane's version of the show, while still entertaining, was a lot more informative and with less panto.

But still that 1% of the audience—the handful of smarts—thought the show should be tailored even more towards their own tastes; the niche companies like America's exciting new independent promotion Ring of Honor or the Japanese circuit. They resented what they saw as Simon's 'dumbing down' of wrestling, so they slammed him every single Saturday night on the forums. I had some sympathy for him. I've never been a particular fan of American independent wrestling or the Japanese scene either. I've always been a WWE man myself. No wonder the smart marks never warmed to me!

Simon wasn't the only one getting stick from The Internet. At the time, Alex himself was receiving waves of unfair criticism for his on-air bias towards the FWA. Many forum fans accused Shane of using Talk Wrestling as a two-hour advertisement for his own company.

Indeed, Alex would regularly talk about upcoming FWA events and invite FWA wrestlers in as guests. However, he didn't do this at the total exclusion of other British companies. If TWA, All-Star, Premier Promotions or WAW did something newsworthy, he would plug it. But understandably, he gave the lion's share of coverage to his own baby, because he truly believed FWA was the best representative of modern-day British Wrestling. And if you'd have been in his shoes, with a captive audience of thousands of weekly listeners, wouldn't you have done the same?

That night at the talkSPORT studios was the first time I'd ever spent a lengthy period of time in Alex Shane's company and I observed him closely before the show went on-air.

Alex Shane is unquestionably the most charismatic man I have ever met. Such was his overwhelming personality that he completely overshadowed even the FA Cup-winning football manager Lawrie McMenemy, who appeared on a soccer show at the talkSPORT studio that evening. McMenemy is a larger-than-life figure, renowned for masterminding lowly Southampton's victory over mighty Manchester United at Wembley in 1976. But Alex had such a commanding presence, I barely noticed he was there.

On early impressions, Alex was like a 6ft7in, 18 stone hyperactive child. The Showstealer just couldn't sit still, as he paced up and down the studio floor in his black leather jacket, mobile glued to his ear, talking into it at a million miles per hour.

I also noticed how Alex liked to do things 'on the fly'. Pre-planning for the Talk Wrestling show consisted of him saying: "So, what shall we talk about this evening?" about 15 minutes before going on-air. This was my first experience of Alex as what I call 'The Denis Norden of Wrestling'. His attitude was 'It'll be all right on the night' and preparation was always last-minute. I would later learn that he adopted a similar ethos when organising wrestling shows.

Alex reminded me of the cool kid in the school playground, with such an aura about him that everyone else wanted his attention and approval, myself included. At first, he didn't speak directly to me that much and I found that a bit deflating. Alex Shane was *the man* in British Wrestling, and I really wanted to impress him. In fact, over the years, I would *constantly* find myself trying to impress him. When it came to British Wrestling, I saw Alex Shane as the in-crowd. And I wanted to be on the inside, instead of the outsider looking in.

I reckon my desire to be accepted by Alex had a lot to do with my difficult childhood. People who know me today might be surprised to read this, but I suffered years of alienation and bullying as a child and used to struggle with the demons from those dark days. As a result, when I first got involved in wrestling, I was just like the teenage Alex had been. I was desperate to be liked . . . to *belong*. Popularity was something I'd never had as a kid and desperately craved as an adult.

School was a living nightmare. I was the class brainbox, the vulnerable and unpopular victim, an outspoken but sensitive child who was always the target for bullies. 'Swot' and 'softie' were two of my regular nicknames. I was never a part of the in-crowd, in fact the in-crowd mocked and ostracised me. Having my bag stolen, suffering incessant name-calling, being excluded from playground games and going home with bruises covering my body from punches and kicks were as much part of my daily routine as Maths lessons.

The worst incident came at primary school when a gang of older kids attacked me on the school field, forced me onto my back then tried to stuff a worm into my mouth. It was a degrading and terrifying ordeal which even made headlines in The Visitor at the time, because the ringleader was the last child to ever receive a caning from the head teacher.

The bullying even continued when I went to study English and History at Keele University near Stoke-on-Trent in 1990. It was the height of 'rave' culture, and I was lumped into a Halls of Residence with a bad crowd of drug-takers and dealers. Because I shunned their self-destructive lifestyle and refused to drop acid or pop ecstasy pills, as many of them did several times a week, I was treated like a pariah. It was a long and lonely four years.

In my final year, one of my flatmates broke into my room, rummaged through my drawers and found all the private correspondence I'd received during my university years . . . personal letters from friends, family, even my then-girlfriend Sharon. Not only did the bastard read them all, he *set fire to them,* leaving only the charred remains. I was heartbroken by this callous violation of my privacy.

Life was hard as an outcast, but things finally began to turn around at the age of 21, when I got a seasonal job on the games stalls at Morecambe's fairground. This cheesy little country and western theme park called Frontierland was where I learned how to work a microphone.

I spent the summers of 1993 and 1994 doing the whole 'Roll up, roll up!' spiel, coaxing crowds of punters to throw bin bags at tin cans and lob basketballs through hoops in the hope they might win an enormous cuddly tiger. It was hard graft and pre-minimum wage, so at the height of summer season I was working 60 hour weeks, coming out with just *£110* after deductions.

But I found fairground life totally empowering. I was good at the job and this earned the respect of my work colleagues. For the first time in my life, I'd been accepted by my peers. This gave me the confidence to come out of my withdrawn shell, as I gradually become more outgoing and sociable, and ended up having a whale of a time spending most of my meagre earnings on beer after closing time in the park's Ranch House Bar.

Over the next 10 years, I gradually developed a wide and diverse circle of friends. By the age of 30, married and with a young son, and working for the local paper at the heart of my community, I'd finally achieved the social acceptance I'd wanted so badly. But I still wanted more.

So when an hour into my Talk Wrestling debut, Alex introduced me to the talkSPORT listening audience by saying: "We are joined by 'The Truth' Greg Lambert, and he indeed does speak the truth" . . . I can't tell you how good it felt to hear The Showstealer acknowledge me like that straight away.

I did a good hour's stint on the show, and Alex and Simon seemed pleased enough. So much so that on November 23 2002, I was invited back to the studios—this time for the full two-hour stint. The regular baddie on the show, FWA's Manager of Champions 'The Twisted Genius'

Dean Ayass, was unavailable that Saturday so I stepped into his place. Our paths would cross soon enough.

My confidence level was higher on that second live appearance on talkSPORT because I knew what to expect. So I contributed far more to the on-air discussion, which centred around the previous weekend's WWE Survivor Series. I've always been a big admirer of Shawn Michaels, believing him to be the greatest wrestler ever to lace up a pair of boots. So I expressed my delight that Shawn had won the World Heavyweight Title at the pay-per-view. In fact I intentionally went on and on about how great 'The Heartbreak Kid' was, to the point of annoying overkill.

I also delivered an on-air rant about the smart marks, delivering my real opinions that there was a minority of Talk Wrestling listeners who went to wrestling shows just to be over-analytical internet critics instead of simply to enjoy a night out. Since becoming acquainted with the UKFF in early 2002, I'd read many vicious personal comments written about Shane, Lilsboy, other British wrestlers and promoters, even other forum users. They reminded me of the hurtful jibes from the bullies I'd had to deal with in life.

I've met so many warm and wonderful wrestling fans over the years. And at times, I find the UKFF quite an entertaining read. It's interesting, both as a promoter and a journalist, to find out the views of wrestling fans. I enjoy discovering what they like, and what they don't, and the UKFF is the easiest place to find this information. Remember, hardly any media outlets cover British Wrestling. It's not like we can pick and choose where to go to find reviews of what we do.

I've found, though, that there is a minority of wrestling followers, indeed a minority of wrestlers and promoters who are secretly members of the UKFF under various aliases, who would rather feed their own insecurities by using the forum to spew out the vilest of bile. They revel in going online to abuse others, instead of utilising the UKFF as a vehicle to positively promote the British Wrestling scene. It's not exclusively a wrestling problem, I've seen this happen on football supporters' forums too.

Online bullying is one of my biggest pet hates. Vermin spitting out personal insults they would never *dare* to say to their victim's face. It's the problem with the internet. It gives everybody a voice . . . and gives cowards an anonymous one.

But that night on Talk Wrestling, live on radio, I used my anger with the UKFF to my advantage. Channelling that pent-up bitterness from my younger days, I unleashed an over-the-top, wrestling promo laying into the smart marks in an attempt to impress Alex and provoke a reaction from the masses . . . just like I'd seen from Robbie Brookside at Dawn of a New Era. And it worked.

"How dare these wannabes write about wrestling?" I ranted. "They don't know what they're talking about. They don't get paid to give their opinion, not like me! I'm The Truth. I am it, I speak it, and now you've all got to face it. I'm Britain's number one wrestling journalist, I'm the foremost authority on pro wrestling today and if you mess with The Truth, you will face the consequences!"

Following my speech, I was called every name under the sun by the UKFF. And I got such a buzz out of being in control of the situation, of making a group of people respond exactly as I wanted them to. I think Alex took notice of my ability to get under people's skin and he later told me my performance on Talk Wrestling was a successful audition for my later career in the FWA. So thanks for motivating me, UKFF. For that, I'll always have a love-hate relationship with you!

While on the subject of Alex, I should mention one other important part of his personality that I got to know during these visits to London. That being Alex Shane—the party animal.

I never arranged anywhere to stay overnight when I travelled down to London, basically because I didn't know if I'd ever actually get to bed before my train journey home the following day. You see, Alex liked nothing better than to finish the radio show at 10pm on a Saturday night, grab a Chinese meal and then go out with a group of hangers-on until 6am on Sunday morning . . . sometimes even continuing the party all day Sunday and into *Monday* morning.

Now, I enjoy going out on the town and having a drink as much as the next man. I also like to think of myself as being fairly broadminded. But my rustic Lancashire style of socialising resembles an evening in with cocoa and slippers compared to what became known as a 'Showstealer Night Out'. As Alex himself explained during our December 2002 interview: "I do have an element of wildness and freakiness to me."

Alex, who once worked as a nightclub doorman in London's West End, seemed to know just about everyone in our nation's capital. So whenever we went out in London, he was able to negotiate us onto just about any guest list. But his taste in nightspots was nothing like the basic pubs and clubs I was used to in Morecambe.

Alex's favourite was called The Wayout Club. And it was indeed 'way out', because it was a popular hang-out for transvestites and transsexuals. Alex is a red-blooded heterosexual for sure, but he was also very much at home in The Wayout Club and was on first name terms with many of its regulars. For me, it was one hell of a weird experience to be stood at a bar watching butch moustachioed blokes in dresses snogging while dancing to 'You Spin Me Round'.

Alex still ribs me about the time when we arrived at The Wayout Club and I was bursting for the loo. The Showstealer quipped: "Ooh Greg, you don't want to be going to the toilet in The Wayout Club!" so I decided to pee in an alleyway. Unfortunately, two London policemen spotted me while I was relieving myself. Alex was shaking with laughter as I meekly suffered a good telling off for urinating on London's sacred streets.

The end of a Showstealer Night Out usually involved me trying to ask Alex for some money to cover my train fare—which was never straightforward, because getting cash out of Alex was often like the proverbial blood and stone. Then he would sort me out a place to crash for a few hours. To his credit, he always looked after me and even though he was usually planning on staying out, he managed to persuade one of his many mates to put me up at short notice.

After my successful slot on November 23 2002, I was looking forward to further appearances on Talk Wrestling. But then less than two weeks later, completely out of the blue, the only wrestling chat show on British mainstream radio was pulled off the air. It was replaced by an easy listening programme for an older market called Champagne and Roses presented by '70s TV star Gerald Harper.

At the time, British Wrestling fans were stunned. There was quite an outcry on the internet. There were even a few petitions set up. Quite a few of the fans who'd slated the show were now furious at its cancellation.

In an interview with WrestlingX in 2004, Simon Lilsboy explained why the show was canned.

"We left talkSPORT on good terms," said Simon.

"Bill Ridley phoned both me and Alex up and told us it was because they couldn't sell advertising to the under-16 market. It was a business decision."

Simon remained the wrestling reporter for The Sun until 2009, developing the paper's wrestling website into the most popular in the country. Former ECW boss and WWE manager Paul Heyman became a regular contributor and during its peak, there were interviews with WWE superstars every single week. Simon got to go to WrestleMania every year all expenses paid and then later went to work for the second biggest wrestling company in the world as head of TNA's UK media operation. Good for him, he deserves it.

As for Alex, he reckons the real reason Talk Wrestling was cancelled was because one of Kelvin MacKenzie's golfing buddies hated wrestling and said he wouldn't tune in on Saturday nights anymore unless he swapped the show for easy listening. Being a Liverpool fan, I now have two reasons to hate MacKenzie, who published lies about the Hillsborough disaster when editor of The Sun. Now there's the kind of scumbag who gives journalists a bad name.

Alex had this to say about Talk Wrestling's cancellation, during our WrestlingX interview just two days after the decision was made:

"Ridley told me basically because of the ratings dropping and not being what they'd expected they were taking the wrestling show off. The ratings thing I knew straightaway was rubbish ... they were actually in the process of getting sponsorship for the Talk Wrestling show because of the fanfare it was getting.

"We all know it's a ridiculous decision. Everyone I've spoken to thinks it's a joke. But I'm still a total believer that we will be back on talkSPORT some time soon."

But that never happened. Talk Wrestling never returned to talkSPORT. First Bravo, and now talkSPORT had abandoned the resurrection of British Wrestling just as it seemed to be gathering momentum.

So where did that leave me?

It left me about to embark on adventures in the wrestling business beyond my wildest dreams.

CHAPTER 4

NO RING CIRCUS

When I was a teenager, my mum and dad went nuts at me for running up a £130 telephone bill. I blamed Bill Apter.

Bill Apter is the most famous wrestling journalist in the world. A veteran writer and photographer who has covered major events worldwide since the 1970s, the New Yorker was the public face of almost all the wrestling magazines I used to buy as a teenager, like Pro Wrestling Illustrated, The Wrestler and Sports Review Wrestling.

Bill's publications were always targeted at the common fan and refused to break Kayfabe. In other words, Apter and his colleagues covered wrestling as though it was a real sport. But their articles—although often complete and utter fantasy—were nevertheless still very entertaining and a big influence on me as a budding writer.

But as the '90s progressed, and the internet rose in popularity enabling fans to discover more about how wrestling really worked, I was no different. I moved away from Bill Apter's fantasy world and became intrigued by a new English-based wrestling magazine called Superstars of Wrestling, which was relaunched in 1994 under the name of Power Slam. Power Slam contained far more insider news and information than the 'Apter mags' ever had, and a much harder-hitting style of writing.

I loved reading Power Slam so much, I became a regular subscriber and today I am the proud owner of every single issue since its inception. And I became even more attached to this dynamic new publication when I realised PS was based in Lancaster, five miles away from my home in Morecambe.

Power Slam didn't deal in fiction, instead it revealed the truth about wrestling's backstage fights, booking decisions, superstar tantrums, defections to rival promotions, wrestler deaths and drugs use, without fear or favour. It celebrated the good workers of the ring but absolutely slated the bad ones. The mag even contained real (or 'shoot') interviews with top wrestlers, unlike the made-up ones in Pro Wrestling Illustrated fabricated to help develop wrestling storylines.

It's 2012 as I write, and over 18 years after its inception, Power Slam remains Europe's most successful independent wrestling magazine. I am fiercely proud to work for the mag and for Findlay, who has allowed me the chance to interview greats like Bret Hart, CM Punk, Daniel Bryan, Road Dogg, AJ Styles, Raven, Konnan, Fit Finlay and so many more.

But while Bill Apter and Findlay Martin were chalk and cheese when it came to their philosophies on wrestling journalism, they did have one thing in common. They both, at one time, ran their own premium rate wrestling information hotline that I phoned behind my parents' backs. "Please get the person who pays the phone bill's permission before you use this service," Bill and Findlay would warn me at the start of their respective messages. I usually ignored them.

How incredible that these two gentlemen whose work I so admired and who both influenced my writing style, would go on to play such a big part in my wrestling career—Findlay as my boss at Power Slam for the past 10 years, and Bill Apter as my storyline arch-rival on two of the biggest live events in recent British Wrestling history. More on this later.

I first met Bill Apter at Revival. He was now working for the London-based Total Wrestling magazine, which ironically, was Findlay Martin's direct competition. At the time, I was touting for any kind of journalism work in the wrestling business. Bill told me to send him some examples of my writing. I did, but never heard back from him. No matter, he's a busy man . . . and besides, Total Wrestling's loss turned out to be Power Slam's gain! Findlay hired me just a few months afterwards and I've worked for him ever since.

My next encounter with Bill Apter was at an international wrestling show at the Preston Guild Hall on Saturday, July 6 2002. I was there with Mark Kay to watch the event as fans, and Apter was there as a guest of the organiser, who happened to be a fellow wrestling journalist and one of Bill's colleagues at Total Wrestling. This was just one week prior to Dann Read's Dawn of a New Era and in a similar vein, the young promoter of 'Global Wrestling Force Battle of the Champions' aimed to capture the smart market by running a supershow mixing the new breed of British wrestlers with international names. The promoter's name was Jon Farrer.

Farrer, a 20-year-old writer from Preston, had assembled an all-star cast of talent for his event. He advertised former ECW guys like Steve Corino, Little Guido (later Nunzio in WWE), Chris Hamrick and Julio Dinero, and also Taylor Matheny (a female wrestler who had been runner-up in WWE's Tough Enough reality show), Ron 'The Truth' Killings (later R-Truth in WWE), up-and-coming US independent prodigy Trent Acid and the infamous Jake 'The Snake' Roberts.

On the day of the show, only Guido, Roberts and Acid showed up. The others had either withdrawn in the weeks leading up to the event or, in the case of Ron Killings, didn't even bother to get on his flight that Jon had arranged and paid for. See, you should never trust anyone called The Truth.

A number of advertised British grapplers like Doug Williams and Flash Barker also weren't there. It wasn't a great start for a new promoter wanting to gain the trust of the fans. Had one of the advertised wrestlers no-showed for good reason, it would have been understandable. But more than seven of them? That was refund territory.

I'm not sure if anyone did ask Jon for their money back though, because the eventual show was certainly entertaining enough to justify the £10 ticket price. Mark Kay and I had a memorable day at Battle of the Champions, that's for sure, mainly because it was the first time we'd ever met one of our all-time heroes of wrestling, Jake 'The Snake' Roberts.

But you know what they say. You should never meet your heroes.

One of the biggest superstars during the WWF's glory years of the 1980s, Jake had come over to the UK in 2001 to live, wrestle and mainly to avoid some kind of bother he was in back home in the States. By that time, I'd seen Jake looking a mess on the famous Beyond The Mat documentary and knew all about this former WWF legend's descent into drug and alcohol addiction. I'd even heard stories of his various backstage misdemeanours on shows since he'd been over in the UK.

Still, this was a guy I'd grown up watching . . . a legend whose intense interviews and compelling WWF feuds with Randy Savage, Rick Martel, Rick Rude and Ted DiBiase had utterly entranced me as a teenager. So when Mark Kay and I arrived at the Guild Hall that day for a 'Fan Fest' (a pre-show event where some of the wrestlers signed autographs and met the fans) and we saw Jake, I just had to go over and say hello.

The man who wrestled The Honky Tonk Man at WrestleMania III in front of a purported 93,000 people cut a bored figure as he sat—or rather slumped—at an autograph table and signed for a handful of grateful fans. It was interesting to see the contrast between Jake's complete lack of enthusiasm and the boundless energy of Jody Fleisch and Jonny Storm, who seemed to be perpetually joined at the hip in those days, having not long returned from their first tour of America together.

"Jody is one of my best friends, both in wrestling and away from wrestling," said Storm, the real-life Jon Whitcombe, in 2012.

"We met at Hammerlock in the mid-1990s. He was really acrobatic even back then, because he had a martial arts background.

"Then he went to work for Scott Conway. Back then, Andre Baker wasn't allowing any of his wrestlers to work on any other shows, so Jody never came back to Hammerlock. Then we met again about a year later, hooked up outside of wrestling and that was it. We still speak to each other every week.

"We wrestled each other all the time back then, but not as many times as people think. People come up to me and say: 'You must have wrestled Jody thousands of times!' No, it was more like hundreds. Promoters felt it was a good match to showcase the best of British Wrestling."

In Preston that day, the best pals happily posed for pictures nearby for a considerably longer queue of customers than the one waiting to meet 'The Snakeman'. I wondered if this was a testimony to the growing popularity of British wrestlers, or because people were scared of going over to talk to Jake.

Incidentally, Roberts had travelled to Preston from that FWA show in Telford the night before. Jake had been special referee in a match between Scott Parker and former FWA Champion Justin Richards. The Master of the DDT had delighted the FWA faithful by producing his trademark giant snake from a bag. He then hurled it on top of the terrified referee Steve Lynskey.

Jake was a lot bigger than I expected and he wore an unkempt pink and purple Nike shellsuit. To be honest, he looked a shell of the man who had lit up WWF arenas six years before. I asked him how Telford had gone. "OK," he growled in a husky whisper. "It was nice to make someone else miserable." No, Jake didn't seem all that thrilled to be in rainy Lancashire that day.

Still, he did pose for a photo with me, because the £7.50 cost of attending this Fan Fest included a free Polaroid with a wrestler of your choice. Later we watched as Jake rounded up Little Guido and one or two others and slithered off to Preston city centre. In search of liquid refreshment? I couldn't possibly say. But Jake's moonlight flit was rather annoying for Jon Farrer, who had wanted his biggest name to stick around for a Q&A session with the fans. Unfortunately for Jon, The Snake was a law unto himself.

The highlight of the Q&A was Robbie Brookside, who is without doubt the best storyteller in British Wrestling. I was captivated by his monologues on such topics as his long-time friendship with WWE's Fit Finlay and William Regal, and his early days wrestling under the bizarre name of Quasimodo at Blackpool Pleasure Beach. Now *there's* a guy who should write a book. Listening to The Wildcat tell his absorbing tales was worth the Fan Fest admission price in itself.

Or at least, it was for me. Mark did nothing but grumble his way through the entire afternoon, because he *hates* Fan Fests. And he learned to loathe them even more in later years when he had to organise them. More on that later.

As I said before, Battle of the Champions was a pretty good show, although the Guild Hall was nowhere near full. The results were as follows:

Mark Sloan and Graham Hughes battled to a no-contest, James Tighe beat Justin Richards, Little Guido beat Jody Fleisch, The Zebra Kid defeated Robbie Brookside and Jack Xavier in a three-way, Michael Kovac downed Paul Sloane, Jonny Storm pinned Trent Acid, Little Guido pinned James Tighe, Jonny Storm beat Michael Kovac, Shak Khan pinned Lee Butler in a hardcore match, and Jonny Storm pinned Little Guido in a tournament final to become the first GWF Champion.

So what was Jake The Snake's role in all this? To this day, I'm still not really sure. He cut an incomprehensible promo, a shadow of the chillingly cerebral speeches he excelled at during the '80s, shuffled around at ringside during Little Guido's win over Jody Fleisch and then, while carrying the Full Blooded Italian on his shoulders back to the dressing room, managed to crack Guido's head on the Fire Exit sign above the entrance door. I have no idea if this was accidental or intentional. One thing I do know is that Jake didn't really do a lot to justify whatever Farrer was paying him.

The storyline of the show was that Kovac, Richards and Guido were a heel alliance intent on winning the GWF Title. Roberts was their 'spiritual inspiration'. But it was the group's heel manager who really caught my eye. In fact, I'd go so far as to say this tiny, irritating weasel of a man was probably the most captivating performer on the show. His name was Ross 'The Boss' Gordon.

Ross Gordon had been around the British scene since the mid-1990s and was involved in a number of projects which attempted, although ultimately failed, to put British Wrestling back on the map.

The wee Scotsman had started out in wrestling as editor of a fanzine then took his first dip behind the curtain when he worked as a cameraman and general go'fer for a promotion called EWA. The EWA, run by wrestler Jason 'The Dirtbike Kid' Harrison, was ahead of its time in many respects because it was a British promotion catering entirely for the smart mark audience.

On July 7 1995, Harrison brought over ECW legend Sabu to headline in front of 150 fans in Walthamstow. It was unusual for a British promoter to bring over one single overseas star for a one-off show and unheard of to charge £20 a ticket. One of the referees that day, incidentally, was a 15-year-old trainee called Alex Shane, who himself would later raise the bar still further when it came to ticket prices for a British Wrestling event.

After a follow-up show in 1996, Harrison flew in Sabu and his fellow ECW stars Mikey Whipwreck and Rob Van Dam—then arguably the most exciting wrestler in North America—for what turned out to be his last Walthamstow event, St Valentine's Day Massacre on February 14 1998. I remember this show because Power Slam covered it with a two-page colour feature. Fin Martin had rarely written about British Wrestling up to that point, so St

Valentine's Day Massacre was clearly a big deal. Unfortunately the trailblazing Dirtbike Kid was unable to follow up on this initial impact, and eventually quit the business in 2000.

But Gordon moved on to work for the Ultimate Wrestling Alliance (UWA) as a TV commentator. UWA was run by former WWF TV editor Andrew Martin and ex-Sky TV employee Dan Berlinka, who managed to negotiate UWA a regular slot on obscure soft porn-dominated cable channel L!ve TV. Sadly neither had much of a clue about how to run a wrestling company.

In Issue 58 of Power Slam, a superb wrestling writer named Rob Butcher reviewed UWA's first TV taping on Sunday, April 11 1999—known as British Resurrection. And he absolutely slated it.

"Despite the barrage of mainstream publicity, the Ultimate Wrestling Alliance came nowhere near close to filling the Crystal Palace Indoor Arena," wrote Rob.

"And while the UWA production team had really gone to town, fashioning a visually impressive entranceway and individual laser graphics for each wrestler, the grappling content was sorely lacking . . ."

After a second taping at Blackpool's Ice Arena in summer 1999, UWA folded. The company had ploughed thousands into advertising, spent far more than they could afford and so when ticket sales for their live events were less than expected, the inevitable happened. By going for huge TV spectaculars immediately rather than starting small, UWA had tried to run before it could walk. And yet another British Wrestling project disappeared after so much early optimism.

The same happened the following year with another new promotion called UCW, despite some fantastic shows. With Ross Gordon in charge of the booking, UCW's Wrestling Xplosion II event at the Coventry Skydome on October 7 2000—headlined by American 'The Fallen Angel' Christopher Daniels and Japan's Shinjiro Ohtani—received a rave review from Power Slam, Rob Butcher describing it as one of the best cards he'd ever viewed in person.

But despite getting the critical side spot-on, UCW, like EWA and UWA before them, failed to get to grips with the commercial aspects of the wrestling business. They had big plans, having signed some of the British wrestlers to contracts (Alex Shane included) and wanted to build on the Skydome success by touring other decent-sized arenas. But once again, financial concerns led to their demise after just two shows, in yet another false dawn for British Wrestling.

EWA, UWA and UCW. Gordon had seen them all come and go. Now he was in Preston working for Jon Farrer's GWF, hoping this time things would be different.

I knew of Ross 'The Boss' from his 2002 appearances alongside Alex Shane and Simon Lilsboy on Talk Wrestling. Gordon came across as a right know-all on the radio and portrayed a similar big-headed character at GWF Battle of the Champions. And I thought he was brilliant at it.

I watched, impressed, as Gordon gave a masterclass in ringside cheerleading and cheating reminiscent of great American Wrestling managers like Bobby 'The Brain' Heenan and Jimmy Hart. Everything about him was designed to get heat both for himself and for his men, even his horribly over-the-top mustard jacket.

Ross was sneaky, cowardly, devious and boastful on the microphone. He was like the obnoxious kid at school who hides behind the bigger lads and gets them to do his dirty work. And the Preston crowd absolutely despised him for it.

"The idea of a heel manager, ultimately, is to make money and put bums on seats," explained Dean Ayass, top UK wrestling manager, in 2012.

"A manager has to be able to make the people want to pay money to see him and his wrestler get beaten up. He has to touch a nerve, to rile up people, to make them think of somebody they don't like in real life . . . like their boss, or their ex-boyfriend or girlfriend, or their next-door neighbour.

"As a manager, you are there to represent your wrestler, to talk on his behalf. In storyline, the manager is taking a percentage of the wrestler's wage, manipulating the wrestler by telling him 'I'll give you the benefit of my advice and knowledge . . . I'll take you to the top!' So you want the fans to think: 'Why the hell is this big tough wrestler associating with this idiot?' I've always been lucky enough to get to manage top wrestlers like Paul Burchill, Flash Barker, Drew McDonald and Christopher Daniels. So the fans always wondered why on earth they needed me.

"A manager is also not a wrestler, not a physical threat, so the fans always feel like a manager doesn't belong anywhere near the ring, which makes them hate him all the more when all he does is cheat and take short-cuts."

Now I have never met Ross Gordon personally, but I identify with him. Like me, he started in wrestling as a writer, then became a commentator, a booker and a manager. And his ringside antics that night in Preston made a big impression on me. In the ensuing years, I think I modelled a lot of my own heel manager style on Ross 'The Boss'.

You may wonder what Ross Gordon is doing now? Well he's not involved in wrestling any more. GWF Battle of the Champions would be the first and last time I'd ever see him in managerial action. He got out of wrestling soon after . . . and stayed out. I heard he'd had a falling out with Dino Scarlo. But whatever the reason, you may sense a pattern forming here.

But despite the fact that Battle of the Champions set him back £14,000, Jon Farrer *didn't* give up on his wrestling dream. Instead, he announced GWF's second show, Aftermath, for the King George's Hall in Blackburn on Sunday, February 2 2003.

Learning from his mistakes the first time around, Farrer drastically reduced his overseas expenses for the second GWF show and flew in only three Americans. The first was Trent Acid. Trent had looked exceptional at Preston against Jonny Storm. But it turned out he was a troubled young man. Acid failed to live up to his potential in the coming years and, like so many in the wrestling business, eventually met a tragic end. I met Trent backstage at the King of Europe Cup show in Liverpool in 2007 and he looked like a human ghost. Three years later he was dead of a drug overdose, aged just 29.

Also on the GWF show was Acid's tag team partner Johnny Kashmere and a little-known hardcore wrestler called Ian Knoxx. The American trio had been booked to attract the smarts. Jake The Snake was back to draw in the WWE fans and was scheduled to wrestle Brookside.

It was just prior to GWF Aftermath that I spoke to Robbie Brookside for the first time, for a telephone interview for WrestlingX. This was something I approached with trepidation, due to an incident a few months earlier.

Scott Conway had brought TWA to my hometown venue The Morecambe Dome on July 29 2002 for a summer show. As any good promoter should, Conway contacted the local newspaper asking for some free editorial publicity and ended up in conversation with of all people, yours Truth-fully.

Scott then hooked me up a phone interview with Drew McDonald. I was surprised to discover the man who threatened to defecate down Ryan Hewson's throat was actually a charming conversationalist when he was in a good mood, and the resulting feature article gave Conway's show some decent advance local press, probably helping to sell some tickets. Scott also offered me complimentary press seats to watch the show, which is standard practice for the promoter of any entertainment event.

But I didn't enjoy the show. TWA's product was nothing like the more adult-friendly style of Revival, Dawn of a New Era or Battle of the Champions, and was instead tailored for kids. It just wasn't my cup of tea.

In my review of the event, I wrote:

"The action had an incredibly dated feel to it—with public warnings, a huge reliance on cheesy comedy and an incessant amount of slow and boring matwork. The cutting edge, fast-paced and highly dramatic 'new school' style of British Wrestling was nowhere to be found.

"But having said all that—such a style would have been lost on the Morecambe audience. The 200 fans packed into The Morecambe Dome—mostly kids—absolutely lapped up the TWA show as they cheered their heroes and booed the villains to their little hearts' contents. The Dome crowd reacted far more to an eye poke or a yell of 'shut up!' from a heel than they would have done for more complicated moves like a somersault plancha or a Michinoku Driver."

I thought my review was fair and balanced. But Conway didn't see it that way.

TWA returned to Morecambe on September 4 2002 and on the day of the event, I phoned The Dome to see if everything was OK for me to get press tickets once again and spoke to the manager Simon Armstrong, who apologetically told me Scott didn't want me to attend the show because he hadn't liked my review of the last one.

Thinking this was a ridiculous situation, Mark Kay and I confronted Scott at the door of The Dome to discuss his grievances face-to-face. We had a perfectly amicable conversation, agreed to disagree, shook hands and he actually let us in. This time, although the crowd was much smaller (around 70) I thought the action was far superior to the previous show. This was thanks mainly to the efforts of Jonny Storm and a solid main event between Robbie Brookside and 'The Page 7 Model' Paul Tyrrell. My review of this show reflected the improvement.

A few weeks later, I read a blog on Brookside's official website. He didn't name me in person, but it was pretty clear he was referring to my less-than-flattering review of the first TWA show. Robbie wasn't happy with my criticism of TWA—one of his main employers at the time. The gist of his on-line rant was that I'd never been in the ring so I had no right to judge. I didn't really understand why he of all people had taken my views so personally, especially as

I'd said Brookside's win over Japanese masked wrestler Kendo Ka Shin was the best match of the night.

So when I called Brookside for the interview, I nervously expected a right Scouse ear-bashing. It soon became clear he didn't have a clue I was the same guy he had an issue with. I always prefer to be upfront and honest in these situations, so I bit the bullet and explained to Robbie that it was me who'd written that review he hated so much.

To my surprise Robbie was cool with my explanation. It turned out he hadn't actually read the review personally. Conway had told him about it and Brookside hadn't been given the full story. We quickly cleared the air, Robbie gave me the interview and, just like at Battle of the Champions, it was a pleasure to listen to his tales. He also explained to me why he feels the way he does about internet fans.

"Fifteen to 20 years ago when I started, computers weren't the in-thing," Brookside told me.

"These fans on the internet used to stand at the back of the hall.

"I do have a website, but I have a guy run it for me. I made it clear to him from the start that I wasn't going to phone up with inside scoops and what-not. In the years that I've been in this job, to me the dressing room is a sacred place and no matter what, that's where it all ends. There are certain people who come into the job in England who take it upon themselves to be the first one out of the dressing room, get on the internet and say all this crap.

"I don't think it's just in wrestling. I've got friends in the music business and apparently it's just as mad. I've got friends who are footballers as well and there's plenty of rumours and s__te that gets stirred up.

"I've survived without the internet so far and I think I can survive without it in future. I don't do a backflip off a top rope and I don't do combinations coming out of my arsehole. I'm a professional wrestler and I just like to be judged on the fact, first and foremost, of how long I've been in the job and the fact that I'm still in the job. That speaks leaps and bounds.

"If these people on the internet are so good and so opinionated, let them get themselves a pair of boots and see what they can do. It's very easy sitting behind a pen-name in their little bedrooms and making comments on what they think is professional wrestling, because professional wrestling changes every three or four years in style.

"If you write an internet thing then I'm sorry if you're playing it by the book, but to me it's easy to slag someone behind a computer monitor. If you can't say nothing decent then don't say nothing at all. I think it's negative to slag people off and I don't like slagging people off. But this is what we have to deal with now and I've had a lot of harder people to deal with in the ring than someone saying negative English behind a computer."

Brookside's words struck a chord with me for the future. But sadly that wasn't the end of the matter. Conway held a grudge about my review and over the next couple of years, as I became more involved with the FWA, he took frequent pot-shots at me on various internet forums, ironically. Scott accused me of journalistic bias towards the FWA (despite the fact I'd never worked for the FWA nor even *seen* a proper FWA show until *after* that first TWA event in Morecambe) and said I didn't belong in the business because I hadn't 'paid my dues'.

Conway quit the British Wrestling business in 2004 and moved to Thailand—yet another promoter to bite the dust. Although I had personal issues with Scott, from a professional standpoint I think his departure was a loss to the British scene. Mark Kay and I learned a lot from observing Scott's approach, which was entirely geared towards attracting families and very different to what we'd seen from Tommy Boyd, Dann Read and Jon Farrer. And it was a philosophy that clearly worked, otherwise Conway wouldn't have lasted as a wrestling promoter for a very respectable 18 years.

Returning to the subject of Farrer, I managed to get an interview with him for WrestlingX two weeks before GWF Aftermath. He came across as a bit cocky but with a good mind for wrestling, very enthusiastic and positive, and with clear goals in mind for the GWF.

Farrer claimed to be an idealist who believed backstage egos, politics and any differences between the British Wrestling veterans and the new generation could be resolved with a pragmatic approach.

He said: "I get on with everybody really well. I try to be a nice guy. I give the old school all the respect in the world and the new school all the respect in the world, and I try to bring all these people together under one roof for one night only, try to mix it together and produce something the fans have never seen before in British Wrestling. If you look at the card for Aftermath from top to bottom, there is something for everybody.

"We're not competition to anybody. We're not competition to Brian Dixon because he's running 30 shows a month. We're not competition to FWA because they are off doing their own thing. We're just trying to have fun."

Sadly, February 2 2003 would turn out to be anything but 'fun' for Jon Farrer.

Mark Kay and I arrived at the King George's Hall in Blackburn at around 3.30pm that day. We immediately saw a crowd of queuing fans outside the building and Farrer on the door, looking harassed. Rather disturbingly, but not entirely unexpectedly, the young promoter was flanked by members of the Lancashire Constabulary, who were frisking fans for weapons as they entered the venue.

You see, Jon had advertised a 'Fans Bring The Weapons Match' between Ian Knoxx and one of Britain's most violent wrestlers, Isaac 'Iceman' Harrop. For such a match, the fans—some of whom were young kids—were encouraged to bring their own household objects to the show for the two wrestlers to use to attack each other.

This was a common practice in ECW and other ultra-violent wrestling promotions in America. But the idea of youngsters bringing such items (which included baking trays lined with stuck-on drawing pins and baseball bats laced with barbed-wire) to a 'family entertainment event' in Lancashire, understandably did not appeal to Blackburn police. It turns out they had been tipped off about Farrer's plans and made sure they were there to confiscate every single one of the homemade weapons.

Then things went from bad to worse for Farrer.

At the afternoon's Fan Fest with the wrestlers (who aside from those already mentioned, included Jonny Storm, Jody Fleisch, Doug Williams, The UK Pitbulls, Five Star Flash, Dirk Feelgood, Johnny Phere, All-Star's James Mason and Mark Sloan) it was noticeable that the wrestling ring had not been set up in the arena. Thinking nothing of it, we left the Fan Fest just after 5pm and headed to Mark Kay's favourite place in the whole world . . . McDonald's, where I was heckled by a gang of wrestling fans while ordering a Big Mac. Yes, my Talk Wrestling notoriety had even spread as far as Blackburn.

But when we returned to the King George's Hall at 6pm for the actual wrestling show, Farrer emerged again and announced to the queuing hordes that the ring hadn't actually arrived. He told us the van driver who was supposed to be bringing the ring had broken down on the motorway. But, claimed the stressed-looking Jon, a replacement ring was on its way, and we should all return at 7pm when the show would *definitely* start as planned.

Mark and I duly killed an hour in the pub, then headed back to the venue and took our seats in the balcony overlooking where the ring was supposed to be—but still wasn't. In yet another surreal twist, instead of the wrestling we'd all come to see, we were then treated to a spur-of-the-moment performance from local comedian Ted Robbins. The star of TV's Phoenix Nights was supposed to be there to watch the show as a wrestling fan. Now the poor guy found himself on the King George's Hall stage, having been roped in to tell jokes in an attempt to entertain an increasingly impatient crowd of 600 wrestling fans who were starting to bay for blood.

By 8.15pm, there was still no sign of a ring. Instead Trent Acid, Johnny Kashmere and Ian Knoxx were in the middle of the arena, improvising a 'war of words' with Storm and Fleisch to hype up their scheduled matches, matches the fans were starting to think would never actually happen. At one stage Farrer sat down at a table, Trent Acid climbed on top and crashed through it, then Knoxx took a swig of whisky and cheered drunkenly as Acid lay motionless. As for Jon, he looked like he wanted the ground to open up and swallow him whole.

"I was backstage that night, and it wasn't particularly tense amongst the wrestlers . . . the only one freaking out was Farrer," said Doug Durdle, aka Doug Williams, in 2012.

"The rest of us were thinking: 'Well, if the ring doesn't turn up then we'll get what we can and then we'll go.' Personally speaking, I'd driven for six or seven hours to get there, but you know what most wrestlers are like. A lot of them would rather have *not* wrestled and got their money.

"In the end, Farrer was going around paying the wrestlers he knew would give him trouble if he didn't pay them. I think I got paid about half what I was supposed to."

At around 9pm, over two hours after the scheduled start time of GWF Aftermath, Jake Roberts came out on stage and told the fans that he was "hissed off". He wasn't the only one. By this time the audience's mood was turning ugly. Then Farrer re-emerged and gave the announcement we had all been expecting. Neither the original ring nor the reserve ring was going to arrive. The show was cancelled.

The fans were livid. Boos and loud abusive chants rained down on Jon Farrer, who cut a forlorn figure as he stood meekly on the King George's Hall stage. In an attempt to pacify the baying mob, Farrer allowed Jake to body slam him hard on the wooden floor, where he laid down to accept a massive leg drop across his chest from the 33-stone Bulk of The UK Pitbulls tag team. It was a fate most of the angry audience felt the young promoter thoroughly deserved.

At this, the bitterly disappointed crowd of fans slowly drifted away, grumbling in discontent, some demanding refunds, others feeling totally, utterly dejected. As for Mark and I, who as members of the press, hadn't paid to get in, we just found the whole episode startlingly surreal.

So that was GWF Aftermath. A big non-event. A debacle. A 'no ring' circus, if you will.

Almost exactly one year after Revival, which had been a day of great hope for the future for the British Wrestling scene, GWF Aftermath saw it hit absolute rock bottom. Newspapers picked up on the story and mocked the wrestling show where the ring failed to turn up. As more information emerged about the ring's mysterious non-appearance, accusations began to fly between wrestlers, fans and promoters on the UKFF and other internet forums, which only served to make the British Wrestling scene look sleazy, cheap and corrupt, and further away from a mainstream TV deal than ever before.

Not long afterwards, Jon Farrer lost his job with Total Wrestling and quit the business. The Dirtbike Kid, Ryan Hewson, Ross Gordon, Tommy Boyd, Scott Conway and now Farrer. All had such big dreams and hopes for the resurrection of British Wrestling. All of them had left it behind either by choice, or following some kind of disastrous failure. It seemed to me the British Wrestling scene had a nasty habit of chewing people up and then spitting them out.

Why on earth did I still want to be part of it?

It was because about two months prior to GWF Aftermath, Alex Shane had offered me the opportunity of a lifetime.

CHAPTER 5

NEW FRONTIERS

In December 2002, about a month after Talk Wrestling was taken off air, Alex Shane telephoned me and asked if I would like to debut in the FWA not as a commentator, not as a writer, not as a radio presenter, but as an actual *performer*. He said he thought I could be "an awesome heel manager". I was knocked sideways by the offer. Naturally, I accepted.

At the time, the FWA was the talk of the UK industry. In amongst all the false dawns, the FWA looked like it really could take British Westling to new heights.

Alex had become 'managing director' of the promotion while sidelined with the neck injury he suffered in March 2002. With the help of Dino Scarlo, Mark Sloan, Elisar Cabrera and others, he began planning a follow-up event to Revival, to be called FWA British Uprising. Alex intended for this event to become so big, it would be a regular fixture on the British Wrestling calendar . . . a much smaller-scale UK equivalent of America's WrestleMania.

To create a big-show aura surrounding this event, FWA hired the famous boxing venue The York Hall in Bethnal Green, London. And they continued the policy of booking overseas performers to get the smarts excited, this time bringing over former ECW stars Balls Mahoney and Jerry Lynn, and an exciting new American talent who went by the name of AJ Styles.

In their most controversial and daring move, they hiked front row ticket prices up to £50 a seat, five times more than the ticket price for an average British Wrestling event. Other promoters, fans and even some of Alex's more sceptical colleagues like Mark Sloan scoffed at this plan. "No-one will ever pay that!" was the general consensus. But they did. It looked like the FWA's high-risk business plan to tailor their product for those smart marks who *were* prepared to shell out for such expensive seats, was paying off after all.

As for me, attracted by the lure of seeing the next step in British Wrestling's rejuvenation, I took a few hours off from a weekend break in London with Sharon and my son Owen to see the show. Like Revival, FWA British Uprising had been hyped up on Talk Wrestling as a simply unmissable happening. And it did not disappoint.

So on Sunday, October 13 2002, I was amongst the rabid crowd of 900 assembled in the historic York Hall. Although it was chilly outside, inside the building the temperature was red-hot. The fans were cramped close together inside this sweatbox and it made for an electric atmosphere, without a doubt the loudest and most raucous crowd I had ever been part of in my life to that point.

I was especially struck by the deafening chants of "F-W-A! F-W-A!" throughout the night, and that there were even more FWA T-Shirts amongst the passionate throng than there had been at Revival. No other British Wrestling promotion had ever been able to sell its own branded merchandise in such numbers. Such was the crazed, almost religious fervour in the audience, I can only imagine this was the closest British equivalent to being inside the ECW Arena in Philadelphia.

"The FWA was indeed British Wrestling's answer to ECW," said Dann Read, who joined me in the crowd that night.

"American Wrestling was at its hottest in 2001 and 2002, and that's when the FWA came around. Wrestling needed to be that hot, to create the number of 'hardcore' fans who made FWA successful. For there to be a subculture in anything, there always has to be a thriving main culture. The audience for British Wrestling is niche, but it was a bigger niche back then because the wrestling audience was bigger overall.

"Plus FWA was new and fresh. That kind of indie wrestling hadn't yet been overexposed over here, like it is now. Everyone around the world was trying to remake ECW. And FWA was like that, with its emphasis on stand-offs and hardcore brawls. Wrestlers used to swear on promos in the FWA. When did you ever see wrestlers swear on a Dixon, a Conway or a John Freemantle (Premier Promotions) show?"

The production values for Uprising, with a proper entranceway and ramp, professional lighting and pyrotechnics, were also rare for a British Wrestling event. And the show itself was an incredible spectacle. Results were as follows:

James Tighe beat Raj Ghosh and Jack Xavier in a three-way, Alex Shane returned in a segment with Dean Ayass and The Old School, The Zebra Kid retained the All-England Title against Hade Vansen, The UK Pitbulls retained the FWA Tag Team Titles against The New Breed after Paul Burchill ran in and destroyed The Breed, Drew McDonald battled Robbie Brookside to a double disqualification in a TWA rules match (Scott Conway was referee), Doug Williams pinned Jerry Lynn, Paul Travell downed Nikita, Ulf Herman beat Balls Mahoney in a No-DQ match, Jonny Storm pinned AJ Styles, Jody Fleisch beat Flash Barker in a ladder match to win the FWA Heavyweight Title.

Although FWA British Uprising only drew half the fans that Revival did, it was a superior event in terms of action. This was helped in part by the red-hot atmosphere generated by the crowd that spurred the combatants on to reach peak form.

The opening three-way, featuring a trio of FWA's brightest young stars in Tighe, Xavier and Ghosh, set the tone with its blindingly-fast, innovative exchanges. Powerhouse newcomer Paul Burchill, a tall, well-muscled and frighteningly agile trainee from the FWA Academy who was yet to have his first proper match, was booked to look like a monster as he annihilated Ashe and Curve of The New Breed in one of the most impressive run-ins I have ever seen. Doug Williams' match with Jerry Lynn was a marvellous display of holds and counter-holds. Wild men Balls Mahoney and Ulf Herman tore the house down with a typically insane ECW-style arena-wide brawl. Jonny Storm and AJ Styles both looked magnificent in their super-slick encounter.

But match of the night honours went to Fleisch and Barker. A phenomenal evening was rounded off with the perfect 'feel good' ending of the FWA's most beloved and talented young star lifting the big title. That night, Jody Fleisch was simply amazing—a human highlight reel of flexibility and athleticism. And he stole the show by performing the most incredible manoeuvre I have ever witnessed live.

Halfway through the match, the Walthamstow daredevil clambered onto the York Hall balcony and then soared off backwards with a moonsault to come crashing down on top of the bullish Barker, who was standing in the middle of a delirious crowd of fans, which included myself. At one point I thought The Phoenix would land on top of me, but he hit the move perfectly on Flash and our section went completely mental in appreciation, chanting "F-W-A! F-W-A!" It was a hell of a moment.

Afterwards, I wrote a review for WrestlingX, which concluded:

"The only problem now is—how can the FWA top this?

"The only way to go one better is to finally achieve that elusive television deal and I certainly hope they do. Mainstream TV audiences deserve to see the FWA in their living rooms as long as they can continue to produce superb quality shows like British Uprising. And the FWA itself deserves such success because everyone in the entire company, from the backroom staff to the boys (wrestlers) out front, works damned hard to create the best possible product for its fans."

I was so impressed, I became a huge FWA supporter overnight. And most who had experienced British Uprising followed suit. In the wrestling press, the show earned rave reviews. Total Wrestling and Power Slam covered Uprising with big colour photo-spreads and gave the event a huge thumbs-up.

Following the success of British Uprising, the rest of the wrestling world began to sit up and take notice of the FWA. Alex Shane had begun negotiations with Ring of Honor, a small but dynamic Philadelphia-based wrestling company that was already building a considerable cult following in the States, to bring over its stars for a huge inter-promotional event back at the York Hall in May 2003. But more on that later.

To cement that FWA was becoming an international wrestling promotion that transcended the UK, Alex Shane pulled off another bold stroke just two weeks after Uprising. In the main event of the FWA's London Calling event on October 25 2002 at Walthamstow, he switched the FWA Title from Jody Fleisch to the acclaimed US independent star 'The Fallen Angel' Christopher Daniels in a three-way main event also including Doug Williams.

Having a bona fide international star as champion like Daniels, who had wrestled for WWE, WCW and New Japan, and would later make his name in TNA, enabled Alex to label his main title as not just the FWA British Heavyweight Championship, but the FWA *World* Heavyweight Championship. Daniels' involvement increased the prestige of both the belt and the company. Plus the sheer unpredictability of the American's win, as virtually everyone thought Fleisch would retain, had FWA's core fan base, yep—those pesky internet smart marks—absolutely buzzing.

The FWA squeezed in another event just before Christmas, the creatively-titled Seasons Beatings on December 15 at Broxbourne Civic Hall in Hertfordshire. Jerry Lynn made a shock return just before the end of the show to defeat Doug Williams and AJ Styles in a triple threat main event. Again, reviews were glowing.

Thanks to British Uprising and these two follow-up shows, the FWA had put British Wrestling right back on the international map. And all of a sudden, it was cool for a wrestling fan to be a *British* Wrestling fan.

So when Alex Shane gave me a chance to be a part of all this, it was a no-brainer!

We concocted an unusual plan to prepare for my debut, scheduled for FWA New Frontiers at Walthamstow Hall on Saturday, February 8 2003, designed to play off the heat I had on the UKFF following my rants on Talk Wrestling.

The idea was that Alex and I would have a war of words on the internet. During my regular blogs on WrestlingX, I would blame Alex for the demise of Talk Wrestling and even start a campaign to get the show back on-air with me as the host. Then, feeling betrayed, he would fire back during his 'Shane's Shooting Gallery' column on the FWA website, where he would say I wasn't welcome any more at FWA events.

This would lead to my shock debut on February 8 as new manager of The UK Pitbulls, whom The Showstealer and his tag team partner Ulf Herman had beaten for the FWA Tag Team Titles at London Calling. This had been Alex's comeback match from his supposedly career-threatening neck injury, which—ahem!—had turned out not to be career-threatening after all.

Launching a new storyline on the internet was a very 21st Century approach and also a controversial and risky one. But Alex again wanted to break new ground and I thought the idea fitted perfectly with The Truth gimmick. It was only natural that an egotistical journalist would take written pot-shots at a big and dangerous wrestler from the safety of behind his keyboard. The fans certainly seemed to buy it as a 'shoot'. In other words, many believed Alex and I had fallen out for real.

Alex and I spoke regularly on the phone in the lead-up to New Frontiers 2003. In fact the first person I called after leaving the King George's Hall in Blackburn on the night of GWF Aftermath—six days before my scheduled FWA debut—was Alex Shane. He answered straight away, yawning, and said I had woken him from a nap. But he listened as I recounted the events of GWF Aftermath and seemed genuinely shocked at what had transpired.

I also telephoned Jon Farrer in the days following Aftermath, just to see how he was. He was, understandably, at a low. His name was mud, he was the laughing stock of the UK scene, he had various creditors on his back, and his life had basically collapsed around him.

The day after the Blackburn farce, fans on the UKFF were out for blood and looking for someone to blame—with Farrer as number one scapegoat. While I sympathised with those who had travelled long distances and spent hard-earned cash to see a show that never happened, I also felt sorry for Jon. He had lost a whole lot more—psychologically, financially and in terms of his reputation. He had experienced a wrestling promoter's worst nightmare. He had entrusted someone to deliver the ring and that person had failed him.

That someone was FWA referee and wrestling ring owner, Steve Lynskey.

In the days following Aftermath, all kinds of rumours were flying around the internet about why Lynskey hadn't made it to East Lancashire. At the time, the rotund ref was adamant his van had broken down en route and his mobile phone had conked out. But some believed there was a more sinister explanation for his absence . . . that others were involved . . . others who wanted to sabotage the show.

Meanwhile, the unforgiving UKFF responded with outrage towards both Farrer and Lynskey. Things became so heated that Scott Conway, that great protector of the UK scene, posted the disgraced referee's mobile number on the Forum for fans to ring for refunds!

"Nobody ever did call me though," Lynskey told me in 2012.

"And it's not like people in the business stopped talking to me either. Within a week Conway phoned me and asked: 'Can you come and do Weymouth, pal?'"

But there was certainly a furore on the forums. During all this online kerfuffle, the FWA posted a statement inviting any fans who'd had tickets for GWF Aftermath to come to New Frontiers for free. They also announced that Lynskey was suspended from refereeing duties and would not be at the show. Basically, the FWA positioned themselves as the knights in shining armour, willing to pick up the pieces from GWF Aftermath to save 'the good name of British Wrestling'.

The day before New Frontiers, Alex called me to inform me of a change in plans. I would still be debuting as manager of The UK Pitbulls. But I would not be alone. Joining me as their co-manager would be, of all people, *Jon Farrer.*

I had a sinking feeling in my stomach. I would have to share my big debut with someone else. Perhaps Alex didn't have that much faith in my abilities after all.

But Alex explained that Farrer had so much heat coming out of Aftermath, it would be foolish not to capitalise on it by introducing him as an FWA character. It also made sense for Britain's two most controversial wrestling writers (from rival magazines) to form an alliance.

The night before New Frontiers, myself and Mark Kay stayed overnight at our old school friend Paul Grace's flat in Watford. I hardly slept a wink that night, I was so excited.

I remember feeling overawed as I set foot inside an FWA venue for the very first time not as a fan, but as a part of the show. After all, I was an outsider. A newcomer. A non-athlete. Someone who had just walked into British Wrestling's best-known company, untrained, whose only prior experience of working on a live wrestling event was my radio commentary stint in Ipswich and who (yes, you're right, Mr Conway) hadn't paid his dues. A 31-year-old married father, actually setting foot into this bizarre fantasy world after years of being mesmerised by its magic.

I was also a real-life journalist. Surely the wrestlers would be extremely wary of me? Maybe they would think I didn't deserve to be there? Maybe they would wonder if my real motive for being there was to dish some dirt for Power Slam? As all these thoughts raced through my head that Saturday afternoon in the Walthamstow Hall, I was prepared for the possibility of receiving a hard time from the FWA workers. Maybe even rejection

I knew the 'done thing' for any newcomer to a wrestling promotion was to go around the building and shake hands with absolutely everybody. It's accepted 'dressing room etiquette'. So that's what I did. As crew members bustled around setting up the ring for the evening's entertainment, I remember saying hello for the first time to FWA performers Raj Ghosh, his then-girlfriend Jenna (Buttercup the maid), James Tighe, Jack Xavier, Andy Simmonz, Ulf Herman, Paul Burchill and Paul Travell.

I also said hello to people I'd met before like Dane 'The Duke of Danger' Hardie, 'The Messiah' Brandon Thomas, Tony Giles, FWA's music guru Ralph Cardall, Ian 'DaSciple' Da Silva and of course, my new charges The UK Pitbulls—two behemoth brothers from Norfolk called Mike and Dave Waters who used the ring names Bulk and Big Dave. The 'UKP' billed themselves as 'Europe's Largest Tag Team' because they tipped the scales at a mammoth combined 55 stone. Everyone seemed friendly enough and happy to accept me. I breathed a huge sigh of relief.

I was also welcomed with open arms by my fellow heel manager, Dean Ayass. Dean, a jovial 26-year-old from Brighton who had also been recruited into the wrestling business several years earlier by Alex Shane, told me to relax and have fun. This was also a big night for Dean, who would be in the corner of Mark Sloan and Flash Barker during their FWA Tag Team Title match with Alex Shane and Ulf Herman.

The climax to this match, ending the long-running rivalry between Dean's Old School faction of veterans and the New School upstarts led by Alex, called for The Twisted Genius to take a steel chair shot to the head. As a non-wrestler, this wasn't something he was used to, and he had to be concerned. So for him to take time out to make me feel at ease was very much appreciated.

Alex, meanwhile, had a distracted look about him, as if his mind was racing at a million miles an hour because he had a million and one things to do. But he broke off from a conversation with his then-girlfriend Nikita (real name Katarina Waters, or Kat for short) to explain the plan for my debut.

Talking in his usual dazzlingly-fast patter, he told me I would interrupt himself and Ulf after they had successfully defended their titles, cut a promo on them and then introduce Farrer. We would entice Alex to come after us, only it would turn out to be a trap. The Pitbulls would jump The Showstealer and give him a beating. It sounded good to me.

By now I was starting to feel at home in my strange new environment, as I explored every nook and cranny of the Walthamstow Hall. I even entered the wrestlers' dressing room for the first time to be overpowered by the soon-to-be familiar icy-sweet smell of heat rub and the sight of Pitbull Bulk's 33 stone bare backside as he got changed. This vision of Big Mike's wobbly derriere almost scarred me for life . . . as did a rookie error which, looking back now, makes me cringe with embarrassment.

The actor 'Bomber' Pat Roach, star of the hit TV show Auf Wiedersehen, Pet and a former top grappler from the World of Sport era, had been invited to New Frontiers as the FWA's new storyline authority figure or Commissioner. After getting wind that I was about to meet the legendary Mr Roach, a work colleague from The Visitor had asked me to get his autograph.

So I waited for what I felt was an opportune moment backstage during the show, and approached the former Raiders of the Lost Ark baddie, hoping to acquire his signature. But as I politely introduced myself, Roach completely fobbed me off and made me look a right fool. That will teach me for still acting like a fan, when the rules had now changed.

I never did get that autograph. Sadly Pat Roach died of cancer the following year.

Time ticked on, into the second-half of the show. In a cramped corridor backstage at the Walthamstow Hall, Jon Farrer and I must have worn out the floorboards, so frantic was our pacing up and down in the moments before we went out in front of the FWA crowd.

We repeatedly recited our lines both to each other and then to ourselves. I was cocooned in concentration as I muttered my promo over and over again from written notes, so much that I barely noticed former WCW star Juventud Guerrera warming up in the corner in readiness for his match with Jonny Storm, and Jerry Lynn putting me to shame by cutting a snappy improvised promo to camera, in just one take.

All I kept thinking as I went over and over my planned speech, was that I couldn't afford to mess this up. I *had* to get this right. Alex was showing so much faith in me. I didn't want to let him down.

All kinds of thoughts and memories flooded my brain . . . from my first ever live wrestling show at the Central Pier in Morecambe as a 12-year-old kid watching the likes of Big Daddy, Jimmy Breaks and the amazing deaf wrestler Alan Kilby, to sitting ringside at The Morecambe Dome every Thursday night during a British Wrestling summer season with Mark Kay and my other teenage cronies, to pestering Sharon to ask her Uncle Mick to tape WWF Summerslam 1989 for me, because he was the only person we knew back then who had Sky TV.

I then recalled actually sitting down at Mark's house to watch Summerslam '89, our first experience of a televised WWF pay-per-view, and being blown away by the the the action, the razzmatazz, The Ultimate Warrior's superhero physique, the crisp technical excellence of Bret Hart, the freakish size of Andre the Giant, the speed and co-ordination of The Rockers, and the mass hysteria that greeted Hulk Hogan's mere entrance into the Meadowlands Arena.

Then I remembered sitting at Revival, almost exactly a year previously. As a fan. With no ambitions whatsoever to actually step out in front of a wrestling crowd as I was right now with a live microphone, dressed in a black leather jacket, shirt, tie and trousers, carrying a notepad and pen as my journalistic 'props', and absolutely bricking it. This had all happened so fast. It was like being thrown in to the deep end of a pool at my first swimming lesson, without any armbands.

I'm no fan of rap music. But for some strange reason, the words of Eminem's number one hit 'Lose Yourself' popped into my head.

"If you had one shot, one opportunity, to seize everything you ever wanted, would you capture it, or just let it slip?"

The FWA wasn't exactly the WWE. And Walthamstow Hall wasn't exactly Madison Square Garden. But by lowly British Wrestling standards, this was the *big time*.

"Greg, you're on!"

I remember Dino Scarlo telling me it was time to go. Immediately behind the curtain it was dark and foreboding, save for the glimmer of light and the noise of 500 wrestling fans beyond it. I heard the faint echo of Alex Shane addressing the crowd, celebrating his and Ulf's win over Sloan and Barker, their decimation of Dean Ayass and their final, conclusive victory over his Old School faction, after a war that had raged in FWA rings for a full year.

I took a few steps forward. I gulped. Then I stuck my nose in the air, sniffed disdainfully and swaggered towards a gap in the curtains. The microphone was at my lips, ready to interrupt Alex Shane mid-speech.

I sauntered on through the darkness and emerged onto an arena stage swathed in light, in front of a crowd of wrestling fans for the very first time. And I said . . .

"Stop the press! Shut your mouths! And listen . . . to Britain's Number One Wrestling Journalist, Greg 'The Truth' Lambert!"

CHAPTER 6

THE FAMILY WAY

I have never re-watched my debut at New Frontiers 2003 because the show was never released on DVD. But this is what I remember of it.

Greg 'The Truth' Lambert strutted onto the Walthamstow stage and paused, soaking in the atmosphere. I looked up and saw Alex Shane and Ulf Herman, dots on the horizon in the ring about 50 yards away, looking puzzled. I looked down, and saw a row of fans, their faces twisted with hate, making uncouth gestures at me, screaming their disapproval at my very presence. Then I heard a roar that was ear-splitting in its ferocity.

"F___ YOU, LAMBERT!"

Followed by a staccato, football-style clap, clap, clap-clap-clap.

And again.

"F___ YOU, LAMBERT!"

(Clap, clap, clap-clap-clap).

Oh yeah. They knew who I was, all right. And they despised me.

Our internet angle had worked. I was a hated wrestling villain.

The adrenalin pumping through my body, I spat a venomous tirade in the direction of Alex Shane. I can't remember exactly what I said, but it was along the lines of that Alex couldn't keep me away from New Frontiers and I was here to take over, but I hadn't come alone. Most importantly, I didn't stumble over my words. My verbal delivery felt larger-than-life, confident and charismatic. And the crowd continued to give me the desired reaction. They were booing me out of the building.

Then I introduced my cohort, Mr Farrer. Jon arrived to a similar gauntlet of hate and we embraced, with a tight, hammy cuddle, shamelessly ripped off from Vince McMahon and Eric Bischoff's 'hug heard round the world' on WWE RAW the previous summer.

Unfortunately for Jon, he *did* falter during his promo. He stuttered and struggled. Then his microphone conked out mid-sentence. Apparently he'd left his mobile phone switched on in his pocket and someone had telephoned him at that exact moment, causing a power surge that cut the sound feed to the mic. Steve Lynskey would later claim he'd phoned Farrer from home, as a practical joke. The fans jeered the hapless Jon.

Alex's expression changed from one of shocked confusion to what he was really feeling at that moment—frustration that the segment seemed to be falling apart. He angrily gestured from his position inside the ring and even from 50 yards away, I could tell he wanted us to hurry up and finish the promo. The problem was, we still hadn't delivered all of our pre-prepared lines. And we were too inexperienced to improvise. So we carried on talking.

Eventually Alex lost patience, climbed through the ropes and stormed up the rampway to grab Farrer. On cue, Bulk and Big Dave from The Pitbulls ambled down the ramp and flattened The Showstealer, laying him out with their big splash/leg drop combination. I managed to deliver some passable pretend stomps to Shane's back before I stood over him, cackling in triumph as the crowd booed vociferously, before Ulf made the save and our gang fled to the back—our dirty work done.

That was it. Ordeal over. I momentarily felt a sense of total exhilaration.

But when Alex returned backstage, he seemed upset with how the angle had panned out. "Your promos went far too long," he scowled. I felt deflated, while still feeling satisfied with my own contribution—especially considering I was an untried first-timer in that situation.

But I also received encouragement from other members of the FWA dressing room, who told me I'd done well. Even Simon Lilsboy popped his head around the curtain once the show had finished and was his usual positive self. "I didn't know you had that in you!" he laughed.

The full results from Greg 'The Truth' Lambert's debut show were as follows:

Raj Ghosh beat Chris Justice, JX beat Duke of Danger, Hade Vansen and James Tighe in a four-way, Zebra Kid and Robbie Brookside fought to a double-disqualification, Jonny Storm downed Juventud Guerrera, Nikita beat Paul Travell, Alex Shane and Ulf Herman retained the FWA Tag Team Titles over Flash Barker and Mark Sloan, Doug Williams beat Jerry Lynn in an Iron Man Match.

As I collected together my belongings ready to leave, I noticed that a line of wrestlers and staff was forming along the corridor outside the dressing room where Alex and Dino were holding a post-show meeting. This, I would come to realise, was the 'FWA wages queue'. After every single show, FWA wrestlers would wait in a line, then be summoned one at a time into the dressing room to receive a critique of their performance that night before receiving their pay-off for the evening's work. This lengthy process meant that some FWA wrestlers had to wait hours after the show before getting paid . . . assuming they got paid at all.

I didn't get paid for my debut. Just like with Dann Read at Dawn of a New Era, I had not discussed any payment with Alex beforehand. I'd just been flattered to be chosen and happy to be part of the FWA. As a newcomer, I didn't feel comfortable with queuing for money—especially because I thought Alex loathed our angle and would never use me again. Besides, Mark Kay was waiting for me outside. Never one for post-show socialising, Mark was bound to be in a hurry to catch the train back to Watford.

So after saying a few goodbyes, I left Walthamstow Hall, pushing past a crowd of fans who were hanging around hoping the wrestlers would come out to sign autographs. They booed me, so I blanked them. Hey, a good heel stays in character even when the show is over.

As we walked briskly towards Walthamstow tube station, I asked Mark his opinion on how my performance had come across.

Now Mark, my best friend of 30 years, is the not the kind of person to give away his thoughts and feelings too readily. He is very much an introspective and analytical character. He is also reluctant to dish out praise, especially where I'm concerned, because he knows I have an ego that needs stroking. Instead, Mark prefers to chop me down a peg or two where he can, rather than fan the flames of my boastful nature.

"You did all right," came the grudging reply. In Mark's language, that means I must have been brilliant.

About an hour later, I received a text message from Alex Shane. I shuddered at the thought of what it might contain, but was pleasantly surprised.

"You did great tonight mate. You're a natural. We're going to have a lot of fun together."

Heavens above, he actually thought I was good! And he wasn't the only one.

Internet and magazine reviews of my own personal performance were generally positive. Comments on the UKFF included "The FWA's new number one heel was born", "Lambert was full of himself, nerdy and awesomely hammy" and "he was surprisingly great on the microphone". I was also pleased to see a rare review of a British show in Power Slam by my colleague Mo Chatra, who wrote that I "performed well". Now that was praise indeed coming from PS!

I was very proud indeed of the heat I got at New Frontiers 2003, and I'm proud of the fact that we launched the Shane-Lambert feud on the worldwide web. I can't recall an instance of any other long-running and successful wrestling storyline—as ours would develop into—being introduced in that way.

Although New Frontiers 2003 was my wrestling baptism, it turned out to be Jon Farrer's swansong. Jon soon moved to America and has rebuilt his life. I'm pleased. Jon clearly had his enemies on the British scene, but I always liked him. I bumped into him for the first time in eight years at an independent show in 2011 in Preston, of all places, and he greeted me with a warm smile and a handshake. He looked tanned, happy and very healthy. That's what getting out of the wrestling business can do for you.

Much of the other post-show praise from observers was reserved for the top two matches at New Frontiers—Jonny Storm v Juventud Guerrera and Doug Williams v Jerry Lynn. At the time, the FWA was attracting legions of fans mainly because of the high quality of the wrestling matches on the card.

Traditionally, a wrestling match tends to work best when a 'babyface' (good guy) is pitted against a heel. That way the fans have someone to cheer and someone to boo, so they are more likely to get emotionally involved in the outcome of the match.

But as you'll have already noticed, Alex Shane was never a slave to tradition. Instead, he often matched two talented babyfaces against each other. And it worked, especially when a Brit wrestled a well-known opponent from overseas; as in the case of Storm-Guerrera and Williams-Lynn. The sheer quality of the action, combined with the fact that these were usually first-time encounters between guys who had never wrestled each other before, not to mention the UK v USA dynamic, would generate huge excitement in the paying audience . . . and in the British wrestlers too.

"I used to love wrestling the imports, like Jerry Lynn, Juvi Guerrera and Super Crazy," recalled Jonny Storm.

"I've always been a great proponent of British Wrestling and Alex also knew we had the talent in this country. But the Americans were needed to generate that extra bit of interest, to take it to the next level above being just another all-British show. It was great to have the experience wrestling all these different guys, it got us more publicity, and that meant the company made more money and could put on more shows."

One problem the FWA did have in early 2003, though, was a real shortage of heels, especially now Dean Ayass's Old School stable had been conquered and disbanded. There was The Duke of Danger, a snobbish 'English noble from Hampton Court' and his sidekick the butler Simmonz, but they were more comic baddies than really hated villains. But there weren't many others on the FWA roster who the fans truly loathed. Someone who they might pay money to see get their just desserts.

I thought Greg 'The Truth' Lambert could fill that gap in the market. And thankfully, Alex Shane agreed.

A few weeks before FWA Crunch in March 2003, Alex phoned to say he was going in a new direction with me because he'd decided to stop using The UK Pitbulls. As you know, the FWA's core fan base was the smart marks and most smart marks hated the UKP. They thought Bulk and Big Dave were too big (as if anyone in the larger-than-life world of wrestling could be *too* big!) wrestled too ponderously and their style didn't fit in with the FWA. I felt sad that The Pitbulls wouldn't be around, even though it did mean I wouldn't be confronted by Bulk's ample naked posterior in the changing rooms again.

But then Alex explained that he would advertise an FWA Tag Team Title match pitting himself and Ulf Herman against The UKP, with the lovely Nikita as guest ring announcer. I would come out, explain that I'd only used The Pitbulls at New Frontiers as a decoy, and introduce my *real* business associates, The Family, who would then attack Nikita in a heinous act of man-on-woman violence. Under my leadership, The Family would then go on to beat Shane and Herman for the FWA Tag Team Titles.

I was overjoyed. I would be the manager of the tag team champions, in only my second ever wrestling appearance? And of The Family? The Family!

I said earlier that there weren't many effective baddies in the FWA, but The Family was slowly starting to fit that description. Based on the real-life cults led by evil religious fanatics like David Koresh and Charles Manson, The Family was bossed by a lean, long-haired wrestler from Birmingham called 'The Messiah' Brandon Thomas. The Messiah, so-named because of his resemblance to Jesus, had spent the previous few months recruiting members for his Family.

Babyface wrestlers Ian Da Silva, 'Solid Gold' Scott Parker and 'Hazardous' Paul Travell had all been losing a lot of FWA matches. They were lost sheep in the FWA and so needed something—or someone—to boost their careers. So in the storyline they became Ian DaSciple, plain old Scott Parker and 'The Righteous' Paul Travell who one-by-one, turned to the dark side and joined The Family. They now followed The Messiah around, brainwashed to do his bidding. They all wore black T-Shirts with an inverted crucifix logo. At some shows, they even came to the ring carrying burning wooden crosses. Controversial religious imagery, certainly, but it got them attention.

"I was unsure about The Family gimmick at first," recalled Paul Travell.

"I just wanted to wrestle, but Alex said he had nothing for me to do. It was the only way I was going to get on the shows. So I begrudgingly did it, and grew to like it. It turned out to be the best storyline I ever had . . . a very simple concept."

I particularly loved The Family's entrance theme tune, penned and performed by Ralph Cardall. Beginning with the chorus hook from Jesus Christ Superstar, it then morphed into a sinister piece of music containing the lyrics: "We are The Family, we steal your souls and imprison the free . . . kneel before your true Messiah . . . see the light!" Every time I heard the music hit before The Family's entrance, I got goosepimples.

I'm not the religious type. So I wasn't offended by The Family in the slightest. Some people were, though, which is why most FWA venues banned them from doing the burning crosses gimmick. I can kind of understand their view. The whole religious cult thing was meant to be entertainment, but it *was* rather near-the-knuckle.

But it did make perfect sense for such a controversial group to recruit a journalist (an expert in PR) as their manager and mouthpiece. And Alex obviously had enough faith in my verbal skills to put me with them.

When I saw The Family members at Broxbourne that day, they all seemed really enthusiastic to be working with me and very excited about the thought of winning the titles. I got on well with all of them. They were down-to-earth guys who all had a great sense of humour—especially Scott Parker, who I really hit it off with, and who wore the best Hawaiian shirts in British Wrestling.

For the angle, we would also be joined by Paul 'Ashe' Dew—formerly of two-time FWA Tag Team Champs The New Breed. Ashe had turned on his partner Curve that night to join our cult instead. This swelled The Family's number to six. We were a true wrestling stable, almost a British version of WCW's New World Order, and I was the manager! I really had to pinch myself.

In an even more exciting, although slightly daunting twist, the angle called for Nikita to slap me hard across the face.

I'd suggested to Alex that the segment would have more impact if I verbally ripped into Nikita, revealing in a 'Truth World Exclusive' that she was Alex's real-life girlfriend, which had never been announced in FWA's storyline world. I would then accuse her of sleeping her way to the top of the FWA. She would slap me in retaliation, The Family would then attack her and set her up for their patented 'Crucifixion Chair Shot' where two Family members would hold her arms outstretched while another blasted her over the head with a chair—nasty! But Shane and Herman would rescue her in the nick of time to set up the title match.

Here is where my embarrassing lack of experience in such situations got the better of me again. I insisted that Nikita should actually slap me in the face backstage before the show, so I could understand how it felt before doing it in front of the audience.

"Are you sure?" she said.

"Absolutely," I replied.

So she reared back and cracked me hard—only to accidentally catch me square on the jawbone with her wrist. My jaw ached for days afterwards, Kat's one tough gal. But that taught me to have more confidence in Alex's ethos of it'll be all right on the night. By the way, we then had another practice run for good luck . . . and this time Kat nailed me perfectly.

When it came to doing it for real, we executed the angle to perfection. I came out and whipped the Broxbourne crowd into a frenzy of hatred, then—acting like an absolute sleazeball—got right in Nikita's face and basically called her a cheap whore. She slapped me beautifully, so well in fact that my glasses flew off my face and landed in the fourth row right where, miraculously, Dann Read happened to be sitting with Mark 'Five Star Flash' Belton. Dann calmly picked my specs up and handed them back to me later, saving them from being sold by some FWA fan for £1 on Ebay, most probably.

The Family then pounded Nikita down, as planned, before the cavalry of Shane and Herman arrived. At the time, Alex and Ulf had earned the collective nickname of 'The Showswearers' from FWA fans, thanks to Ulf's liberal use of the F-word on the microphone. At Crunch 2003, the foul-mouthed German excelled himself as he launched a furious tirade of expletives at The Family after we fled the ring. Backstage, Ulf was a cool guy. But once in the arena, he was a dangerous, unpredictable weapon-wielding maniac who scared the living hell out of me—for real.

The match itself was my first as a ringside manager. I didn't have any wrestling or managing training whatsoever, which probably makes me unique amongst top-level British Wrestling performers. I just did what came naturally and what I'd seen Bobby Heenan and Jimmy Hart do on TV for years, throwing in a smidgeon of Ross 'The Boss' and a sprinkling of two of my heroes, those charismatic showmen Freddie Mercury and Chris Eubank.

Whenever my team of Paul Travell and Scott Parker gained the advantage, I strutted around arrogantly like a pompous peacock, riling up the fans with a smug grin or a sarcastic comment. But when the much bigger duo of Shane and Herman turned the tide, I raised my eyebrows in horror, twisted my mouth in despair, stomped around with frantic concern for my team and pretended to scribble notes on my writing pad—as if coming up with a new tactical plan on the fly.

By the way, I love Broxbourne Civic Hall as wrestling venue. The Hertfordshire theatre is only small and compact, with capacity for about 450-500 fans, but its closed-in lay-out with tiered seating on either side of the ring generated a fantastic crowd atmosphere. I always really enjoy performing there. Unlike many other sardine tin changing areas at other wrestling venues, there was also plentiful space backstage for the large FWA contingent of performers to spread out, across a corridor of four dressing rooms. Alex and Dino always took over the far dressing room at Broxbourne, which doubled as the FWA office while the rest of the performers milled around in the corridor, rehearsing their upcoming matches.

I also loved my mutual relationship with the Broxbourne fans. They loved to hate me, and I loved to hate them too.

The match on March 16 2003 was a riotous brawl and gripped the spectators from beginning to end. At one point The Showswearers and The Family actually left the ring and fought into the Broxbourne crowd. Taking some pre-match advice from Dean Ayass, I climbed into the ring to keep out of the way for my own safety, and watched as Paul Travell climbed to the top tier of the Civic Hall seating area then hit a picture-perfect flying DDT on Shane, driving him head-first into the wooden stage. I then winced as Ulf, who as a former ECW star was an expert in the Extreme, smashed poor Ashe in the head with 'the hardest chair shot in pro wrestling'. There was no illusion here. Ulf smacked Ashe full force in the cranium.

The finish called for Alex to set up a table and drag me into the ring. He then hauled me onto his shoulders, hoping to splatter me through the wood with his finisher the One Night Stand. Thankfully Scott Parker saved me as planned, before Travell picked Alex up and drove him through the table with a spinebuster. With Ulf having been taken out by the rest of The

Family, all that remained was for 'The Righteous One' to nimbly ascend to the top rope and dive on Alex's chest with his 'Bloodshot' flying splash. Cockily, Parker made the cover with just his fingertip—because Alex wanted The Family to get a dominant win to establish the group as a real threat.

One. Two. Three. The FWA had brand new Tag Team Champions.

Afterwards, we were all really happy with how the match had gone. I was particularly impressed with the chemistry between Alex and Paul Travell, who although deadly rivals in the squared circle, were great mates away from the ring.

In fact, the whole show was a belter, which many fans rated as one of the best FWA events ever. Full results of Crunch 2003 were:

James Tighe pinned Hade Vansen, JX beat The Zebra Kid to win the All-England Title but the decision was then reversed when JX was revealed as the suspended Jack Xavier, Juventud Guerrera downed Jody Fleisch, Simmonz pinned Raj Ghosh, Doug Williams pinned James Tighe to earn a shot at the FWA Title, The Family beat Alex Shane and Ulf Herman to win the FWA Tag Team Titles, Jonny Storm pinned Jerry Lynn to win the XPW European Title then turned heel on Jody Fleisch.

There were other talking points following the show. Everyone was concerned for the health of Phil 'Flash' Barker, who was rushed to hospital after being taken ill in the dressing room before his scheduled match with Doug Williams. Thankfully, Flash—a very popular veteran who everyone in the FWA admired—was OK. Young James Tighe stepped in to face The Anarchist and did his future prospects no harm with his solid performance.

We also marvelled at the popularity of Andy Simmonz, the wrestling butler. Simmonz's role as The Duke of Danger's manservant, who wrestled in a waistcoat, bow tie and trousers, was intended as a mid-card comedy attraction. Yet the stocky sidekick managed to elicit the biggest ovation on the entire show. This unexpected devotion of the FWA fans was christened 'Simmonzamania'.

The continuing development of Paul Burchill was also creating a stir. At 6ft4 and over 20 stone, Burchill (who worked as a primary school teacher away from wrestling) had the kind of power and physique that most British wrestlers simply didn't possess. But what made the 23-year-old rookie stand out was his ability to execute jaw-droppingly agile moves like a standing moonsault and a running shooting star press.

At Crunch 2003, Paul used this spectacular arsenal to absolutely cream Steve Lynskey, who had been welcomed back into the FWA fold with open arms after his one-show suspension. The disgraced official was an understandably popular choice of victim with the fans. The FWA faithful went berserk for this latest Burchill intervention, chanting his name over and over. Remember, the guy hadn't even wrestled an actual match yet. A fantastic example of FWA booking brilliance, and testimony to Steve Lynskey's ability as a referee the fans loved to hate. Just like American referee Earl Hebner in 1997 after he cheated Bret Hart out of a WWF World Championship match in one of wrestling's most notorious incidents, the unrepentant villain of the No Ring Circus used his new-found notoriety to transform himself into one of the biggest heels in British Wrestling.

I was actually present that night for a brief backstage exchange between Alex and Lynskey which seemed a little odd. Shane walked past as I was introducing myself to Steve, who caught the FWA booker's attention and said: "Thanks for having me back, Alex!" The Showstealer furrowed his brow in confusion at first, then grinned and replied: "Don't worry about it."

Jonny Storm's own heel turn on his pal Jody Fleisch also got the fans talking and Alex hoped their ensuing feud would last for at least a year. Then six days after FWA Crunch, Doug Williams reclaimed the FWA Title from Christopher Daniels on a Ring of Honor show in the USA. The championship changing hands on foreign soil was another major happening that increased the global prestige of the FWA. These were certainly exciting times.

As for me, I was now an integral part of Britain's most talked-about and revolutionary wrestling promotion in years. And I even bravely took my place in the FWA wages queue outside Alex and Dino's dressing room after Crunch had ended, meaning that I received my first pro wrestling wage packet. My pay-off was a measly £20. But at the time, I wasn't complaining.

As manager of the FWA Tag Team Champions, I felt on top of the world.

CHAPTER 7

THE PROMOTER

Every Thursday night during the summers of 1991 and 1992, Mark Kay and I went to The Morecambe Dome to watch wrestling with our gang of best mates Daniel Stembridge, Jason Brown, Robert Dent and Paul Grace. The six of us were inseparable back then, in fact we're all still good pals today, and we'd join forces on those wondrous Thursday nights to boo the heroes and cheer the villains, basically doing everything a wrestling fan *isn't* supposed to do in some kind of cocksure attempt to get ourselves noticed by the performers. We christened ourselves 'The Rulebreakers' Posse', we behaved like big obnoxious kids and I have to shamefully admit, we had a whale of a time doing it!

I have such great memories of those Thursday night summer shows . . . . like getting an autograph from future WWF superstar Steve 'William' Regal . . . Belfast wrestling legend Dave 'Fit' Finlay and his then-wife Princess Paula propping up the bar after his match . . . the mammoth Giant Haystacks telling me to "Eff off, four eyes!" . . . booing Big Daddy (who still gave us a big smile and a thumbs up, bless his heart) . . . ridiculing a smiley Irish babyface called Tony Stewart every single week for the crime of daring to wear a girlie pink singlet . . . and the incident where we finally went too far, and our insults and general disdain for the good guys enraged one wrestler so much, he demanded we meet him outside The Dome for a *real* fight.

His name was Johnny Angel. But more on him later.

A tiny coastal resort 25 miles north of Preston and an hour's drive from Manchester, Morecambe had been steeped in wrestling folklore for decades. In the 1960s, ITV World of Sport's weekly wrestling slot sometimes aired from the town's Winter Gardens ballroom, including a show broadcast on July 27 1966 just days before England won the football World Cup (headlined by Albert Wall v Ian Campbell and Jack Dempsey v Vic Faulkner). One popular competitor at the Winter Gardens in those days was the Canadian wrestler and true Mohawk Indian chief Billy Two Rivers. Whilst visiting Morecambe, this war-dancing warrior romanced a local girl and they had a child who grew up to become famous international designer Wayne Hemingway. Morecambe is also the place where the fearsome British Wrestling villain Steve Logan, famed as the tag team partner of Mick McManus, lived out his final days before his death in 2003. There is so much wrestling history in my tiny coastal home town.

"I can remember coming to Morecambe quite a lot as a child and I always have fond memories," Robbie Brookside told me in 2011.

"Me dad would bring me because Blackpool was more expensive. People can call Morecambe the poor man's Blackpool all they want, but I had so many happy times there.

"I remember wrestling Mike Bennett in 1983 at The Carleton in Morecambe and my eye came up like a plum. I also got a cauliflower ear wrestling Keith Martinelli in Morecambe once. Me mum wasn't too pleased about that. I used to wrestle at Pontins at Morecambe too. We used to do an afternoon show there and it used to be heaving. It's where I learned how to work a crowd, in places like Pontins and The Carleton.

"And even when I was going down the 'dark path' with the FWA in Morecambe, I always really enjoyed it. It's a special place. The Dome was a really great place for me to wrestle. I think I started there the year it first opened (in 1980) . . . Orig Williams was the promoter back then."

Throughout the 1980s and '90s, this funny little Dome-shaped venue by the sea continued to attract the biggest names in the wrestling biz. We saw Daddy, Haystacks, Regal, Finlay, Marty Jones and even the late 'British Bulldog' Davey Boy Smith, arguably the biggest British Wrestling star of all-time, who headlined at The Dome in summer 1994 just two years after he main evented WWF Summerslam at Wembley Stadium in front of 80,000 people. And when Brian Dixon brought All-Star to The Dome a few times at the turn of the century, one October 2000 event featured an appearance by the near-600lb former WWF Champion Yokozuna. Just days later, the mighty 'Sumo Champion' was found dead of heart failure in his Liverpool hotel, aged just 34.

Then in January 2003, came the chance for two best pals from Morecambe to, incredibly, add our *own* names to this who's who of Dome wrestling history, thanks to Alex Shane. I could scarcely believe the speed in which I went from being plain old Greg Lambert to Greg Lambert—wrestling journalist, radio reporter, performer . . . . and now promoter!

It all happened when Alex phoned me up and explained that in order for the FWA to continue its growth, the promotion had to expand its fan base across the UK. That meant putting on more shows away from the London area. In other words, he wanted to go out on a nationwide tour.

At the time, the FWA was primarily known for its stand-alone, monthly shows in the south of England. Critics of the FWA said it could never be recognised as Britain's top wrestling company unless it got out of its comfort zone and promoted more extensively. After all, All-Star put on well over 100 events a year up and down the country, albeit with hardly any internet or media fanfare because the slower-paced family-friendly style of wrestling. But still, Brian Dixon was running pretty much full-time. The FWA already beat Dixon for quality, but now Alex wanted more *quantity* too.

Alex asked me if I knew any suitable venues for wrestling near where I lived. I immediately touted the virtues of The Morecambe Dome. Then Alex hit me with a question that would change my life . . . again!

"Greg, how would you like to be an FWA regional promoter?"

Going into his usual salesman's overdrive, Alex told me I was one of a few intelligent and trustworthy people in British Wrestling whom he thought capable of promoting a show for the FWA. He then explained how it would work.

He wanted me to pay for the FWA to put on a show in Morecambe. I would also have to hire the venue and do all the promotion by putting up posters and getting the event newspaper and radio coverage in the local area, while Alex would do everything else, such as arrange for the wrestlers and the wrestling ring to travel up on the day. We would split any profits from the event 50-50.

My head was spinning as I listened to Alex's sales pitch. On one hand, I was very open to the idea of becoming a promoter. Bringing the FWA to my hometown really appealed to me. It would be another exciting challenge and, having already come so far by getting a foot in the door of the British Wrestling business, I didn't really want to turn Alex's offer down in case it stalled my momentum.

But on the other hand, I was very confused about whether this was actually a good deal for me, and very conscious of what happened to Dann Read in Ipswich. So, not being a particularly business-minded person, I insisted to Alex that I would only come on board if Mark Kay was my partner, because Mark works for HSBC and understands finance inside out.

Mark looked over Alex's offer and concluded it was a great deal for the FWA but a terrible one for us. We would finance the entire show and do all the donkey work? While the FWA would just roll up on the day, contribute nothing financially, but have the chance to sell merchandise and film the event for video release? Therefore guaranteeing them profit regardless of how many tickets were sold? The FWA had nothing to lose, but we could potentially lose *big* if a Morecambe event failed to draw enough fans.

This was my first experience of being caught between Mark and Alex, who have always been two opposite ends of the spectrum when it came to their vision of how much money to spend on a wrestling show. Mark looks at wrestling as a business first and foremost. He often says that any fool can put on a great wrestling show by spending loads of cash, but it takes skill to put on a great show within a budget. Over the years Mark the Banker has hammered three words into my brain. "Control your costs." So he's not exactly a man for taking financial risks.

In contrast, back then Alex wouldn't have known a budget if he'd tripped over the Chancellor of the Exchequer's briefcase.

I've always been somewhere in the middle. Making money has always been secondary to enjoying the experience of being involved and trying to promote and develop the British Wrestling scene. I've never been all that bothered about getting rich from British Wrestling, because I'm a realist, and I know there's very little money around . . . although I've certainly never wanted to end up skint through the wrestling business.

So Mark and I conferred, then told Alex we couldn't charge the usual high FWA ticket prices for this proposed event. The Morecambe public simply wouldn't pay anything more than £15 for a ringside seat. So we'd be far more comfortable if the FWA paid for half the show costs. We also wanted some control over who wrestled on the show, to ensure costs were kept as low as possible. We stressed that we were keen on the project, but were desperate to learn from Dann's experience and not lose pots of money.

But in standing firm, Alex revealed something about the FWA that would eventually lead to its demise. He explained that the FWA, for all its high-profile and big talk, actually had no money behind it.

That's right, the FWA had no cash whatsoever.

The FWA, supposedly the company putting British Wrestling back on the map, was completely skint.

"There was never any money . . . almost every single big show FWA did back then was paid for out of my blagging," Alex told me recently.

"British Uprising 1 was financed when Dino got a money backer but from then on, I'd just get sponsors and people to pay to have merchandise tables. I'd just tell them that if they didn't, they'd miss out on the biggest event ever in British Wrestling. With me saying it, and with Dino behind me validating every word I said, everybody believed it.

"If we did make any money, we'd spend it on another foreign import or pyrotechnics, or pay the boys more."

At the time, the FWA was paying its top stars like Jody Fleisch, Jonny Storm and Doug Williams about three times as much as they got working for All-Star and other promotions. The average wage for a British wrestler was usually £40-50 per match.

"The philosophy was, well if Jody throws himself off a balcony at British Uprising 1, we'll pay him £150 plus a £20 bonus from Dino," continued Shane.

"Basically, we were learning how to run a company on the fly. We weren't running a business. We were spearheading a *movement*."

So the only way Alex's planned 'British Breakout Tour' would happen, in fact the only way most of the FWA shows *ever* happened, was if investors, such as ourselves, were willing to take a financial plunge and become part of that movement . . . the crusade for The Holy Grail.

Alex was willing to negotiate a little on the overall costs but he flat out refused to go halves. He guaranteed that the FWA name and its reputation for high quality wrestling would sell tickets. Because of this, he refused to allow us too much influence over who would actually wrestle. We wanted a mix of the FWA regulars and some trainees, maybe even some cheaper talent from other UK promotions. But Alex wanted the show to blow the Morecambe fans away. This meant it would cost more.

Should we have turned Alex down flat? After all, the Frontier Wrestling Alliance may have meant something down south, but most people in Morecambe had never heard of the FWA. In fact there was nothing to stop myself and Mark from running our own wrestling show at The Dome, cutting out the FWA altogether (which, four years later, we eventually did.)

But back then, we didn't have the contacts, the confidence nor the experience to 'cut out the middle man'. We politely argued with Alex until we were blue in the face, but in the end, we gave in. Besides, Alex was *unbelievably* persuasive. There is an old saying, "he could sell sand to the Arabs". Well Alex Shane could sell sand, sun, camels and probably pork to the Arabs too.

Alex had an answer for every concern we raised. He expertly convinced us that we were becoming a major part of the biggest thing to happen to British Wrestling in years, that was on the verge of making huge money and could potentially make us all rich. So we grudgingly agreed to a deal.

But the show ended up costing much, much more than the price Alex originally agreed with us. A few weeks later, Shane told us Juventud Guerrera would be headlining the tour. We didn't mind this too much, because we knew Guerrera would be a ticketseller. But then Alex added former ECW star Chris Hamrick. Then other hidden costs mysteriously appeared as show time approached. Surely we could have avoided the spiralling wage bill had we signed a contract with the FWA, I hear you cry? But that's not how things work in the amateurish world of British Wrestling, where much is done on verbal agreements and therefore, trust.

You're probably thinking how naïve we were. But the truth is, we really, really wanted to become wrestling promoters. That's why we allowed Alex to get his own way, and spend more and more of our money. We could have said no. We just didn't want to. And in the back of our minds, we knew that if we could sell out The Dome, or come close to it, we would make a profit anyway. Flushed with enthusiasm and seduced by the buzz surrounding the FWA, we were confident we could draw a big enough crowd to make money.

Mark and I had a lot of fun promoting that first show. We were so proud that we were going to bring wrestling to our hometown, the place where we've both lived all of our lives.

In many respects, the recent history of Morecambe is startlingly reminiscent of the trials and tribulations of British Wrestling. The North West resort, famed as the birthplace of the comedian Eric Morecambe and the home of the royal family's favourite potted shrimps, enjoyed a booming heyday in the '50s and '60s, just like British Wrestling. Morecambe wasn't just a popular destination for cheap and cheerful holidays back then—it was one of *the* live entertainment capitals of the north. Even The Beatles and The Rolling Stones played in Morecambe. Honest, they did!

But then in the '70s and '80s, the resort fell gradually downhill as Brits began to look elsewhere for their entertainment. Tourist numbers plummeted and many of the town's attractions closed down.

Nowadays Morecambe still has so much going for it. We have a rising pop band called The Heartbreaks, whose brilliant album Funtimes was one of the best debut releases of 2012. Then there's Morecambe FC, who earned promotion to the Football League for the first time in their history five years ago after a dramatic play-off win at Wembley Stadium, boosting the local economy and the feeling of civic pride in the town. We also have a stunning promenade view across the Bay towards the Lake District, miles of golden sandy beaches and the gorgeous 1930s art deco Midland Hotel, a striking building which gleams, as if carved from white marble, resplendent on our seafront.

Contrasting with this dazzling natural beauty, though, are Morecambe's many ramshackle buildings, derelict former attractions and empty shops. The town has needed a major overhaul for 30 years, and its aspirational residents keep on hoping that the next regeneration idea or new tourism project will be the one to catapult the town back to its glory days. Instead, there have been many failures and false dawns in Morecambe over the past three decades. Followers of British Wrestling will find that depressingly familiar.

But I am one of Morecambe's biggest fans and supporters. I love promoting my hometown and I'm proud to be what they call 'a true sandgrown'un'. In fact, cut me open and you can bet your life I'd bleed . . . well . . . sand.

I'm also eternally optimistic that Morecambe will rise to become significant once again, just as I was becoming convinced that British Wrestling was heading back to its halcyon days. And I felt inspired and privileged to play a tiny part in that renaissance by bringing the Frontier Wrestling Alliance to town.

Mark and I went on to work very well together as a promotional team for the next eight years. My best pal means the world to me. We met at primary school when I basically gatecrashed his home in 1981 and invited myself into his garden to play football . . . even though I didn't actually know him at the time. But Mark being the easy-going chap he's always been, he kind of shrugged his shoulders and allowed this bossy kid from down the road to come in and take over the game, and we've been best friends ever since. Mark was best man at my wedding, he's Owen's godfather, and in many ways he's like my brother, although Alex felt there were times we bickered more like an old married couple!

Our business partnership was a success because we counterbalanced each other, each bringing different skills to the table. Mark looks at everything from a detached, commercial and often cautious perspective. I'm more emotional and energetic, the public face of the double act. In a nutshell, Mark was the brains of our duo, and I was the mouth.

Another major reason for our success is that we built an exceptional team of unsung heroes who have helped us behind-the-scenes at Morecambe shows over the years. I'm talking about Mark's mum Jennifer Kay, a stalwart of our merchandise table; our production wizard Bryan Fulton, who has been a crucial cog in the Morecambe wrestling machine for many years; my wife Sharon (who puts her hatred of wrestling to one side on show nights) and her best friend Claire Barrett, who ran our ticket box office; our dedicated ring crew of wrestling trainees, particularly Kyle 'Jynkz' Paterson (always the first to arrive and last to leave, an example to all young wrestlers); our sponsors from Morecambe businesses such as my good mate Colin Smith from Ma Murphy's pub, the Bailey family from Westgate Tyres, the late and much-missed Steve Weatherhead from Rita's Cafe and my longtime friends Rob Ellershaw and Debbie Walsh from the Ranch House Bar; and venue managers Simon Armstrong from The Dome (whose biggest wrestling claim to fame was that he once sold Giant Haystacks a sofa), Stewart Aimson from The Carleton and Paul Ineson from Lancaster and Morecambe College. We couldn't have done it without you guys.

My privileged position as a reporter for the town's newspaper has been another major advantage for us as wrestling promoters because I have a wealth of local contacts who have been of great assistance.

There was a chap called Jack Robinson who ran the swing boats and go karts next to The Dome. One day, he offered to put some posters up for us around the caravan park where he lived. After we got talking, I realised this little old fella was actually the former European Lightweight Champion *Jackie* Robinson, a big star from the TV era of British Wrestling. I used to enjoy chatting to Jack about his heyday, and would regularly give him complimentary tickets to watch our shows at The Dome. Jack left Morecambe a few years ago to retire to Stockport after selling the miniature passenger train he used to drive up and down the promenade. I should also mention that his cousin Billy Robinson was also a fantastic wrestler and an international star in both America and Japan.

Now from the sublime, comes the ridiculous. We also had help for that first ever Morecambe extravaganza from an invaluable but utterly barmy source . . . the town's most outrageous radio personality, DJ Pep.

Driven by his mate Paul Travell, Alex Shane visited Morecambe two weeks before our event to see The Dome (which he fell in love with at first sight—seaside venues were in his blood, remember?), do a photo-shoot on the promenade (which got us a full-page spread in The Visitor) and even conduct a live interview from the studios of our local radio station The Bay. This memorable night brought Alex face-to-face with 'The Pepster'.

Pep is a friend of mine and was then the host of a fast-moving, irreverent Saturday night show on The Bay, which I'd guest hosted with him on a few occasions. A wacky, wisecracking self-publicist with flamboyant fashion sense and a liking for shameless promotional stunts—"like Timmy Mallett on speed" is how Alex described him—Pep was an ideal character to get involved in professional wrestling. So he had been only too happy to agree to make an appearance at the show and hype it up on the radio beforehand.

When Alex and Pep went on-air, their chemistry was fabulous to behold. They were like twin sons from different mothers, and got on famously. Their radio interview was an absolute classic, as they bantered back and forth, seamlessly exchanging hilarious jibes to promote the FWA's arrival in Morecambe. If anything, Alex was slightly bewildered by Pep's over-the-top nuttiness. I've never seen anyone bamboozle Alex in a bout of verbal fisticuffs, either before or since. Only Pep had the gift of the gab to take on The Showstealer!

Pep was also about the only human being in the Western hemisphere with the balls to play a practical joke on Alex Shane. After our second show in Morecambe the following August, The Pepster invited myself, Alex, Mark, Doug Williams and other FWA wrestlers to Brooks nightclub in Lancaster, the nearest city to Morecambe—where Pep was the resident DJ. A good time was had by all and a fair few drinks were sunk, and Alex—who can be camper than Christmas when he wants to be—treated us all to some dancefloor moves to 'I Think We're Alone Now' by Tiffany.

But then came a cheeky announcement over the microphone from the grinning Pep. "Is there an Alex Spilling in the house? Could Alex Spilling come to the DJ stand?" Now Alex had a real bee in his bonnet about people using his real name. We all knew this. So did Pep. Not that this stopped him. Alex had a face like thunder as he demanded to know who'd told Pep his real name! I think he did eventually see the funny side, though.

On the night of the first show, Alex had massive reservations about Pep's involvement, thinking him to be a loose cannon who had no idea about pro wrestling (and he was right!). Some of the FWA's hardcore fans also criticised us for having a cheesy radio DJ do an angle on the show. But the publicity Pep brought us was vital in getting locals interested in our first event in Morecambe. And I thought The Pepster's performance on April 21 2003 was actually rather good.

Clad in a tatty Superman outfit and a baseball cap, the self-styled 'Morecambe Mayor of Fun' wandered out to the ring to address the fans with his usual shtick, only to be interrupted by The Family. Pep pricelessly responded to their intrusion by calling Paul Travell, Ian DaSciple and Brandon Thomas "Cockney tossers!" This was especially hilarious because Travell was from Portsmouth, while DaSciple and Thomas were proud Brummies.

My angry cult responded with a typical Family beatdown until, just as typically, Alex and his tag team partner Nikita—whose gimmick in the FWA was that she was good enough to wrestle the men—heroically saved the poor Pepster from a mauling, setting up Alex and Kat's match with The Family later that night.

Although Alex liked Pep personally, I think his unpredictable antics aged Alex by several years. So Mr Spilling decided to abandon plans for The Mayor of Fun to be in his corner for a rematch with The Family at the follow-up August show. Pep did a brief promo that night and further angles with Alex on our Morecambe shows in April and May 2004, but then never appeared for the FWA again.

In 2003 Pep gained national notoriety by proposing to his girlfriend at a Robbie Williams concert, live on Radio 1. In 2007 he was voted the UK's Nightclub DJ of the Year and was presented with his award by his hero Peter Stringfellow, and then in 2011 appeared as a contestant on hit Channel 4 show Come Dine With Me. I was made up for him, because he loves the limelight. Pep can irritate with his madcap ways, but he's still a top bloke.

The Morecambe show turned out to be the third leg of the FWA's first nationwide tour. British Breakout commenced in Ware (Where? It's in Hertfordshire!) on April 19 2003, then moved hundreds of miles up the east coast to Cleethorpes on April 20, came down to us the following day, then on to Bolton on April 22, Sudbury in Suffolk on April 23, Acton on April 24, Portsmouth on April 27 and finally Newport on April 28.

British Breakout was also a significant milestone because so many of our fellow regional promoters went on to bigger and better things on the UK wrestling scene.

Sanjay Bagga, a well-dressed and confident teenager from London, promoted the Acton leg. At the time Bagga had just turned 18, was a big wrestling and FWA fan, and was an outspoken and rather unpopular member of the UK Fan Forum who used to hang around FWA shows, looking to get involved.

Mark and I admired Bagga's entrepreneurial spirit and his haphazard attempts to get noticed by The Internet. He loved winding up the online crowd and still does to this day, so he seemed to be a man after our own heart. We saw something in Sanjay, so we took him under our wing. Although he wasn't a great writer, he was keen as mustard, so we recruited him to pen articles for WrestlingX—mainly because he was hated on the UKFF and acted like an egomaniac. That made him all right in our book.

Bagga ran a stall at FWA shows selling programmes and a fanzine called Frontier News. I christened Sanjay 'The Del Boy of British Wrestling' because he always had some money-making scheme or other on the go. Little did I realise how far his wheeling and dealing would take him in the coming years. Sanjay later became head of one of Britain's top promotions, LDN Wrestling.

Three wrestlers from the North West—Lee Butler, 'Dangerous' Damon Leigh (DDL) and Mike Bishop—were in charge for a solid little show at the Horwich Leisure Centre in Bolton, where I managed The Family in a tag title defence against Alex and Ulf. Shortly afterwards, Butler formed the Wigan-based Garage Pro Wrestling (GPW) but soon left the wrestling biz. After Butler departed, GPW became one of the top companies in the UK under new booker Johnnie Brannigan.

Damon and Mike would enjoy a much brighter future in the business than Butler. DDL went on to become GPW's top star, an FWA regular and in 2009 when I opened a wrestling school in Morecambe, I appointed him my first head trainer. 'Bish' gave up physically wrestling and instead became one of the country's most respected referees. Mike's a top lad, who continued to come along to support our Morecambe shows even after he retired from the business.

Then there was Dann Read, back in the promoting game in charge of the Sudbury show, after Alex worked his persuasive magic on him too. I would love to be able to report that Dann made money this time. But the truth is, he ended up in the red once again.

Still, Sudbury Leisure Centre saw a great show, headlined by Jonny Storm beating Zebra Kid for the All-England Title in a belting match. Sudbury was also an auspicious occasion because it marked the first time I ever shared the ring with Dann as part of a wrestling angle, as he stepped into the DJ Pep role as The Family's sacrificial lamb for the evening. It was great to be part of Dann's hometown show, even if it didn't have the desired financial outcome for him. Apart from Mark Kay, Dann had become my best friend in the wrestling business.

Finally, there was Stevie Knight . . . no relation to Ricky, by the way. The real-life Steve Pendle was already a name on the UK front, a great in-ring entertainer and talker with a self-deprecating sense of humour, who'd wrestled for both the UWA and UCW until injury temporarily stalled his career. But now 'The Shining Light' was itching to get back into the business. Promoting the Cleethorpes event, assisted by his friend Richard Young, was his first step towards an in-ring comeback.

I met Stevie and 'Youngy' for the first time when they came up to watch the Morecambe show the following day, and I really liked them straight away. Youngy was a down-to-earth and cheerful lad who was keen as mustard, while the blond-haired Stevie was a right character, with the most prominent cheekbones in British Wrestling. But little did he realise that day, how much The Morecambe Dome would shape his future.

"I'd actually wrestled at The Dome about 10 or 12 years before, for Max Crabtree . . . possibly against Johnny Angel," Stevie told me in 2009.

"I was probably about eight stone and just getting knocked about. I was the young sacrificial lamb back then.

"I used to do all around the Morecambe area, Pontins at Blackpool, different holiday camps every week. When I stopped doing them I'd go off and do shows for Brian Dixon and Crabtree. It wasn't like it is now, where people do four shows a month. I was doing 10 a week. It was crazy. I think that's a contributing factor as to why I'm so beat up now. And back then, I did proper matches with big guys who really threw me about."

Manoeuvring a gang of wrestlers, a wrestling ring, production set-up, merchandise and TV cameras around the country for this intensive schedule of British Breakout Tour shows required tip-top forward planning. Unfortunately, I quickly discovered that organisation was never FWA's strong suit. The chaotic night before our first ever show in Morecambe was a prime example.

Mark and I picked up The Zebra Kid from a motorway service station 30 miles from Morecambe—where he'd been dropped off after another show up north. Then we took him out to a pub for a drink and a game of pool (and yes Roy, you beat me!) before delivering him to Mark's mum's house where he was staying. Then we had to wait up for the rest of the wrestlers and staff to arrive. Alex had informed us they would be travelling straight to Morecambe from Cleethorpes in a minibus and would land at around midnight. Oh, and by the way, they would then need overnight accommodation in a hotel. Yes, one of those extra costs Alex had neglected to mention in our initial negotiations!

Midnight, he'd said. But Alex had a notoriously poor grasp of geography. Bless him, he probably thought every town 'oop north' was just a few miles apart, but Cleethorpes is a good three hours from Morecambe. To make matters worse the minibus got lost en route. 4am came and went. Mark and I were sitting in my living room, yawning, waiting for the phone to ring.

Just before 5am we got the call that the bus had rolled up in Morecambe. We drove out to the pre-arranged meeting place and saw a bleary-eyed Ralph Cardall at the wheel, looking like he hadn't slept for a week. Juventud Guerrera, Chris Hamrick, Paul Burchill, James Tighe, Elisar Cabrera, Steve Lynskey and quite a few others were crammed in the back of the bus. They looked like escaped refugees who had endured the trip from hell.

We then had to despatch this group of tired, bruised, grumpy wrestlers to different parts of Morecambe. I guided the bus to a seafront hotel opposite The Dome while Mark bundled Juventud and Hamrick into his car and dropped them at his parents' house, where they slept almost right up until show-time.

The following day, Alex turned up at The Dome in the passenger seat of a car, having stayed overnight in Cleethorpes, looking fresh as a daisy. The boss's prerogative, I guess. The rest of us were knackered already.

I'll always remember walking into the empty Dome that afternoon with Jack Xavier, an extremely talented grappler from Birmingham whose swarthy Anglo-Italian looks, colourful ring attire, chunky underdog quality and willingness to take big bumps were really establishing him as a cult favourite with FWA fans. Renzo Divattimo (that's his real name) looked around, soaking in every part of The Dome . . . the spacious stage, the curved brick walls, the grandstand seating area and the Waterfront Bar. Then he said: "Whoah, I'm going to love wrestling here." That was a typical reaction of the FWA wrestlers and staffers that day. They thought The Dome was ideal for pro wrestling.

Alex loved The Dome too, although he said that from the outside, it looked like "a giant breast". Typical Showstealer. If he wasn't thinking about wrestling, back then he was usually thinking about the fairer sex.

The results of our first FWA show in Morecambe were as follows:

James Tighe pinned Raj Ghosh, Flash Barker defeated Jack Xavier, Chris Hamrick downed The Zebra Kid to win the FWA All-England Title, The Family retained the FWA Tag Team Titles beating Alex Shane and Nikita, Simmonz beat Hade Vansen, Doug Williams wrestled Juventud Guerrera to a draw.

I asked Alex if I could refrain from accompanying The Family that night, not wanting to play a baddie in front of my hometown crowd. This was a bit snobby of me, in hindsight. But it did give me the chance to step in as ring announcer for the first-half, when regular Master of Ceremonies, the mild-mannered young man with the most ironic nickname in British Wrestling, 'Hardcore' John Atkins, was delayed. The chance to compere an FWA event was another string to my wrestling bow and meant I had the best seat in the house to observe how the Morecambe fans reacted to the FWA's debut.

The show started with Tighe v Ghosh and Barker v Xavier, both FWA babyface v babyface matches. The standard of wrestling was strong. But there was one problem. The crowd was a little subdued at first. I remember a young boy sitting behind me during the Barker-Xavier match asking: "Who do we cheer for, dad?" This was not your typical FWA audience of smart marks. The Dome was full of families and kids who desperately wanted somebody to hate. The wise Steve Knight used to sum it up best for me. "Most wrestling fans just want to see cowboys v Indians."

Then the third match saw British 'cowboy' The Zebra Kid take on American 'Indian' Chris Hamrick for the All-England Title. They had had a traditional good versus evil match, with some awesome wrestling and great entertainment thrown in. Both men were brilliant. Hamrick beat Roy for the title in one of my all-time favourite Morecambe matches. The unpopular result aside, it was exactly the kind of match our audience wanted to see. I made a mental note for the future, and ever since then my Morecambe events have been tailored towards the family audience, but also peppered with the kind of new school wrestling the smarts can appreciate.

After The Family had retained the FWA Tag Team Titles in a typical Family v Alex brawl, The Showstealer angrily threw Steve Lynskey through the ropes and he took a really bad bump on the outside. Steve just lay there on the wooden floor, not moving. I felt sick to my stomach. On our very first show, one of our guys looked like he was seriously hurt. But in the end, Lynskey was able to limp away to the dressing room and eventually left The Dome under his own steam. A lot of the wrestlers actually thought slippery Steve, a wind-up merchant extraordinaire, was already fed up of conditions on the tour and was faking his injury so he would be sent home. I couldn't possibly comment!

It was an incredible buzz to see The Dome full of enthusiastic fans that night because of something *we'd* done. People we knew were telling us "Great show!" as they left after the superb main event between Williams and Juvi. Even Findlay Martin popped along to watch and complimented the FWA wrestlers within the pages of Power Slam. And everyone seemed in agreement that Morecambe was the best show of the entire Breakout Tour.

But, just as at Dawn of a New Era, critical success was not matched by commercial wealth. Mark and I had done everything possible to promote the FWA's visit to Morecambe. With Juventud on the bill and Pep pushing it like a maniac on the radio, posters everywhere across the town and its neighboring district and excellent coverage in the local press, we managed to draw a respectable crowd of 250. Nowhere near a sell-out but not bad for a live entertainment show in Morecambe—and certainly better than anything Conway managed the previous year.

But the problem was, Scott's shows cost him a fraction of what it was costing us. So we ended up losing close to £1,000.

Afterwards, Alex saw our long faces and tried to console us by saying: "You've got to speculate to accumulate" and "Everyone loses money on their first show." But at the time, we were extremely deflated and rather miffed with Alex for making the event so un-necessarily expensive. We saw ways in which costs could have been cut, without reducing the quality of the show. Silly things like not paying for a ring announcer to travel up from London, because I could have compered the whole night for free!

But unlike other British Wrestling promoters who threw in the towel after big financial losses, we didn't quit. We also kind of realised that Alex and the FWA now needed us more than we needed them. If they wanted to continue using the mecca that was The Dome, they would have to make concessions. So—having paid our 'promoting dues' and further earned Alex's respect—we were able to alter the terms of the deal for future shows, making the agreement more favourable to us.

With hindsight, though, we can't feel too bitter at The Showstealer about losing money on that first show. Mark and I are grown adults and we knew what we were getting ourselves into. We took the risk, we invested in the FWA and it backfired . . . . temporarily. But at least Alex gave us the chance to run our own wrestling show in Morecambe. No-one else would have done. We would never have become promoters, if it wasn't for his faith and influence.

And long-term, losing money on that first show became a blessing in disguise. By spending the extra cash on having Juventud, Hamrick and a really strong line-up of British stars on April 21 2003, it meant the quality was far superior to any wrestling show in Morecambe previously. That meant we established a fan base for FWA in Morecambe right off the bat. A lot of those fans have come back again and again over the years.

And we certainly never lost that much money on a Morecambe event after that. On our third show in April 2004, we turned in a profit. And by 2005, profitable Morecambe shows were becoming a regular occurrence.

Becoming a promoter also gave me an entirely different perspective on the FWA. To outsiders, the FWA was an exciting big-time wrestling promotion with potential to crack the mainstream. Scratching under the surface made me realise the company was actually a badly-organised, under-financed, poorly-structured mess. But it somehow kept achieving great things thanks to the unyielding focus, vision, drive and patter of one Alex Shane.

The FWA was held together by the thinnest of strands. And inevitably, at some point in future, that strand was bound to snap.

CHAPTER 8

FIRST BLOOD and BARBED WIRE

Looking back now, I can see just how incredible it was to be part of the FWA in 2003-4.

Not only were the shows top-notch and the fans' reaction very positive, but all the workers got on like a house on fire. You hear stories about all the backstage 'politics' in the WWE and how certain wrestlers backstab their colleagues to get to the top. There was none of that in the FWA dressing room. Coming to work on an FWA show was so much fun and we all had such a good craic backstage. My regular trips down south became the highlight of my month.

That's not to say that we messed around, far from it. Rarely did any FWA wrestler step out of line or give anything other than 100%, and that was thanks to Alex and Dino. Both commanded such respect.

Alex exuded a potent mix of intimidation and intelligence. He was bigger than almost everyone else in the FWA, so no-one wanted to cross him, and also had such a sharp wrestling brain which came up with so many excellent creative ideas. Dino had vast experience and knowledge, but also a reputation in real-life as someone not to mess with. So nobody wanted to get on Mr Scarlo's bad side either.

"Dino was a tough guy to figure out," said Hade Vansen in 2012.

"He was a nice guy, but he definitely had an edge to him. I personally found him quite straightforward, though. If he liked you, he would take time to teach you. But if he didn't like you, he wouldn't give you the time of day.

"As for Alex, I like him a lot. I think he's a very decent person and on the whole, has a good heart. No-one can deny his passion for wrestling and I certainly can't argue that he's got his own vision for the business. I think that *he* thinks a lot of what he's doing is the right thing . . . but whether it's always in the best interests of those around him is disputable."

Alex and Dino both did an amazing job of making the FWA roster feel like we were part of something special. There were times when they rounded everyone up and gave us pep-talks before the show. They hammered it home that everyone in the FWA was hand-picked because they were the best in the country. They would tell us that FWA was set to achieve great things, meaning that although most of us were earning a pittance for working the shows, we would eventually earn big money, and told us how lucky we were to be part of the company.

Such speeches made everyone feel desperate to please Alex and Dino. Their motivational abilities were similar to how American promoter Paul Heyman (one of Alex's heroes) would rally the troops in ECW and gained similar results. In 2003 almost everyone in the FWA felt a great sense of loyalty to Alex and Dino and would have done just about anything to make them happy. The roster would have walked through walls to achieve The Holy Grail of mainstream success for British Wrestling. That's partly why FWA shows were so good.

"The American wrestlers talk about ECW like it was their favourite time in wrestling, and the FWA was the same for me," said Jonny Storm.

"There was so much hype about it. There was a lot of good booking and it was like a family backstage. Everybody got on well. They understood we had something special. The FWA will always be remembered as the resurgence of the glory days of British Wrestling.

"Alex and Dino were pioneers, and when people look back on the recent history of British Wrestling, what they did should be remembered."

One of the most memorable of their shows came on Saturday May 17 2003, the inter-promotional one-night tournament between FWA and ROH known as Frontiers of Honor. This was massive at the time but looking back, and remembering some of the talented American names who competed that night at the York Hall, it seems even bigger now.

There was Samoa Joe, Low Ki, Christopher Daniels, AJ Styles, Paul London . . . it was like wrestling's answer to Before They Were Famous. What a terrific line-up of future WWE and TNA stars.

"I remember meeting most of these guys for the first time when I was booked on a 'King of Indies' tournament on the West Coast in 2001, only the second time I'd wrestled in America," recalled Doug Williams.

Held on the weekend of October 26 and 27 2001 in Vallejo, California, what a watershed moment in American Wrestling history *that* event was. There was Doug, Samoa Joe, Low Ki, Daniels, Styles, Frankie Kazarian, Brian 'Spanky' Kendrick, Bryan Danielson (Daniel Bryan) . . . all competing in a two-night indie tournament right at the outset of their careers. A few months later, Ring of Honor debuted with the same nucleus of talent. The energetic and radical wrestling action on display caught the imagination of fans, wrestlers and promoters worldwide . . . including Alex Shane.

"Most of the Americans who came over back then were young guys who didn't know much about the importance of the old World of Sport era of British Wrestling," continued Doug.

"But they enjoyed working in the UK because they would make a trip out of it and sell a lot of their own merchandise, and the FWA was well-received by them because we were drawing big crowds so they got to wrestle in front of 500-plus people, compared to the 150-200 they would get on many American indie shows. I can't remember the Americans saying *anything* negative about the British scene back then.

"The guys who stood out to me back then were Samoa Joe and Chris Daniels; Joe because he was so different from most of the other American indie guys, and Daniels because whenever we wrestled each other, he always had a clear view in his head of how the match would go. He'd come up with 100 ideas he wanted to do in the match, and nine times out of 10 they would work. He was so brash and loud, a real character."

At Frontiers of Honor, this 'Golden Generation' of American up-and-comers would all compete on the same night in front of the British smart fans who'd grown to adore them from watching videotapes of their progressive, hard-hitting bouts in the States. Once again, Alex Shane conjoured up money 'out of thin air' and turned an ambitious vision into reality.

And on this, the biggest night in FWA history, I nearly blew it.

First of all, I went out the night before the show to a Queen tribute concert at The Dome, had a skinful and woke up with a pounding hangover. Then, during the arduous five-hour train journey down to London, I received a phone call from a furious Alex.

Earlier in the week, to further my storyline feud with The Showstealer, I'd published a parody of his Shane's Shooting Gallery column on WrestlingX.com without asking Alex's permission first. In this cutting piece of satire, I'd re-named Alex The Show*squealer* and taken the mick out of his long-winded writing style and lack of geographical knowledge, among other things.

It seems my parody had cut too near the bone for the boss's liking and the boys who'd read it were having a good laugh at his expense. So he called me and gave me a right tongue-lashing for making him look a fool.

So when I arrived at the York Hall a few hours before the show, I half-expected Alex to punch me in the mouth and fire me from the FWA for good. Instead, he forgave me, saying he had more important things, like Frontiers of Honor, to worry about. Next time I should check with him before publishing anything that might cause him grief. I breathed a huge, stale beer breath of relief. Then I gathered round a portable TV set to watch the 2003 FA Cup Final with some of the other boys, while keeping one impressed eye on Samoa Joe and Low Ki as they engaged in a friendly but intensely competitive UFC-style grappling contest in the ring. Joe and Brandon looked like they were trying to rip each other's limbs off—and this was just a warm-up.

Later that night, around 1,000 fans transformed the York Hall into a cauldron of bedlam as the best of the Brits fought the crack American squad in a series of dream inter-promotional bouts. Mouthwatering matchups like James Tighe v Paul London (who signed for WWE weeks later), Flash Barker v Low Ki, Zebra Kid v Samoa Joe, Jonny Storm v AJ Styles and Jody Fleisch v Christopher Daniels, all took place on the same show! Full results were as follows:

James Tighe pinned Paul London, Jack Xavier pinned Mikey Whipwreck, Paul Burchill trounced Ross Jordan and Raj Ghosh in a handicap match AJ Styles beat Jonny Storm, Samoa Joe made Zebra Kid tap out, The Family downed Alex Shane, Ulf Herman and Nikita, Flash Barker drew with Low Ki, Christopher Daniels pinned Jody Fleisch.

Aside from the tournament, which the Americans won 3-2 after Jonny Storm stabbed Team FWA in the back to help Daniels beat Fleisch, there were two 'proper' FWA matches added to Frontiers of Honor too. One saw Burchill make his actual wrestling debut, and continue his killing spree by wiping out the team of Ross Jordan (real name Ross Jones) and Raj Ghosh in a handicap squash match. The prodigious rookie was accompanied by his new manager, Dean Ayass, who surprisingly received a hefty cheer from the York Hall as he smugly brandished the microphone and addressed Burchill's hapless victims before the match.

"Mr Jordan? Mr Ghosh? You are entering this ring at your own risk! Mr Burchill and Mr Ayass will not be held responsible for any . . . broken . . . bones!"

The 'Burchill disclaimer', Dean's pre-match warning of impending pain for Paul's adversaries, eventually became one of the most popular catchphrases in the FWA.

"I actually came up with the idea for the disclaimer one day while crossing the road to get a sandwich during my lunch hour from work," said Dean in 2012.

"I told Alex about it and he flashed me that grin he always had whenever somebody had a good idea.

"I used the disclaimer for a few shows and the crowd wasn't reacting. I was going to stop using it but Alex told me to persevere, saying sometimes it takes the crowd a while to get used to new things. Eventually, I had 1,500 people chanting along with the entire thing at British Uprising 3. They even put it as a slogan on a T-shirt."

I was involved in the other non-tournament match at FOH. A six-person tag team war pitting Scott Parker, Paul Travell and Brandon Thomas against Alex, Ulf and Nikita was yet another instalment of the awesome 2003 feud between The Family and The Showswearers. In my opinion, these ECW-style hardcore brawls set a standard for brutality and creativity that has never been matched in British Wrestling. And I had the best view in the house as my gaggle of religious misfits and our deadly enemies continued to find new, innovative, and often downright insane ways to inflict pain on each other.

The FOH bout is most remembered for the stunning moment when Nikita climbed to the second tier of the York Hall and dived a full 15 feet off the balcony on top of The Family. And the moment when Shane grabbed a staple-gun and proceeded to—OUCH!—acquaint it with The Messiah's nether regions. And the moment when poor Ashe, in a planned interference spot, completely botched a springboard dive and fell flat on his face in the ring. Thankfully, amongst the breathtaking chaos of this unforgettable scrap, my awful promo before the match has been all but forgotten. Until I reminded you, just then. Oh well . . .

Struggling with my hangover and taunted mercilessly by a deafening crowd who loathed the ground I walked on, I could barely hear myself think above the din of "F__ YOU LAMBERT!", "ASSHOLE!" and "SHUT THE F___ UP!" chants. One fan had even brought an inflatable doll wearing a T-shirt with the logo 'GREG LAMBERT'S WIFE'—which Ulf proceeded to flatten with a piledriver! FWA fans were thoroughly charming human beings, weren't they? I gabbled some pointless nonsense over the microphone, couldn't make myself heard, and then gave up.

Heaven knows what the watching officials from Ring of Honor thought of me, this geeky-looking Englishman who had just displayed all the verbal skills of a doorknob. But afterwards Dean Ayass, as always, had words of encouragement. He told me I should take the fact that the fans drowned out my promo as a compliment. "They're supposed to hate you, "said The Twisted Genius. "The more they heckle you, the better you are doing your job."

Dean was right. A bad guy's boos are really his cheers. The worst crowd reaction in wrestling is the sound of silence. You can love me or hate me—it doesn't matter as long as you care passionately either way. The fact that one fan cared enough about my character to create an inflatable sex doll of my wife to taunt me with, proved that I was doing my job properly as a villain.

The FWA definitely brought out creativity in the fans like no other British Wrestling promotion before or since. One group of devoted FWA followers even produced their own witty fanzine called 'Shiny Pants', so-named because a lot of the FWA wrestlers back then, including Alex Shane, performed in shiny pleather trousers.

My favourite column in Shiny Pants was called 'Mrs Lambert's Journal', a spoof look at what would happen if all the members of The Family lived with me. It painted a picture of my wife as a long-suffering Florence Nightingale figure who treated The Family's various wounds with sticking plasters and antiseptic cream as they hung around the house playing with kitchen knives and hiding drawing pins.

I found it hilarious. For her part, Sharon found it rather disturbing.

I was also amused when Shiny Pants described me as "a man more evil than Skeletor". The FWA faithful really believed I was a nasty piece of work, so I was clearly doing something right. They were paying their money to see me get my come-uppance. But that didn't happen at Frontiers of Honor. Instead, The Family won when Ian DaSciple interfered. Unlucky, smart marks! Chalk another one up for The Truth!

Overall, Frontiers of Honor was another fantastic success for the FWA. The show received yet more plaudits from wrestling fans and media. A two-part video of the event sold like hot cakes on both sides of the Atlantic. There was talk of further collaborations between ROH and FWA in the future. Our disorganised wrestling promotion with no money behind it was—to the outside world, at least—on an absolute roll.

In fact, aside from my dodgy promo, the only other thing I recall going wrong that night was when a panicking Christopher Daniels rushed out of the dressing room after the show and asked me: "Have you seen my onk?" I stared at him blankly, not knowing what an 'onk' was. Daniels was frantic. "You know, my chain, my ONK!" I didn't have a clue what he was on about, believing 'onk' to be some strange American word. Eventually I realised the exasperated Daniels was talking about his *ankh*, the Egyptian hieroglyphic symbol he wore around his neck. Turns out The Fallen Angel had removed this precious item before his match but it had disappeared from ringside.

The chain had great sentimental value to poor Chris, so Dean Ayass and I quickly searched the emptying arena. Sadly we never found the ankh. To my knowledge, the onk never turned up either.

The FWA's momentum showed no signs of stalling at the next event, Vendetta on June 22 2003, back at lovely Broxbourne Civic Hall. The results were:

Nikita pinned Raj Ghosh, The Zebra Kid beat Mark 'Five Star' Belton, Jonny Storm pinned Super Crazy to retain the XPW European Title, The Family retained the FWA Tag Titles in a First Blood Match against Alex Shane and Ulf Herman, James Tighe defeated Jody Fleisch by countout, Flash Barker beat Jack Xavier, Burchill crushed Simmonz and Mark Sloan, Doug Williams beat American Dragon (Daniel Bryan) to retain the FWA Title.

Vendetta saw the latest twist in the Family-Showswearers saga, a match where the first team to bleed would be the loser. The show also saw The Family seek a new member, 18-year-old Raj Ghosh. Raj was on a losing streak that went from bad to worse in the opening match of Vendetta, as he lost to Nikita, a mere girl! As Ghosh remained despondently in the ring following this embarrassment, The Family emerged to confront him.

Unlike my York Hall disaster, this time I absolutely nailed my promo. Although Alex and Dino thought it went way too long, I still consider it one of my best ever.

I advised the wayward Raj to join The Family to turn his career around. But Ghosh refused and my boys attacked, only to be sent scattering by The Showswearers' cavalry. Then Ulf cheerfully vowed to make us "piss blood from our heads and s__t our pants!" In the morally-bankrupt world of wrestling, such profanity made the Giant German the biggest babyface in the FWA. The fans then roared approval as The Inflatable Mrs Lambert was forced to take an Alex Shane legdrop!

76

The First Blood match was utter anarchy. As I watched on in mock horror from my ringside position, Ulf used all manner of bizarre objects to beat Parker senseless inside the ring—a broom, a cheese grater, a chalkboard, a computer keyboard, even a garden gnome! Meanwhile the ever-so-slightly unhinged Travell went back and forth with Alex in amongst the fans. I look back now and marvel at how Scott and Paul put their bodies on the line. They acted like human crash test dummies for the onslaught of the much bigger Shane and Herman.

The finish came when Ulf busted Travell open, seemingly winning the FWA Tag Titles back for The Showswearers. However, moments earlier referee Andy Coyne had been inadvertently knocked out by a stray chair shot. Meanwhile, Ian DaSciple sneaked into the ring and switched places with Travell. So when that paragon of virtue Steve Lynskey arrived as Coyne's replacement and checked DaSciple, there was no blood to be found.

I then grabbed a 'crystal decanter' (in reality, a fake glass cup) and crept into the ring. With the fans going ballistic in fury, I went to smash it over Ulf's head. But then Raj Ghosh reappeared and snatched the decanter off me. I cowered in the corner as Ghosh looked for all the world like he was about to smack me one. But instead he turned around and shattered the glass over Ulf's cranium. A swerve! The Giant German bled, Lynskey saw the crimson and he called for the bell. Once again The Family had thwarted the fan favourites through a sinister plan, perfectly booked by Alex Shane and Dino Scarlo, and executed superbly by everyone involved.

This exciting First Blood match was the highlight of another crackerjack FWA show—a show that had something for everyone. For example, if you liked classic scientific wrestling, you had Doug Williams v 'American Dragon' Bryan Danielson.

Danielson was a pleasant young man with exceptional talent from Aberdeen, Washington who at the time, competed on UK shows wearing a Stars and Stripes-patterned mask. In the States for Ring of Honor, he usually wrestled without the mask. So the smart marks weren't happy to see him under the hood that night. They heckled The American Dragon, demanding: "TAKE THE MASK OFF!" Bryan took great delight in refusing to oblige, riling the crowd up perfectly by deliberately not doing what they wanted.

"I remember being really tired that night because I'd just come back from Germany, so I just kind of let all the mask stuff pass me by," said Doug Williams.

"Bryan was a really nice guy but to me, he didn't really stand out from the other Americans as a wrestler back then. The mask gimmick was the start of the character work he'd later show in the WWE . . . and he was mainly developing this by working in Britain on All-Star shows."

Sure enough, seven years later The American Dragon would morph into Daniel Bryan, WWE World Heavyweight Champion and one of the most entertaining personalities in the business today. YES! YES! YES . . . he did.

As I was saying, that Vendetta show had a bit of everything. If you liked a fast-paced match with lots of near-falls and high-flying, there was Jonny Storm v Super Crazy. If you were a fan of comedy, there was Duke of Danger and Simmonz—whose rib-tickling double act was really getting over (starting to resonate) with the FWA fans. If you liked sexy ladies, there was Nikita. If you liked hard hitting, there was Zebra Kid versus Mark 'Five Star' Belton. Yes, the former Five Star Flash had been accepted into the fold under a new ring name, which was a big achievement because the FWA rarely brought in 'outsiders' back then.

And if you liked blood, guts and nutty brawling, there was The Family versus The Showswearers.

Looking back, Vendetta 2003 was probably the apex of the Family-Showswearers feud. Although I loved being involved and couldn't wait to participate in the next instalment, some FWA fans expressed concerns that the Shane/Herman-Family saga might grow stale through overkill. After all, the two teams had fought each other to a standstill on every FWA show since March. Some fans wanted to see something different.

So Alex tried to freshen things up when the FWA ran its second nationwide tour in August 2003. This was called the Northern Exposure Tour. This time the FWA only visited three towns, as opposed to the seven on British Breakout. I guess only three regional promoters (including myself and Mark) could afford to work with the FWA again so soon after April . . .

At our second Morecambe show on August 2 2003 headlined by Doug Williams v Christopher Daniels for the FWA Title, The Showstealer introduced the comebacking Stevie Knight as his temporary partner in Ulf's absence. The Shane-Knight duo then beat Travell and Ghosh to win the Tag Titles, before dropping the belts back to The Family two days later in Cleethorpes.

Ulf was back in time to face The Family again at FWA Hotwired in Broxbourne on September 21 2003, where the violence levels were upped still further in British Wrestling's first ever Double Barbed Wire Baseball Bat match. By this time, I had serious concerns for the mental and physical well-being of Paul Travell.

In character, The Righteous One was a tortured soul who appeared to like receiving pain as much as inflicting it. In real-life, Paul is a cool guy—funny and great company. But the intensity of the feud changed him.

Travell was always trying to out-do whatever he did in his last match. This meant coming up with even crazier stunts, even bigger bumps, even more dangerous ways to keep the fans interested in the feud. I felt the pressure Paul put on himself was causing him to become unbalanced, like his character, and he often took more punishment than was good for him. At times, I was worried he might go too far and get seriously hurt.

"I think there were many factors about why I used to do the hardcore stuff," said Paul, as he reflected on his career in 2012.

"Part of it was my youth. I thought I was invulnerable, as you do at that age. I certainly wouldn't be doing those things today, at 32.

"I was so dedicated back then. I had a lot of passion for wrestling. But it wasn't like I was another Abdullah the Butcher, with scars all over my head. When I bled, I'd cut myself with a tiny blade, a one millimetre cut, and get a lot of blood coming out for what was really nothing. It looked worse than it was, that was the illusion of wrestling. And when I was being power bombed on the drawing pins, I had so much adrenalin going through me I didn't think about not being in control.

"Look, I'm no big tough guy. I'm a small guy and I did a lot of this stuff because I felt under pressure to be remembered. It's wrong. I watch a lot of UFC now, and there's welterweights and flyweights, smaller guys than me who are proper hard men, they'd beat the s__t out of most wrestlers.

"I think wrestling is really dated with its emphasis on size. It's part of the reason why I fell out of love with wrestling. People think you have to be a big guy. That's why Eddie Guerrero and Chris Benoit felt under pressure to take steroids to get bigger. Wrestling ruined them. They were perfect as they were."

Paul Travell was the least of Alex and Dino's worries at Hotwired. The talk of the dressing room that night was the shock retirement of 'The Phoenix' Jody Fleisch.

At the time, Alex and Dino had big plans for Jody's feud with Jonny Storm, which they were meticulously building up to climax with a grudge match at British Uprising 2 that October. But, a few weeks after he'd wrestled on the Northern Exposure Tour and looked as good as ever, Jody quit wrestling. It came totally out of the blue, and nobody could believe it.

We heard so many different stories as to why Jody needed a break. All we knew for certain at Hotwired was that his big Uprising match with The Wonderkid was off. This was a major setback for the FWA, and one of many that would accumulate and contribute to its eventual demise. The promotion had lost its most popular and talented performer.

Jody wasn't the only absentee at Hotwired. The Family also suffered a major casualty, 'The Messiah' Brandon Thomas. As in the case of Fleisch, the departure of Brandon was clouded in mystery. For whatever reason, Thomas simply didn't want to wrestle for the FWA any more. I can't understate how big a blow this was for The Family. Although Brandon was not the best wrestler, he played his role as our spiritual leader to a 'T'. Without his holy presence, The Family never quite had the same aura.

I don't know how much Jody's premature retirement affected matters, but Hotwired 2003 did not live up to the high standards the FWA had set in previous months. But this was another problem with the FWA. The fans were spoilt. So if the FWA produced merely a *good* show, rather than a great one, it failed to meet their expectations. Then the knives came out on the internet forums.

Results were:

Jack Xavier beat EZ Money, James Tighe defeated Flash Barker, Simmonz beat Mark Sloan, Zebra Kid went to a no-contest with Flash Barker, Jase the Ace beat Lee Darren, Jonny Storm defeated Chris Hamrick by DQ, FWA British Tag Team Champions The Family beat Alex Shane and Ulf Herman in a double barbed wire baseball bat match.

Perhaps the biggest talking point coming out of Hotwired 2003 came at the end of the first-half, when out of the blue, Hade Vansen stormed the ring and angrily seized the microphone.

As far as the fans were concerned, Hade wasn't even meant to be on the show. His wrestling career was on the slide, he'd been losing a lot of matches, and was so far off management's radar he'd only been used at Hotwired as part of the FWA's security crew.

But then Vansen downed tools and stunned the Broxbourne crowd by cutting what is called a 'worked-shoot' promo. This was a speech designed to make the fans think he had spontaneously interrupted the event *for real* to disrupt proceedings so he could vent his real-life frustrations about the way his FWA career was heading. What made it look all the more real was that Hade didn't air his dirty laundry at FWA's storyline owner Elisar Cabrera, but instead spilled his guts at the boss in real life, Alex Shane.

The smart marks weren't sure. Was it real or not? Well yes, of course it was. Hade's 'unscheduled' appearance had been pre-planned and his every word scripted.

"The whole thing was Alex's idea," Hade told me.

"We built up to it beautifully. I had been getting jobbed out (losing) and left off shows. There used to be this regular fan night the FWA held in a bar in London called The Job Squad. One night I turned up unexpectedly and started brawling with Alex. People had to jump between us to pull us apart. The next day, the fan forums were on fire. They thought it was real. In fact, Alex and I had planned it, but hadn't told anyone.

"Then I took the mic and started complaining about the way I was being unfairly overlooked for opportunities in the FWA. I said now it was my time to shine, and that I would assert myself by any means necessary even if it meant jumping in the ring to stop the show.

"It was a standard 'worked-shoot' promo. It happens all the time now. But back then the concept was quite new in Britain.

"We intentionally targeted it at the internet fans. You see, the UK Fan Forum had an enormous amount of influence back then. The FWA's success was built on the back of its internet fan base, that sort of demographic. There were other promotions like All-Star who looked down on this kind of internet promotion and just went out and put posters up or got press through the local rags, but the FWA was definitely successful at courting The Internet in a way that nobody else was at the time.

"But I wonder if in the end, it worked against them, and its biggest strength became its biggest weakness."

As for my involvement at Hotwired 2003, it turned out to be minimal in the end. I was initially excited to be involved in the main event of an FWA show, but then Alex told me I would be barred from ringside for the Double Barbed Wire Baseball Bat brawl. So I watched, disappointedly, from backstage as Alex, Ulf, Travell and Raj Ghosh battled all over the Civic Hall, cringing along with the fans as they sadistically used the razor-sharp barbed wire to carve each other open.

I felt the Hotwired match was inferior to the previous Family-Showswearers epics, although Travell was in his element as usual, as he hurled himself around like a lunatic, bled like a stuck pig and even took a One Night Stand, straight through a pile of drawing pins!

But our new member, Raj Ghosh, was not as happy in his hardcore work. In real-life, young Raj didn't seem all that enamoured with being part of The Family. In fact, he often complained about taking the huge bumps and skull-crunching weapon shots that Travell saw as routine. Although the FWA Academy graduate did work hard in the ring, I often felt that the reluctant Ghosh's heart was never in being part of The Family.

The biggest problem with the Hotwired match was the finish. Yet again, Alex and Ulf seemed to have won the titles, but Steve Lynskey disqualified them on a confusing rules technicality. Ending the show on such a flat note was a rare FWA booking mistake, in my view. Alex justified it by saying that because he and Ulf had been screwed yet again, FWA fans would be even more desperate to see them exact revenge on The Family in one final encounter at British Uprising. In reality, the finish of the Hotwired main event just sent people home feeling disappointed and bewildered.

Still, the result provoked Alex into making a challenge. At Uprising, if Alex and Ulf lost, they would leave the FWA forever. But if they won, I would have to take an Ulf Herman chair shot to the head!!!!!

AAARGH!!!!!

So on we rolled to FWA British Uprising 2, held at the York Hall on Saturday, October 18 2003. Despite the absence of Jody Fleisch, the line-up was strong on paper. The obligatory American contingent was former WWE and ECW star Justin Credible, the returning ECW cult figure Mikey Whipwreck, and red-hot US indie prodigies Homicide, Colt Cabana and a highly-touted newcomer making his European debut, who went by the name of CM Punk.

Paul Burchill was set to finally get his hands on the slippery Duke of Danger, who had been dodging 'The Monster' for almost a year. James Tighe, who had been on a winning streak in 2003, was to challenge Doug Williams for the British Heavyweight Title in a battle of the company's two best technical wrestlers.

But arguably the biggest attraction on 'the UK's answer to WrestleMania' was the final battle between The Family and The Showswearers, and the chance that maybe, just maybe, Greg 'The Truth' Lambert would have his brains caved in!

On the morning of the show, FWA held a fan gathering at Lee Hurst's comedy club in Bethnal Green. Fans milled with the wrestlers, obtained autographs, bought wrestling videos from tape trading stalls and listened intently as the FWA stars gave interviews at a press conference to hype up the show. I was impressed by how accessible the FWA was to its fans. It was like one great big club, and I was proud to be a member. Mark Kay hated it though. He couldn't wait to leave.

After the Fan Fest, Kay gave myself, Colt Cabana and none other than the future Straight Edge WWE Champion, CM Punk, a lift to the York Hall in his Corsa-to-the-stars. The then-blond haired Punk was quiet, with an air of sarcastic aloofness to him, but seemed on the whole a decent guy. Cabana was exactly the same as his in-ring persona, a loud and loveable joker with a gleaming smile; reminding me a lot of Joey from the sitcom Friends.

After dropping us off, Mark disappeared with Dann Read and Sanjay Bagga to Tower Bridge, to kill a few hours watching illusionist David Blaine on his 44th day suspended 30 feet above the Thames in a glass box.

David Blaine wasn't the only crazy dude who pulled off a death-defying stunt in London that day, and lived to tell the tale.

Step forward, 'The Righteous' Paul Travell.

CHAPTER 9

. . . BOMBS AND FIRE!

FWA British Uprising 2 was the show where everything that could go wrong, *did* go wrong.

For starters, we had a bomb scare.

Just hours before the biggest show on the British Wrestling calendar, some numptie phoned the police and claimed there was an explosive device in the York Hall. Alex gathered the entire roster and crew on the balcony and told us that although police were confident it was a hoax, we would still have to evacuate. So the entire crew—including myself, CM Punk and all—had to wait outside in the back yard while the authorities searched the building. This meant the start time was delayed, but FWA shows rarely started on time anyway!

Once the area had been declared safe, the fans were ushered in and British Uprising 2 got under way with an introduction by the FWA commentary team of Tony Giles and Nick London, who was former referee Andy Coyne under a different name. Tony and 'Nick' introduced the official Uprising music video on the big screen. The FWA's breathtaking music videos, expertly produced by the creative maverick Ralph Cardall and his band Citizen Smith, really made the FWA stand out amongst the handful of UK wrestling companies plying their trade at the time.

Ralph and other members of the FWA production team like Kieran Lefort, Ian Dewhirst, Mark Sloan and Barry Charalambous spent hours painstakingly editing footage to create either spectacular music videos, or DVDs of the live events or later the FWA television show itself, often for little or no pay. I will at this point also name-check some of the other unsung heroes of the FWA's operation who deserve a mention too; like head of security Rus Rogers, referee Stevie Cox, ring crew member Simon 'King Slim' Cronin, website guru Andrew 'Fozzy' Maddock, photographer Sarah Barraclough, and camera operators extraordinaire Amy Hanifan and Phil Austin. These dedicated team members all played their part in making FWA stand out amongst wrestling companies in Britain at the time.

Full results of the last ever FWA event at the York Hall were as follows:

Jack Xavier pinned Homicide, Nikita beat Mark Sloan, CM Punk beat Colt Cabana, Ulf Herman and Mikey Whipwreck beat FWA British Tag Team Champions The Family in a non-title Apocalypse Grudge Match, Jonny Storm pinned Justin Credible, Hade Vansen beat Flash Barker by submission to win the FWA All-England Title, Paul Burchill beat Hampton Court in a handicap match, FWA British Heavyweight Champion Doug Williams beat James Tighe.

The last ever FWA event at the York Hall? That's right.

After British Uprising, management at the Bethnal Green venue banned the FWA from promoting there ever again. This was mainly due to a terrifying incident during the biggest match of the show and the biggest match of my short wrestling career to that date.

The Paul Travell fire incident.

I mentioned before that Travell felt an obligation to make his next stunt even more dangerous than his last. So the loveable nutter agreed to the most life-threatening stunt of all at British Uprising 2.

He agreed to be slammed through a burning table.

After the first two matches, tension was high backstage. I've never seen Alex so tetchy. He had taken himself out of The Family v Showswearers match so he could concentrate on overseeing and co-ordinating the show. He was already stressed due to the bomb scare, was uncharacteristically snapping at people, and now Uprising 2 wasn't going as well as he'd hoped.

Although Jack Xavier and Homicide opened with a decent little outing, the fickle FWA fans were unhappy with the result. When the chunky Brummie beat the Brooklyn tough guy, they simply didn't buy it. So they booed. Not a good start.

Nikita's match with Mark Sloan followed, and it was average at best. Mark's wrestling style was never my cup of tea. The problem, in my opinion, was that while The Specialist possessed an arsenal of innovative, spectacular-looking manoeuvres, his matches looked too choreographed and lacked emotion or personality. It was usually too obvious that he was running through a sequence of moves from memory rather than participating in a believable fight.

Then CM Punk had an entertaining scrap with his best pal Colt Cabana, finishing him off with a Pedigree from the middle turnbuckle. But even so, this was not turning into the blow-away show FWA fans had been conditioned to expect.

Backstage, Ian DaSciple was nervous, because he had been given the job of setting the wooden table alight. I was on edge too, as I went around everyone who would be involved in the match, making sure I knew everything that was supposed to happen. I knew if we pulled everything off as planned, it would tear the house down. Everything I'd done in the FWA over the past eight months had built up to this no-holds-barred 'Apocalpyse Grudge Match'. And a lot was riding on it. We simply had to get it right.

The storyline was that Alex was 'injured', so was forced to withdraw. Instead, Ulf had a surprise partner, who turned out to be Whipwreck. Their opponents were Travell and Raj. I patrolled ringside with Scott and Ian, jawing at the fans.

The match definitely suffered without Alex. His chemistry with Travell had held many a Family-Showswearers brawl together. Even so, the action was brutal. It was violent. And the fans loved it.

At one point, Ulf pressed Travell above his head and dropped him in a pile of drawing pins. The German monster then stepped on Paul so the tacks became embedded in his body. What a loon, I thought. And the worst was yet to come.

The moment came for DaSciple to set up the table, pour lighter fluid on it and then flick a cigarette lighter to ignite the blaze. As the flames took hold, Travell and Ghosh set Herman up on the top rope, only for the Giant German to overpower Paul with a choke slam, sending 'The Righteous One' plummeting to his fiery doom.

"WOOOOOOAAAAHHHHH! HOLY S__T! HOLY S__T!" roared the astonished fans.

But as Paul went through the table, the fire had all but gone out. So when he lurched to his feet, there was just a tiny flicker of flame on his T-shirt.

Seeing the stunt hadn't created the desired effect, Mikey Whipwreck then grabbed the bottle of lighter fluid.

"I remember it all perfectly," said Travell, recalling the incident.

"I met with the pyro guy before the match, and he showed me a special gel. He told me he'd put some wax on my back, then some of this gel on my shirt, and then when I went through the table, my shirt would catch fire but I would be protected before I felt any heat at all . . . but only for about a minute.

"The problem was, when Ian DaSciple set the table up, he only squirted a tiny bit of lighter fluid on it, because he had never done anything like this before. Then he kept squirting it with lighter fluid while it was on fire, which only succeeded in setting the top of the lighter fluid bottle on fire.

"When I went through the table, the impact put the fire out. The only thing that was on fire was the lighter fluid bottle, so Mikey picked up what was basically at that point, a flame thrower. And I'd told him I had protective gel on my back . . ."

Which would only protect Paul's skin for about a minute, remember?

Whipwreck squirted the lighter fluid right at Paul's back. At this, The Righteous One went up like an inferno.

I was standing barely three feet away. As Travell staggered about, screaming in terror, his back ablaze, I froze. I hesitated. I didn't know what to do.

Being honest, I wasn't exactly sure if this was supposed to happen. Was it part of the show? Or had the stunt gone wrong? In those few seconds of madness, I honestly wasn't 100% certain. That's inexperience for you.

I was wearing a new knee-length black woollen coat, a garment that would later inspire wrestling fans to chant "HARRY POTTER!" at me. A thought raced through my mind. Should I take off my coat and smother Travell with it?

Too late. Whipwreck had dived on Travell, breaking character for a second or two, and was rolling on top of him in an attempt to put him out. Then I knew for sure. The stunt *had* gone wrong.

Panicking FWA officials threw water on Travell until the fire was completely extinguished. A medical crew gathered around Paul as he writhed on the floor in agony. And the fans barely noticed as Ulf superplexed Raj off the top rope and covered him for the one, two, three.

After months of the most violent feud in British Wrestling history, and after months of my stable squeezing out controversial victories by the skin of our teeth, and after months of build-up, twists and turns, Ulf Herman had finally scored a convincing win over The Family right in the middle of the ring.

But nobody cared.

That's because everyone's attention was on the stricken Travell, as he was helped backstage.

But I couldn't show concern for Paul. It was now time for my big moment.

As a result of the match stipulation, I now had to take the hardest chair shot in professional wrestling from Ulf Herman. Not bloody likely. So as Parker and Whipwreck brawled to the back, and as Herman double choke slammed DaSciple and Ghosh out of their boots, the cowardly Truth bailed out and retreated down the ramp. But my attempted escape was thwarted by Alex Shane, who emerged through the curtain, grabbed me by the hair and frog-marched me roughly back to the ring.

The fans were right back into it as Alex and Ulf tied my hands to the ropes with gaffer tape, ironically in the crucifix position. Ulf even wrapped some tape tight around my eyes as a makeshift blindfold. I didn't have to pretend—it hurt like hell.

I struggled desperately and screamed a high-pitched girlie scream of terror, but there was no escape. The end looked nigh as Ulf prepared the steel chair, ready to bash my skull to oblivion.

The FWA fans who hated my guts stomped their feet and clapped in delight as the salivating German lifted the destructive weapon high in the air, all set to bring it down upon my unprotected, helpless head . . .

. . . until the last possible second, when I was saved by a most unlikely source.

Alex Shane seized the chair from Ulf and smashed his own tag team partner in the head with it. The crowd gasped.

As I untied myself and fled, The Showstealer assaulted Ulf mercilessly, cracking his elbow repeatedly with the chair. I darted back through the curtain, sweating profusely and filled with adrenalin, to hear the muffled chants of "F___ YOU ALEX!" from the outraged audience.

Alex Shane had turned to the dark side, in what was unquestionably the highlight of FWA British Uprising 2. The watching Bill Apter later told me he thought it was the greatest heel turn he'd seen in over 30 years of covering wrestling all over the world.

As I went backstage, I immediately sought out Paul Travell. But he had already been taken to hospital, suffering from third degree burns.

"I don't blame Mikey Whipwreck, it's not his fault," continued Paul.

"Everyone in that match takes joint responsibility. Nobody said they didn't want to be involved in it.

"I might have felt differently if I'd been permanently scarred. But it honestly wasn't as bad as it looked. And I made a career out of it. It's what I'm most remembered for."

But when Alex got backstage, he was livid. The management of the York Hall were equally furious. They weren't happy about the fire stunt, not at all. There were bound to be recriminations.

It's easy to say with hindsight, and certainly I didn't say it to the FWA powers-that-be at the time, but perhaps authorising Paul Travell to fall through a burning table at a wrestling show wasn't the brightest idea they'd ever had.

The rest of the show passed in a blur. The second-half definitely had its moments and British Uprising 2 did get some good reviews. But it was nothing compared to the Uprising of 12 months earlier, when the FWA had raised the bar to a level never seen before in modern-day British Wrestling, and one that, despite all our efforts, the FWA never quite met again.

I didn't speak to Alex for two months after British Uprising 2. The Showstealer went into hiding and stopped answering calls altogether. He later told me he had fallen into a deep depression after Uprising. He said he'd lost thousands of pounds of his own money on the show. And he lost the York Hall as a venue, which was another monumental blow to the FWA.

In fact, Alex spent those two months seriously considering if he should close down the FWA for good.

Alex Shane and me with the FutureShock and XWA Title belts in 2010.

The American contingent backstage at Frontiers of Honor 2003 . . .some
recognisable faces for sure!

'The Phoenix' Jody Fleisch, with that York Hall balcony in the background.

We are The Family! Left to right: Ashe, Scott Parker, 'The Messiah',
Paul Travell and The Truth.

'The Highlander from Hell' Drew McDonald.

The Duke of Danger with his maid Buttercup.

The Morecambe Dome—a magical place.

'Wonderkid' Jonny Storm just after winning the FWA All-England Title at
Sudbury in April 2003.

The lovely Nikita, aka Katie Lea, aka Winter.

I had a love-hate relationship with the FWA fans.
We loved to hate each other!

Jake 'The Snake' Roberts battles 'Rowdy' Ricky Knight.

Sanjay Bagga, the kid from the fanzine stall who became one of the
UK's top promoters.

The great Robbie Brookside in action for All-Star Promotions.

A formidable team: Mark Kay, Dann Read and me backstage at Universal Uproar.

Christopher Daniels and AJ Styles: two of American indie wrestling's
'Golden Generation'.

Brian Dixon, the daddy of all British promoters.

YES! YES! YES it's Daniel Bryan, aka Bryan Danielson, backstage during Ring of Honor's UK tour in 2006.

Joe Legend and D'Lo Brown were the coaches on the ill-fated Celebrity Wrestling show. Here they square off at Universal Uproar.

My favourite British wrestler 'Psychotic Warrior' Johnny Phere with some of the fantastic Morecambe wrestling fans.

Robbie Brookside visits my training school in Morecambe, January 2011.

Alex Shane didn't rate Johnny Phere...until he wrestled him in this match in Morecambe in June 2010.

Two of British Wrestling's best young talents competing in Morecambe in July 2012; Joey Hayes (in mid-air) and Bubblegum.

The one and only Stevie Knight is his usual charming self before a show at his second home, The Morecambe Dome.

British ex-pat Nick 'Magnus' Aldis with fellow TNA star and frequent UK visitor Samoa Joe.

Steve Corino, Mick Foley and The Sandman during the eight-man tag at
Universal Uproar, November 12 2005.

Kendo Nagasaki – British Wrestling legend.

In my opinion, the best all-round performer in British Wrestling of the past decade—'The Wonderkid' Jonny Storm.

Former Pro-Wrestling:EVE Champion Saraya-Jade Bevis, currently under contract to WWE as Paige.

Alex Shane proved his credentials as a world class wrestling performer in his
2005 feud with Mick Foley.

The brilliant 'Rock Star' Spud, star of TNA British Boot Camp, with his
XWA cronies Axl Rage, Stallion and JD Sassoon.

Backstage with Ulf Herman after the FWA show in Sudbury, April 2003.
This giant German wanted to hit me hard in the head with a steel chair.

January 30 2010: The scene at the end of the final wrestling show ever at The
Morecambe Dome before it closed and was demolished.

The FWA and IPW:UK crews united after Final Frontiers on March 25 2007. Back left to right: Johnny Phere, Steve Lynskey, Doug Williams, Flash Barker, Scott Parker, Andy Quildan, Greg Lambert, Dean Ayass, Dann Read, Declan O'Connor, Sam 'Berry' Gardiner, JC Thunder, Jack Saunders. Middle left to right: Ross Jordan, Max Voltage, Luke Phoenix, Dave Moralez, Joey Hayes, Martin Stone, James Tighe, Dirk Feelgood, Sam Slam. Standing extreme left: Chris Hatch. Standing middle: Paul Travell, Paul Robinson, Spud. Standing extreme right: John Atkins. Lying down front centre: Hade Vansen. Kneeling at front: Daniel Edler.

CHAPTER 10

TELEVISION

"After British Uprising 2 I suffered what I can only describe as a mini nervous breakdown. The bomb scare we had that day led to a chain of events that ended up getting me, not FWA, in a serious amount of debt and the stress of it all led to me shutting down everything for five months.

"Fans said what they wanted to say as usual but for the first time I really did not care. I needed a break from everything and felt physically and mentally exhausted. When we came back at New Frontiers 2004 I felt different. I just was not the same passionate person that I was before our last York Hall show. I would have thrown in the towel then. But I had two more goals left to achieve and more importantly I didn't have anything else!

"I still had two goals—to get a weekly national TV show and to run the Coventry Skydome. Until I had done these I would not be able to stop with FWA."

Alex Shane, March 30 2005

After Alex emerged from his exile in 2004, he managed to achieve both of his two goals. He secured a weekly national FWA television show; then on November 13 2004 he promoted FWA British Uprising 3 at the Coventry Skydome, in front of the FWA's biggest ever crowd.

Unfortunately, both of these achievements would ultimately contribute to the destruction of the FWA.

On March 9 2004, Alex announced the FWA had signed a five-year deal to become the "sole and exclusive UK promotion" on The Wrestling Channel (TWC)—the brand new wrestling-only channel on Sky TV.

"Alongside the FWA's weekly television show, viewers can expect to find everything from highlights of FWA main shows, FWA wrestler profile shows, FWA Unsigned, and FWA home shopping," he said.

"Over the coming year, there are even plans for a fly-on-the-wall documentary series, as well as sit-down interviews with imported foreign talent.

"The deal is exciting news for both the FWA and The Wrestling Channel. For over five years now, the FWA has strived to bring the best homegrown talent into the living rooms of wrestling fans around the United Kingdom on a regular basis. The signing of our first national weekly TV slot is a huge landmark for us as a company.

"Everybody at the Frontier Wrestling Alliance would like to thank the wrestlers, staff, and most importantly the loyal fans, that have helped to make this vision a reality."

What a watershed moment, or at least that's how it felt at the time. It was an incredibly exciting announcement for the FWA performers, including myself. I loved the thought of seeing myself on television, doing something I love, on a weekly basis. Who wouldn't? I also thought it was a positive move for British Wrestling. The FWA was putting on great live shows, with a cast of dedicated and talented wrestlers, with the best production values of any British Wrestling company at the time. Finally, we would have the chance to show a TV audience what we could do.

When The Wrestling Channel launched properly on March 15 2004 after a month of test programming, it created a huge buzz amongst the hardcore British Wrestling fan base. The Americans didn't have anything like this. But we Brits now had our very own channel airing non-stop wrestling from 10am to midnight, seven days a week, featuring everything from old 1970s Memphis footage to cutting edge ROH. It was great.

Particularly popular were the archive matches from the glory days of British Wrestling. TWC aired classics from the World of Sport era of the '70s and '80s as well as 'shoot interviews' with some of the industry's biggest names, and an informative and entertaining news/chat show called The Bagpipe Report.

And on Thursday nights at 9pm, later moving to Fridays at the same time, the FWA TV show had its own one hour slot. Hosted by John Atkins, whose relaxed and professional style was well-suited to the role of anchor man, the programme brought the stars of the FWA (including me) directly into British living rooms every single week. Magnificent.

This really felt like a step in the right direction. We had a weekly British Wrestling programme on national TV for the first time in decades. It really felt like we'd finally achieved The Holy Grail.

Except we hadn't.

Firstly, the mere announcement caused a massive backlash on the UK Fan Forum. The mis-use of the words 'sole and exclusive' upset a lot of people within the British Wrestling fraternity. Many accused the FWA of monopolising The Wrestling Channel—ie stopping other British promotions from having a chance to showcase their own product on TV.

The reality was nothing of the sort. In fact the deal paved the way for plenty of other British companies to follow FWA onto TWC, including Sanjay Bagga's LDN, Ricky Knight's WAW and IPW:UK. Alex even organised a special TV taping in Bolton on April 9 2004 called FWA Unsigned. This allowed young wrestlers from several other British promotions the chance to wrestle in front of the TWC cameras for the first time. FWA Unsigned gave non-FWA talent (at the time) like 'Dangerous' Damon Leigh, Joey Hayes, Dirk Feelgood, Johnny Phere and Declan O'Connor their first big televised break.

Alex didn't have to do this, but he did it to give young talent a chance. And as he pointed out at the time, if other British promotions were so upset that FWA was getting on TV and they weren't—then why hadn't they tried to make it happen for themselves instead of just moaning?

Irish Whip Wrestling, a promotion based in the Republic of Ireland, was another to receive airtime on the new all-wrestling channel. IWW's biggest star was a raw and powerful newcomer with bright red hair, milky white skin and an awesome physique. His name was Seamus O'Shaughnessy.

On December 2 2004, Alex Shane went over to Ireland to wrestle the real-life Stephen Farrelly, this talented rookie strongman known as S.O.S.

"I watched how Seamus carried himself, he was the most *professional* professional wrestler in the UK and Ireland at that time," said Alex.

"Seamus had his own agent. He was diplomatic, polite, likeable, knew how to present himself and was constantly driving himself to improve.

"He was still learning the business so before our match, I talked him through a lot of things and during the match, I did everything I could as the heel to make him look a strong babyface. Afterwards, he said to me: 'That's the first time I've truly believed that I *can* do this.'

"The day before he left for America, he phoned me to thank me for the help I'd given him. That showed a level of class you rarely see in wrestling.

"I respect so much what he's done. No wonder Triple H became his friend. He probably looked at Seamus and thought: 'That's the kind of guy we need more of in this company'."

That's Alex Shane's assessment of Seamus, the genial 'Great White' superhero now known worldwide as *Sheamus*, Ireland's first ever WWE World Heavyweight Champion.

Despite the odd success story, it didn't take long for the stark reality of just what The Wrestling Channel would actually achieve to sink in.

The answer was . . . very little.

For most of the time when British Wrestling was broadcast weekly on ITV in the '50s, '60s, '70s and '80s, there were only three television channels. Part of the reason why the wrestling grew in popularity and home grapplers like Big Daddy and Giant Haystacks became stars, was because of this limited choice of viewing. British Wrestling had a captive audience.

But in 2004, The Wrestling Channel was just one of hundreds of available channels on satellite and cable television in the UK. And in the kingdom of channel hopping, the remote control is king.

TWC also had the added problem of a massive competitor, an established monster who enjoyed a dominant market share of the wrestling viewing audience—namely, World Wrestling Entertainment. In March 2004, WWE averaged 270,000 viewers for its programmes on Sky Sports. TWC programmes, including the FWA TV show, generally only drew a few thousand viewers—despite advertising in the national media including on Sky Sports itself and in a new weekly wrestling column in The Daily Star, written by grapple fan and journalist Patrick Lennon.

As a TV channel devoted to a niche product targeted at a restricted demographic (mainly young adult males), TWC struggled to attract businesses prepared to pay to advertise between its programmes. And without sufficient advertising revenue, the channel was always battling to survive.

TWC bosses also had constant difficulties in acquiring new footage, meaning that it wasn't long before the channel was chock-a-block with repeats. This lack of fresh meat did little for ratings.

With cold hard cash in short supply, TWC bosses were only able to pay a pittance to those—like the FWA—who *did* supply ever-changing programme content. So it usually ended up costing the FWA more to film, edit and produce an episode of the TV show than the eventual pay-off they received . . . a pay-off which only arrived several weeks later anyway, leaving the FWA coffers permanently playing catch-up.

So instead of the planned big splash, FWA's tenure on The Wrestling Channel made barely a ripple. Those big plans for an FWA shopping channel, wrestler profile shows and a fly-on-the-wall documentary, well, they never happened.

In early 2005, FWA TV disappeared off TWC. By then British Uprising 3 had come and gone, the FWA had gone into financial meltdown, and we could no longer afford to produce a weekly television show. So TWC ended the five-year contract less than 12 months in.

FWA wasn't the only casualty as TWC battled to survive. Some of the channel's other flagship programmes—like The Bagpipe Report—quickly disappeared because they cost more to produce than the income they generated. In order to stay afloat, TWC was forced to compromise its content and broadcast mixed martial arts and adult films—because in reality, they drew bigger ratings than wrestling . . . . or to be more accurate, *non-WWE* wrestling.

A young wrestling fan from Ireland named Sean Herbert was the driving force behind TWC. In 2009, during a chat on the UK Fan Forum, he explained some of the problems he'd faced.

"TWC lost a lot of money in year one, which is why our programming kicked ass when we launched. We had everything good that was possible to licence at the time, a lot of which we paid too much for—that, and we overestimated our potential viewership: not a good combination. So we eventually subsidised the channel's income with (adult sex channel) Bang Babes. That enabled us to stay in business and break even throughout 2005.

"We turned a small profit in 2006 and 2007. By the end of 2006 onwards . . . ratings were enough to cover the channel's costs, and we knew how to keep costs at a minimum.

"I know a lot of people moaned about us showing MMA and not showing promotion X, Y or Z anymore. But the fact was that we only dropped shows that weren't financially viable to air, and we only signed deals that made money. If we didn't take that approach, we wouldn't have lasted much into 2005.

"TWC was my idea and my baby and it came to fruition through a combination of aptitude, hard work, and blagging—I hadn't a f___ing clue how to launch a TV channel, but I didn't let it stop me, because I knew I could learn fast and pull it off. And if I failed, so what?

"I negotiated all the licence deals, I put all of the elements in place, I went back and forth to London on my Mam's credit card (I was broke) to meet with satellite companies, I had a meeting with Sky where I was such a noob that I forgot to bring a notepad and pen . . . and I eventually got financial backing and it rollercoastered from there.

"We kept the channel afloat for four years and even managed to turn a small profit and eventually sell the business."

On January 14 2008, the channel was re-named The Fight Network, having been bought out by the Canada-based cable operators of the same name, and continued to air a mixture of pro wrestling and other combat sports. But The Fight Network encountered many of the same difficulties as its predecessor. On December 1 2008 the channel ceased transmission in the UK and Ireland for good.

Sean explained: "The bottom line is that there is only a niche audience for non-WWE wrestling. And it's tiny. And the income you make from the niche audience watching, needs to be greater than the costs of running the channel. And that's tough.

"The Fight Network died after 10 months of trying to do what we did, and they had big money behind them. We had me and three others in a small office in the Dublin suburbs."

I see a lot of similarities between Sean Herbert's TWC during its peak years of 2004-5 and Alex Shane's FWA during its own peak of 2002-4. Both became reality thanks to the drive and vision of a passionate individual with a burning love for professional wrestling and no business background, and both are remembered fondly by wrestling fans even to this day. It's hardly surprising that in 2005 Alex and Sean teamed up to promote the best independent wrestling show held in the British Isles during the noughties. More on that later.

Ultimately, though, both TWC and the FWA were not financially sustainable. And for the FWA, The Holy Grail turned out to be nothing more than a poisoned chalice.

CHAPTER II

THE GREATEST YEAR

The FWA's stint on Sky TV would ultimately end prematurely, but Alex Shane deserves credit for bending over backwards in an attempt to make it a success. In March 2004, refreshed following his five-month hiatus, The Showstealer had redoubled his efforts towards making the FWA product as exciting as it could possibly be, in order to create compelling storylines and wrestling action for television. The result was arguably the most creatively memorable year for any promotion in recent British Wrestling history.

Now banned from the York Hall, the FWA had to find a new London venue for its comeback show and inaugural TV taping. This was Brent Town Hall near Wembley Stadium. It was a decent building for wrestling, but with nowhere near the legacy and ambience of Bethnal Green. Still, fan anticipation for the FWA's return was high, especially when Raven was announced as the headline act.

The former ECW legend and WWE star, then in the midst of a heated rivalry with the fast-rising CM Punk on the US independent scene, was still enough of a drawing card with British fans to attract a crowd of 700 to Brent Town Hall on March 26 2004. Exactly one year later, I witnessed another example of Raven's star power first-hand, when we brought The Flock leader to wrestle in Morecambe and drew our biggest ever attendance at The Dome.

Results from FWA New Frontiers 2004 were as follows:

Mark Belton beat James Tighe, Mark Sloan went to a no-contest with Aviv Maayan, Jonny Storm pinned X-Dream, Burchill and Simmonz defeated Stevie Knight and Jorge Castano, CM Punk beat Raven, Alex Shane beat Jack Xavier, Hade Vansen fought Zebra Kid to a double disqualification, FWA Champion Doug Williams defeated Steve Corino in a two out of three falls match.

New Frontiers also marked Alex Shane's first match since his heel turn. To assist his transformation to the FWA's number one villain, Alex changed his theme music to a more sinister track, adjusted his catchphrase to "it's *time to fear*, because The Showstealer is here" and recruited a gang of muscular trainee wrestlers to dress up as nightclub bouncers and act as his 'personal security force'. This group included three rookies—Paul 'Stixx' Grint, Leroy Kincaide and a rugged Londoner named Martin Harris—whose wrestling name was Martin Stone.

I expected that Ulf Herman would be there as normal, ready to unleash a terribly violent retribution on Alex for his treachery at British Uprising 2. This made sense to me, from a storyline perspective, and a Herman-Shane match was certainly what the FWA fans wanted to see. But on March 26 2004, Ulf *wasn't* there. Instead, Alex brought in a different opponent to act as his new nemesis; in a plot twist which may not have delivered the dream match, but certainly made everybody sit up and take notice.

During what would eventually be broadcast as the first ever match on the FWA's new Sky TV show, Mark Sloan was wrestling the debuting Aviv Maayan—a super-polite and technically proficient young man who was Sloan's star pupil at the FWA Training Academy. The action was developing unremarkably, until a bleached-blond haired figure in a white shirt and tie stomped through the crowd, leaped the guardrail and slid into the ring, bringing the Sloan-Maayan encounter to a halt.

The fans could not believe their eyes. It was former ECW Champion Steve Corino, who seized the microphone and proceeded to call Alex Shane out, leading to a verbal spat between Corino and Shane which had fans buzzing. Corino, nicknamed 'The King of Old School', was the last person the fans expected to see at an FWA event.

Less than a year before, the American had a very public argument with The Showstealer over the Frontiers of Honor extravaganza. It was a silly misunderstanding really . . . Alex thought Elisar had booked Corino for the show, Steve was adamant he was never scheduled to come to Britain, and these two strong personalities ended up trading vicious barbs on the internet. The fans knew there was genuine animosity between Corino and Shane, so there was bedlam in the arena as they anticipated what they thought could turn out to be a real fight.

"Although I don't get on with Steve Corino any more after we fell out over 1PW, we did get on back then and he really didn't like Alex at all," Steve Lynskey recalled.

"It was me who persuaded him to come to the FWA. He said the only way he'd do it was if Alex apologised to him in the dressing room in front of all the boys . . . although that never happened."

But Alex, always one to try to blur the lines between real life and storyline in order to extract controversy, did eventually bury the hatchet with Corino. But because the fans didn't know this, Shane shrewdly realised a feud with Steve would be big box office for the FWA. He also felt his matches with Corino would be better than bouts with Ulf Herman, who wasn't a proficient ring technician and only excelled in a hardcore environment.

Alex also didn't relish the prospect of wrestling Ulf in the kind of violent matches Herman made his trademark. Alex had put his body through hell the previous year during all those wars with The Family and wanted to take it easier for a while. So he put the Herman feud on the backburner.

Although Ulf briefly returned to the FWA at British Uprising 3 and Goldrush later that year, the Shane-Herman feud fizzled out after that. Ulf was owed money from those shows, money he never received as the FWA's financial situation hit the skids, and this pay dispute meant he never again returned to the FWA. That was a shame. I think a properly built up Herman v Shane match could have been a huge deal for the FWA. The company's most popular babyface versus its most hated heel. I'm sad it never happened, and I think the fans were disappointed too. I'd go so far as to say that the collapse of the Shane v Herman rivalry contributed as the fans rapidly lost interest in the FWA in 2005.

But back in 2004, Alex's heel turn had also affected The Family. We were no longer the company's most hated act—Alex was. And although Shane drafted in the intimidating Drew McDonald at New Frontiers to replace The Messiah as the group's new spiritual leader, I felt The Family had definitely lost some steam. But Alex had come up with an interesting storyline with the potential to turn things around.

Since burning himself half to death at Uprising, Paul Travell had gradually gained a lot of fan support. The FWA fans appreciated Travell's sado-masochistic efforts to entertain them. So when 'The Righteous One' emerged at New Frontiers, wielding his new 'sidekick'—a barbed wire baseball bat he'd christened 'Mr Pointy'—he received a booming ovation.

In storyline, I was furious that Travell's head was being turned by the attention of the fans. So I used the powerful presence of Drew McDonald to keep the FWA's 'Hardcore Icon' in check, even when Drew himself couldn't be there in person due to his many other wrestling commitments.

Copying an angle I'd seen Kurt Angle pull off on WWE Smackdown, I even began carrying a large framed photograph of Drew to ringside for Family title defences. Whenever Travell was distracted by the fans' cheers, I would hold up the photograph to remind him that The Highlander from Hell was always watching and implored him to cheat to win matches to keep Drew happy.

"Do it for Drew!" I yelled, as Travell stared back at me with a tortured look on his face, his conscience torn between the growing adoration of the fans and his loyalty to The Family. It was obvious he would eventually turn on us, but the question was when? And how? It definitely made for a gripping plotline.

As mentioned before, CM Punk was back over for that New Frontiers weekend, where he defeated Raven at Brent and James Tighe in Enfield. I had the pleasure of sitting down for a Power Slam interview with the self-assured Punk in the café at the Southbury Leisure Centre before the Enfield show, when he was adamant he would one day be a success in the WWE. Prophetic words indeed.

I thought Punk was all right, but not everybody did.

"I didn't really see eye to eye with CM Punk," said Dean Ayass.

"It stems from an incident while we were driving to Enfield. I was in a car with Punk and Steve Corino, who I've always got on really well with. We pulled up at a retail estate, where Steve and I got out to check out this Chinese buffet place to see if it was worth stopping for food. But it was really manky, so we came out again.

"Back in the car, Steve was taking the mick out of Punk for his Straight Edge thing, how he didn't do drugs, didn't drink, didn't sleep around. He told Punk he wouldn't have liked the Chinese restaurant because you'd have to go from one dish to another like you might go from one woman to another. Then I piped up: 'Yes, it would be like promiscuous eating!' Everybody laughed, but Punk shot daggers at me. It was like: 'How dare you take the piss out of me.' Well pardon me for trying to make him feel welcome in a strange country by having a joke with him.

"But I will say this for Punk. At International Showdown in 2005, I was on the backstage camera. I was filming people as they went up the steps to the ring for one of the video packages for the DVD, and filming promos as the wrestlers came backstage after the match. I asked Punk if he would do a promo, and he delivered this incredible impassioned five-minute speech about his opponent Samoa Joe, completely off the top of his head. I was absolutely blown away."

The night after Enfield, Doug Williams successfully defended his FWA Title against Punk in Newport, Wales.

"It was a decent match with a lot of comedy, as I recall," said Doug.

"But if I'm going to be brutally honest, I didn't see anything from Punk that would make him stand out from any of the other Americans I wrestled at that time. Certainly there was no indication that he would go on to become the biggest star in the business."

By the time FWA Crunch rolled around in Broxbourne on April 11 2004, The Family was looking threadbare. For some reason, Ian DaSciple and Ashe were no longer being used and Drew wasn't available. So there was just Paul, Raj, Scott . . . oh, and the trusty photographic tribute to Mr McDonald at my side, as The Family defeated Mark Belton and Aviv Maayan in a tag title defence.

Later that night, as Simmonz and Buttercup soaked up the adulation of the crowd, I led The Family to ringside. As I had for Raj Ghosh nearly a year earlier, I got in Simmonz's face and cut an impassioned speech in an attempt to recruit the FWA's cult hero to The Family. I pointed out how The Duke of Danger mistreated his henchman, and how he could be British Heavyweight Champion if he ditched the ridiculous butler outfit, dumped his "blonde scrubber" of a maid, and joined our group.

As the FWA's new number one babyface, Simmonz duly refused. This led to the obligatory Family beatdown, which featured the bizarre sight of Raj dropping his own girlfriend Jenna head-first with a DDT. Yes, even domestic violence is perfectly acceptable in the professional wrestling ring where almost anything goes.

But The Duke of Danger scooted out to ringside to make the save, smashing my beloved Drew photograph frame over Scott Parker's bonce in the process. I acted all devastated and furious, and vowed revenge on Hampton Court. This was a cracking little angle, which I absolutely loved.

Results from FWA Crunch were:

The Family beat Mark Belton and Aviv Maayan, All-England Champion Hade Vansen pinned Zebra Kid, Eamon Shrahan pinned James Tighe, Jonny Storm defeated Sonjay Dutt, Alex Shane downed Jack Xavier in a Last Man Standing Match, FWA Champion Doug Williams beat D'Lo Brown.

I have really fond memories of that whole Crunch weekend. On the Thursday before the Broxbourne show (April 8 2004) the FWA brought D'Lo Brown to Morecambe. The former WWE Intercontinental Champion was arguably the biggest star we ever had on at The Dome, and the overseas wrestler I've most enjoyed meeting.

Most of the American stars I've worked with over the years didn't have much to say. They tended to exchange a few pleasantries, keep themselves to themselves and concentrate on their match. So who were the friendliest overseas stars I've ever met? I would say Joe Legend, Steve Corino, Jimmy Hart, Colt Cabana, Terry Funk, Bill Apter, Earl Hebner, Mick Foley and Raven—once I got to know him—and definitely D'Lo, who was an absolute gent.

The big Floridian was also a huge hit with the crowd as he pinned Jonny Storm in a very good main event. TNA star Sonjay Dutt was also over for the weekend too. That night Mark Kay and I actually made a profit for the first time ever as promoters and celebrated by getting 'Down with the Brown' at seedy Morecambe nightclub Crystal T's. I'm not sure Alex Shane and Andy Simmonz recall this evening quite as happily though, given the rough pair of slappers they left with. I swear blind to this day that Simmonz's . . . erm . . . lady friend actually had no teeth.

Alex did have a fulfilling weekend wrestling-wise though, as he put over (lost to) young Aviv in a textbook big man v small man match at Morecambe, which he watched with pride on video the following morning at my house. Then he beat Jack Xavier in a thrilling Last Man Standing match at Broxbourne, which Alex personally rates as his best FWA match ever, with help from his new ally, the All-England Champion Hade Vansen. Now known as 'The South City Thriller', Hade's fortunes in the FWA had really benefited from a turn to the dark side. With his movie star good looks, natural charisma and presence, I saw the cocky Hade as a potential star of the future. He definitely had 'the look' to go far in the business, although his skills inside the ring needed work.

The Crunch weekend was a whirlwind for me . . . we did four shows in four days. It finally seemed like the FWA was stepping things up, quantity-wise. Alex had done an interview with Power Slam in early 2004 where he'd outlined plans to run "six to eight shows per month". The Crunch weekend had been an unmitigated success as far as I was concerned. I could sense momentum really building once again after the blip of Uprising 2.

But then . . . nothing. The FWA didn't return for another six weeks, for our second of five shows that year at The Dome.

May 29 2004 saw an all-British show with no American imports, so we didn't draw as well as the D'Lo event. But creatively, it was another belter, as Jonny Storm cockily put his career on the line against James Tighe, who'd been on a losing streak. And wouldn't you know it, Tighe turned the tables to pin The Wonderkid and send him into exile. In reality, the loss was a storyline cover so Jonny could go and live in Thailand for a few months.

Meanwhile FWA TV kept Storm in the public eye with some hilarious skits of Jonny's supposed misadventures in 'Thailand'—which had in fact been filmed on Morecambe beach. Self-absorbed but loveable, Jonny was really developing into a well-rounded performer by this point, adding verbal virtuosity to his vaunted in-ring skills.

Another grappler with bags of character was Dirk Feelgood. The date of May 29 2004 marked Dirk's FWA main show debut. Although he took a pasting in two minutes flat from the rampant Burchill, this was a breakthrough occasion for the colourful Monk of Funk. It was also a big moment for me.

Real name Andrew Dickinson, Dirk was a regular guy with a great sense of humour. Soon after we'd first met at Dann Read's show in Ipswich in 2002, we became buddies and he began to pen a regular column for WrestlingX. Shortly afterwards, Mark Kay and I decided to go and see him wrestle—and so began our monthly Friday night trips down to a working men's club in deepest darkest Longton near Stoke-on-Trent. Known as Bidds, this spit-and-sawdust drinking hole was the home of a tiny promotion called AIWF-GB (formerly GBH) run by veteran wrestler Chris Curtis.

Chris coached a stable of talented young wrestlers including Dirk, Johnny Phere, Five Star Flash and another prospect called Pip Cartner, whose wrestling name back then was Symon Phoenix. Later, Pip would go on to become one of the UK's very best talents under the name of Bubblegum.

While the FWA was thriving on a national scale, AIWF-GB was British Wrestling's best kept secret. They put on their basic but entertaining little shows in the rustic surroundings of Bidds, completely under the radar of even the low-profile UK scene. I can't express just how much Mark Kay and I enjoyed being in the crowd for those cheesy Friday night shows. We'd hang out with the wrestlers after the matches, and struck up a great rapport with the likes of Five Star, Chris, Dirk, Johnny, his brother Simon, Pip and the veteran Stoke wrestler Keith Myatt, a lovely fella who we remembered watching at The Dome as 'Kindhearted' Keith Myatt during the Rulebreakers' Posse era.

"Bidds was just awesome," recalled Mark.

"It was my sort of place, being a country music fan, because it had a mural of country stars on the wall. It was old-fashioned, the drink was cheap and the atmosphere was always rocking.

"The wrestling was of a mixed quality and some of the comedy could be unintentional. But for the fans, the actual wrestling never meant as much as the characters and caring about who won or lost.

"I miss Bidds. I've never seen that kind of thing duplicated anywhere else."

However, Bidds is also memorable for one terrifying night on the M6 coming back from Longton, because it was nearly the death of us. But for this incredibly lucky escape, my involvement in wrestling would never have taken off, and this book would never have been written.

It happened in December 2002 . . . appropriately, on Friday the 13th.

"It was the closest I've come to dying," continued Mark.

"It was raining quite hard. We were approaching some roadworks when suddenly I lost control of the Corsa and we spun 180 degrees.

"Greg was in the passenger's seat and grabbed me in panic. I shoved him off, thinking 'Jesus Christ!' I thought we were goners.

"I remember a big truck blazing past us, missing us by inches. It must have seen us spin and moved lanes at the last second.

"You know how they say in times of extreme crisis, you see things in slow motion? That's what happened to me. There we were flying sideways down the motorway and I can't believe how much time I had to think clearly about what to do. Time stood still.

"When the car came to a halt, we were pointing back towards the way we had come. Thank God it was nearly midnight and the motorway was quiet. Somebody was looking after us that night."

So we lived to tell the tale and to return to AIWF-GB, where Dirk and Johnny formed a hilarious tag team which played off their opposing personalities. The geeky Dirk would act the goat while the maniacal Phere seethed at his partner's tomfoolery. I loved 'Pleasure and Pain' and often found myself crying with laughter at their antics—particularly Phere's OTT temper tantrums and Dirk's delightfully tongue-in-cheek ring introduction before every match, when the nerdy 'playboy' proclaimed himself "The Mister who Kissed Your Sister, The Brother Who Scored With Your Mother and The Altar Boy of Sexual Joy".

Dirk and Johnny were the stars of AIWF-GB. They had something so many other British wrestlers back then *didn't* have . . . *personality*. Too many British grapplers, even today, are more concerned with pulling off spectacular moves than being what they should be; and that's *entertainers.* The big characters are always the ones the public remember, whether it's Hulk Hogan and The Rock in America, or Daddy, Haystacks, Kendo Nagasaki and Les Kellett in Britain. They're also the ones, generally, who make the most money.

Feelgood and JP were also nice guys who deserved a break. The more I went to see them, the more I became convinced they were ideal to step up to the FWA. I just had to convince Alex.

This took some doing. I sent Alex tapes of Feelgood and Phere. It took him months to watch them. Then when he eventually did, he seemed unimpressed with what he saw. Refusing to take no for an answer, I pestered and pestered The Showstealer until he eventually put Dirk and Johnny on the FWA Unsigned bill of April 2004, and then agreed to give both try-out matches on FWA events in Morecambe. And after Dirk's selfless display in helping to grow Burchill's reputation as a monster, Alex was finally sold on the abilities of The Monk of Funk and he became an FWA regular.

Dirk now had his feet firmly under the FWA table and I was sure Johnny Phere could soon join him. After all, Phere was the more dedicated of the two. And unlike Dirk, who looked like an ordinary bloke in spandex . . . albeit dazzling lime green spandex with a yellow smiley face on the chest . . . Phere also had 'the look'. With his chiseled movie star features, tattoos and toned body, he had all the physical tools to be a somebody in the wrestling business. He also ate, slept and breathed wrestling and had real fire in his belly to make a career out of his obsession.

"My younger brother Simon and I used to wrestle everywhere as kids," said Phere, speaking in 2012.

"We'd wrestle in parks, in the backyard and in the playground. We'd just have matches against each other at random: barbed wire matches, using chairs . . . one time he even swung a garden swing at my head.

"I think it was a release for me. I was a shy and withdrawn child. The physical pain masked the mental pain I was going through.

"I found Chris Curtis' gym through the internet. August 26 2001, it was, when I attended my first session.

"There were so many established wrestlers there and they brutalised us. It was horrendous. We just did hour after hour of bumping on hard mats.

"But me being me, while others dropped out, I just worked harder. I would bump while carrying weights. I would bump even before training started, just to do more than the others. I wasn't the best wrestler, but I was by far the most passionate."

I had the same desperation for Johnny to succeed. That's why on the day of his FWA try-out—July 31 2004 at The Dome, also against Paul Burchill—I encouraged him to do everything he could to shine and impress Alex. I even suggested that Johnny show off one of his best moves, the snap suplex, which Burchill could then recover from in superhuman style and then polish Phere off with his devastating power arsenal.

The explosive three-minute match progressed exactly as I had planned. Phere looked great and Burchill, in winning, looked even better. I was delighted with Johnny's performance. But Alex wasn't. The Showstealer thought JP did too much and his aggressive style made Burchill look weak. He also didn't like Johnny as a person, thinking him moody and ungrateful for the opportunity. The match didn't even make it onto the FWA TV show. I was so deflated that Phere had failed his big audition, when I felt he'd passed with flying colours.

This was the start of what Mark Kay calls my own 'obsession' with Johnny Phere. And over the years, it does feel like JP's career has become almost my personal project. But that's because I see his talent where so many other promoters never have. He's so underrated . . . he simply doesn't get the credit he deserves.

I also see his qualities as a person. The real-life Jamie Hutchinson is sometimes misunderstood, just as Alex misunderstood him that day in Morecambe. You see, Jamie has had a few personal problems in his life. For years he struggled to hold down a regular job, and he found it hard to settle in one place—often moving from town to town. He dedicates his spartan life to a rigorous regimen of physical training and prefers not to socialise with other wrestlers. And he takes wrestling *incredibly* seriously. JP 'lives his gimmick' which has often seen him mocked by his peers in the dressing room who probably feel threatened by his devotion to his art.

Jamie *can* come across as moody to people who don't really know him, but that's just his nature. He's not ungrateful or aloof, in fact he's the exact opposite. He's humble, a real grafter, and has a charm, vulnerability and decency to his character. And he's a *great* performer, with a unique and engaging in-ring persona. He's also a really good singer on the quiet. Check out his renditions of David Gray songs on YouTube, and prepare to be shocked.

All in all, Johnny Phere is, without a shadow of a doubt, my favourite British wrestler. And despite the setback of July 31 2004, I was determined not to give up on him.

"It's funny actually, because Greg was always more bothered about getting me into the FWA than *I* was," continued JP.

"Greg had seen all the different sides to me: my wrestling, my promos and my character work. But Alex hadn't seen the whole picture at that point.

"Perhaps that's always been my problem though. I've never put myself out there to try to impress promoters. So one promotion at a time tends to bring me in, whether it was AIWF-GB, GPW or XWA, and I'd just concentrate on getting to the top of that promotion, rather than try to get work anywhere else. I don't know why I've never relied on more than one company. I guess I just never pushed myself hard enough."

I've always believed that if Johnny *did* push himself hard enough to get a try-out with a major American company, they would sign him on the spot. He's got the action hero look, the intensity and the talking ability they covet so dearly. Whenever he's on camera, he positively bursts through the television screen—he's *made* for worldwide TV. I do think, though, if JP made it to America he would struggle once he got there . . . because Johnny marches to the beat of nobody's drum but his own. He would never kiss anyone's backside, and sometimes you have to play the political game to survive, especially in the dog-eat-dog world of McMahon.

Back to the FWA main shows, and sandwiched between the May, June and July 2004 Morecambe events was FWA Carpe Diem on June 18, back at Brent Town Hall. The results were:

Mark Sloan beat Aviv Maayan, Mal Sanders beat Steve Grey two falls to one, Low Ki beat James Tighe via a knockout, Simmonz beat Burchill by countout, Alex Shane and

Hade Vansen defeated Ross Jordan and Paul Travell, FWA Heavyweight Champion Doug Williams beat The Zebra Kid

The biggest surprise for me on this show was the presence of Jake 'The Snake' Roberts.

Yes, Jake was still living in the UK and still making a nuisance of himself. A few months earlier, Roberts and Alex had been part of a February/March tour of Scotland and the North East with a promotion called WZW. Backstage at an event in Dumfries, a worse-for-wear Jake had goaded Alex in the dressing room and made a disgusting comment about his mother and grandmother, at which the livid Showstealer had slapped 'The Snake' twice across the face, Roberts had retaliated by picking up a whisky bottle intending to use it as a weapon, and the angry pair had to be separated by the other wrestlers. Jake did apologise to Alex the next day though, once he was sober.

Still, we all thought Jake was the last person Alex would have brought into the FWA. Yet there was the former WWE great at Brent Town Hall, as large as life, slumped on a chair in the backstage area.

Desperate times had called for desperate measures. Steve Corino was supposed to be there to continue his feud with Alex, but had been unable to make it due to flight problems. So Alex called in Jake as a late replacement, thinking his 'star power' and a heated in-ring Alex-Jake confrontation—playing off their real-life enmity—would appease fans deprived of Carpe Diem's marquee attraction of Shane v Corino. But unfortunately, Jake showed up 'in no condition to perform'. Alex and Dino had to tell him to go home.

Two months later on August 1, Jake proved his unreliability yet again by no-showing a major event at the KC Arena in Hull promoted by Stevie Knight. This turned out to be a fabulous night's wrestling, headlined by a gripping three-way main event where I managed Paul Burchill to victory over Doug Williams and The Zebra Kid. Who needed Jake? Not Stevie Knight, that's for sure.

Later that month, Johnny Phere was booked in a match with Roberts, while both were working for WAW.

"When I spoke to Jake, I actually found him to be a nice guy and he certainly knew his stuff," said JP.

"But then when you're getting ready backstage, and he has his line of cocaine and his bottle of whisky, and he's offering them to you, it's quite shocking.

"I've always been staunchly anti-drugs and had the willpower to say no, even to someone like Jake. But I bet a lot of other wrestlers at the time said: 'Yeah, sure' because it's their way of being part of the crowd. That's not something that's ever interested me.

"Jake was also in a lot of pain at the time, with his back, so he wouldn't let me slam him during the match. I also heard off Ricky Knight that I was supposed to win the match, but Jake didn't want to lose to this young lad, so he ended up going over (winning).

"It would have been nice to say I'd got a win over Jake 'The Snake' Roberts, but I've never viewed wrestling like that. I do what I'm told to do."

By the end of the year, The Snake was in trouble with the law. On November 2 2004, he was found guilty of animal cruelty after he'd neglected his pet 12-foot Burmese python to the point that it starved to death (you really couldn't make this stuff up, could you?) Jake then slithered back home to America, his bridges well and truly burned in Britain. What a truly sad state of affairs.

Having been let down by the shell of Jake Roberts, Alex and Dino came up with Plan C for the scheduled tag team match—giving a chance to a delighted young Ross Jordan and none other than Paul Travell, who defied my orders to become Ross's partner and thus dip his toes even further into the babyface waters.

Travell and Jordan v Shane and Vansen was a decent little scrap, but the fans were clearly disappointed that the long-awaited first wrestling match between Alex and Corino had failed to materialise. This was a rare example of FWA doing the opposite of Alex's mantra which he'd first unveiled to me at Revival. They over-promised . . . but under-delivered.

Despite this, there were several memorable moments at Carpe Diem. Simmonz ended the winning streak of Burchill thanks to outside interference from Drew McDonald. Why would Drew help Simmonz? Was The Family still trying to recruit the mega-popular butler? This was interesting stuff which added an extra element of intrigue and kept the Family-Hampton Court war simmering ahead of their upcoming clash for the Tag Team Titles.

Aside from McDonald, other British Wrestling veterans made an impact at Carpe Diem. Mick McManus, one of the most famous names in the history of the British ring, made a guest appearance at the show and it was a real privilege to shake hands backstage with the great 'Man They Loved to Hate'. And Flash Barker, who was being forced to quit the ring through injury (which in storyline terms, had been caused by Hade Vansen in their match at Uprising 2) was given an emotional send-off in a ceremony where Doug Williams, Justin Richards and Low Ki—Barker's opponent from Frontiers of Honor—all paid tribute to Phil.

I've always had huge respect for Flash. I've enjoyed chatting to him backstage at shows and absorbing his immense knowledge and love for the business. He was also one of the biggest supporters of the FWA itself, so I was pleased he was allowed his moment of glory.

"Flash was one of my best friends in the business at the time," said Doug Williams.

"We wrestled each other hundreds of times for Premier Promotions, the FWA and All-Star, and we got on like a house on fire. A promoter could always put us together and we'd have a good match, and we did it everywhere we went. It's a real shame he didn't quite get everything from the wrestling business that he wanted to."

The veteran Ricky Knight, or Paddy as he was known backstage, also debuted at Carpe Diem. The Norwich brawler wore an American football shirt in the ring and could still perform at a high level at the age of 51. The fans booed him mercilessly after he cost his own son The Zebra Kid his match with Doug for the FWA Title, committing the ultimate act of evil by betraying his own offspring.

And earlier in the show, Ricky's wrestler wife, the bright red-haired Julia Hamer—whose wrestling name is Sweet Saraya—had also made a shock arrival by blindsiding Nikita, giving her a piledriver. This attack came after FWA's mousey ring announcer Jane Childs turned manipulative superbitch, by revealing she was the person who had placed a bounty on Nikita's head. It was a shame FWA never really followed up on this angle because it certainly had a hot start.

This was my first meeting with the Knights and I quickly developed huge respect for them. British Wrestling's first family are loveable rogues with immense passion for the business. I've always enjoyed working with Ricky, Saraya, Roy, his brother Zak and their sister Saraya-Jade, who signed for the WWE in 2011 and now wrestles under the name of Paige on NXT—their weekly television show featuring the 'stars of tomorrow'. I'm proud to say that all five members of the Knight wrestling family have wrestled for me in Morecambe at one time or another. And although he may have had his problems away from the ring, I've always found Roy, in particular, to be a really nice bloke.

Prior to meeting Paddy and his wrestling family, I'd heard a lot of negative stories about the clan. "The Knights work too stiff," was one popular phrase being bandied about. In other words, some felt that in an effort to make their matches look believable, Ricky, Saraya and Roy sometimes hit too hard inside the ring. But James Curtin, aka 'The Rock Star' Spud, told me this was an urban myth.

"The Knights are very misunderstood, in my opinion," said James in 2012.

"They are unorthodox but they are not stiff. They're just extremely good at making it look real.

"I've wrestled Julia. She's rough but not dangerous. Julia makes the fans believe that she really is this nasty woman. And Paddy is a gentleman in real life. So is Roy. None of them would ever hurt anyone on purpose in the ring."

Meeting the Knights reinforced a belief of mine which I try to live by. Always take people as you find them and don't judge anyone until you've met them yourself. It's become my number one rule when dealing with people in wrestling. I've heard a lot of tittle-tattle about wrestlers and promoters over the years. I try not to listen. Instead, I make my own mind up about people and base my opinions on personal experience alone.

"A lot of people say a lot of things about the Knights, calling us pikeys or whatever," said Ricky in 2012.

"But we will work with anyone and we will help anyone. People meet us and realise that we're not what we're made out to be.

"For example, I've heard it said that I've had my differences with Alex. I have no problems with Alex whatsoever."

The creative machinations of the FWA really fascinated me back in 2004. I loved to try to second-guess Alex and Dino's booking plans, and work out who was going to wrestle who, and why, what was going to happen next, and why things didn't quite work out as I expected. I wanted to learn more about the twists and turns of the creative process behind the wrestling and maybe even get to suggest some of my own ideas for FWA storylines.

So after one of the summer 2004 shows in Morecambe, I told Alex I wanted to become more involved behind-the-scenes in FWA, that I felt I had something to offer not just as a performer and a promoter, but as a booker.

Alex always likes to say that in life, your biggest strength is also your biggest weakness. One of my big strengths is that I'm never satisfied with what I've got so I'm always pushing to better myself, to do more, try different projects, get the most out of life, never standing still.

But that also means that sometimes, I take on too much than is good for me. And joining the FWA management team was one of those occasions.

Alex duly invited me to a meeting with himself and Dino in London, the day before the FWA's big summer 2004 event at Broxbourne Civic Hall, FWA Vendetta. Dino picked me up near Bethnal Green tube station in his open-top sports car and raced me through the East End to Alex's home in Finsbury Park. We ended up in a dingy pub on the Seven Sisters Road near Shane's house where, in a privately booked upstairs room, I listened as Alex and Dino mapped out their plans for Vendetta, and absorbed every bit of their knowledge and expertise as I could.

I was especially fascinated by their layout (script) for the finish of our match, The Family v Hampton Court for the FWA Tag Team Titles. It sounded complex on paper, but if we pulled it off, the Broxbourne fans would be treated to a real emotional roller coaster!

Results from FWA Vendetta on July 25 2004 were:

Mark Sloan beat Jack Hazard, Mark Belton downed Aviv Maayan, Double C (Antonio Cesaro) beat X Dream, Ricky Knight pinned The Zebra Kid, All-England Champion Hade Vansen and Jack Xavier went to a double countout, Hampton Court beat The Family to win the FWA Tag Team Titles, James Tighe beat AJ Styles by DQ.

The thrilling climax of Paul Travell and Raj Ghosh's title defence against The Duke of Danger and Simmonz has gone down in the annals of FWA history as The Simmonz Double Turn. It also created the loudest crowd 'pop' (noise) I'd heard on a live UK wrestling show to that point.

To keep the retired Flash Barker in the mix, the popular hard man was unveiled at Vendetta as the FWA's new authority figure. As the title match unfolded, Paul Burchill turned up, looking for revenge on Drew McDonald for what happened at Carpe Diem. Their brawl led to mayhem in the arena, as Barker and his force of security staff tried to separate the raging 'Monster' and the burly Scotsman. Eventually Flash demanded that McDonald and Burchill both leave the ringside area to restore order and allow the title match to continue. I acted furious at Barker's decision to throw our 'spiritual leader' out of the building—while the rebellious Paul Travell reacted with a sick smile of satisfaction.

Towards the end of the match, Travell appeared to have matters well in hand but once again, preferred to play to the crowd, bringing Mr Pointy into the ring. According to a pre-match stipulation, if Paul used Mr Pointy then I would be fired from the FWA. Irate at Travell's continued insubordination, I could stand no more . . . and I slapped The Righteous One across the face!

Paul's expression immediately changed and he proceeded to go completely psycho. Turning to Raj Ghosh, he hooked his own tag team partner and dropped him face-first with his Sacrificial Slam. Then, as I looked on in utter horror, he seized Mr Pointy and went for me too. So I legged it! With the fans egging him on, Travell's final act as a member of The Family was to chase the frantically backpedalling Truth out of Broxbourne, leaving Ghosh at a two against one disadvantage.

The battered Duke of Danger managed to tag in Simmonz and the fans roared in anticipation of the butler taking advantage of Ghosh's predicament. But instead, Andy charged across the ring and delivered a shocking corner splash to the Duke! The Broxbourne faithful were stunned as Simmonz's expression changed. "I SOLD OUT!" he bellowed, ripping off his butler garb to reveal underneath . . . a Family T-Shirt!

The fans booed for all they were worth. It was a Family ruse all along! Simmonz *had* joined the cult! Surely not? No! NO! The fans were heartbroken in disbelief as the butler beckoned to Ghosh to hold the Duke in place as he climbed to the middle turnbuckle, looking for all the world like the servant was about to attack his boss . . . .

Simmonz leaped off the turnbuckle to deliver his Butler Blockbuster . . . but not to The Duke. Instead, he hooked *Ghosh* with the move, driving Raj with precision into the canvas! YES! Then, in a stroke of marketing genius which had fans rushing to the merchandise stall afterwards, Andy tore off his Family shirt to reveal yet another garment—the brand new Simmonz tee—a T-Shirt replica of his butler's waistcoat and bow tie. The pumped-up Andy flashed a double bicep pose of celebration to the cheering fans, before leaping on top of the fallen Raj as the referee counted one, two, THREE!

At this, the crowd went absolutely potty in celebration. The people were on their feet, hugging each other, applauding and yelling in genuine relief and delight. Simmonz had *not* turned to the dark side, but had pretended to in order to dupe The Family and make sure the tag team championship belts would be Hampton Court's after all!

The booking of this marvellous piece of theatre was classic Alex and Dino. They sent the fans' emotions down one route, then swiftly brought them straight back down another one, to ensure they experienced a rollercoaster of feelings, then POW! They delivered exactly what then spectators wanted at the end. The Simmonz Double Turn proved that although wrestling is not 'real', when done properly it can still provoke real reactions even from those jaded fans who think they are smart to the business.

Vendetta 2004 also saw an appearance in the FWA by a tall and slim Swiss wrestler called Double C. At time of writing, the real-life Claudio Castagnoli is now enjoying worldwide success as the WWE United States Champion, Antonio Cesaro. Alex and Dino sure had a habit of booking the international stars of the future, didn't they?

Another highly emotional situation at Vendetta centred around a real-life family, Ricky Knight and The Zebra Kid. At Vendetta, 'Rowdy' Ricky defeated his own flesh and blood after an exciting brawl when his younger son Zak—then only 12 years old—actually got into the ring to plead with his dad and brother not to hurt each other any more. Zebra listened and stopped fighting, but the dastardly head of the Knight family preferred to use Zak's intervention as a distraction so he could pin Roy for the victory!

This despicable act was supposed to lead to a big blow-off match between Ricky and Zebra . . . but yet again the wrestling gods conspired against the FWA to cut off a bubbling feud in its prime. In September, Roy Bevis was jailed for nine months for drink driving. This meant the planned Knight-Zebra culmination couldn't happen. This was a blow for FWA booking plans, but nothing compared to the effect on Roy and his family. Ricky, who in real life was really close to his son, was devastated by Roy's incarceration, and I really felt for him.

Meanwhile July 2004 was a time of family celebration in the Lambert household as on the 11th, Sharon gave birth to our beautiful second son, Dale. I remember when Dale was three weeks old I got up with him in the middle of the night, switched on the TV and as I fed him, watched unheralded British heavyweight boxer Danny Williams score a stunning fourth round KO over the legendary Mike Tyson.

This shocking upset turned Williams into an overnight sensation, the most talked about sportsman in Britain. So when Alex told me that he'd managed to get Danny—himself a wrestling fan—to appear on the next FWA event in Broxbourne on September 5 2004, it was a *really* big deal. As a long-time boxing fan, I was so excited about the prospect of meeting and working with Danny Williams, and so impressed that Alex had managed to acquire his services. Was there *anything* beyond Alex Shane's extraordinary capabilities as a wrestling promoter?

And what an opportunity this posed for the FWA. The involvement of a genuine celebrity—who had catapulted himself into the consciousness of the entire nation—would surely generate wider publicity, credibility and recognition for the FWA outside of just the wrestling and boxing fraternities. We hoped the national press and TV would cover the story, and in turn, this would get the FWA noticed by a mainstream audience. The Holy Grail, people! The Holy Grail!

And September 5 2004 did indeed turn out to be an auspicious day for the FWA. Hotwired was an incident-packed event, one of our greatest ever. Danny Williams took part in a heated pull-apart brawl with Alex Shane which made the hoped-for headlines in the pages of the national newspapers—The Daily Mirror even devoting half a sports page to a report and photos of their 'fight'. And in the main event, Steve Corino pinned Alex Shane in a bloody and dramatic blow-off which Power Slam described as "the match of Shane's life".

And next on the agenda for the FWA was to be our first ever event in a proper concert arena, FWA British Uprising 3 at the Coventry Skydome. Remember, running the Skydome was one of Alex Shane's big career goals.

It would surely be the perfect end to the perfect year, which would springboard the FWA towards further progress in 2005 and beyond.

But in reality, Hotwired was the peak of the FWA. September 5 2004 was as good as it was ever going to get.

Behind-the-scenes, there were cracks starting to appear. And those cracks were about to become great, yawning chasms.

CHAPTER 12

BRITISH UPRISING 3

Someone was conspicuous by his absence at Hotwired 2004. Dino Scarlo was nowhere to be seen. Here's what happened.

After Vendetta, Alex had told me he was planning a short holiday. After breaking up with Nikita (the two remained good friends) he'd met a Canadian girl and fell head over heels in love. At the time he was convinced she was 'the one' and he wanted to go to Canada to see her. In his absence, Alex asked me to assist Dino with running the FWA, making sure the website was regularly updated, that kind of thing. He gave me one vitally important assignment in particular. I like to call it 'Operation Corino'.

After Steve Corino's transportation problems prevented him from appearing at Carpe Diem, Alex entrusted me with making sure there were no such hitches in flying him in for Hotwired. I had to book his flights, sort out his work visa and arrange a driver and accommodation for him for when he landed in the UK, and then ring Corino at his home in Philadelphia to keep him informed of his arrangements. Oh, and he'd be wrestling for a promotion called BCW in Scotland on the Friday evening . . . even though he was landing at Gatwick Airport, 400 miles away, on the Friday afternoon . . . and at our show in Morecambe on the Saturday, before his big match with The Showstealer in Hertfordshire on the Sunday. Cheers for that, Alex! The pressure was on!

So Alex went off to see his sweetheart and in his absence, I ended up having several telephone conversations with an exasperated Dino. During our discussions, Dino expressed displeasure that Alex had gone abroad in the weeks leading up to such a key event and particularly that he'd lumped Corino's arrangements onto me without sorting them out himself before departing—although I was happy to do it, being eager to do anything to help.

Dino was clearly frustrated and gave me the impression he was losing patience with Alex's whimsical nature. There may also have been other underlying issues I don't know about. But the next thing I knew, Alex phoned me to tell me Dino wanted nothing more to do with the FWA. And sure enough, Dino Scarlo, a man of his word, was never seen at an FWA event again.

I liked and respected Dino immensely. And after he'd gone, I feel he was really missed. He and Alex were a perfect team. Alex was the front man who took most of the credit, but Dino worked in the background, an unsung hero, a voice of reason in the creative process whose simple and logical approach was the perfect counterbalance to Alex's outside-the-box thinking, a positive influence in the dressing room giving worthy advice or dishing out reprimands when necessary.

"Dino always had this aura about him," said Dean Ayass.

"I'd known him ever since he used to do Hammerlock shows with Andre Baker, and always got on really well with him. He was like an overenthusiastic kid if he got excited about something, even after all those years in wrestling.

"He did have a reputation, and I wouldn't want to get on his bad side. But I never saw him get pissed off with anybody. I've seen him have quiet words with people backstage, but that was the extent of it.

"When I did the commentary at Revival, Dino came and sat next to me, taking notes. I guess it was the British equivalent of having Vince McMahon in my ear. But he quietly gave me advice of what to say, and I remember him flashing me a big thumbs up and a big smile when he liked what he heard. He really spurred me on . . . he was really supportive of me."

Dino's departure was a major setback for *everybody* in the FWA. I'd go so far as to say it was *the* single biggest contribution to the promotion's decline. And Alex was devastated. He worships Dino, and he proved it in 2010 when he named an annual award for the best young British wrestler of the year after his mentor, calling it the Scarlo Scholarship.

"I think Dino was getting tired of wrestling politics in general," Alex told me recently.

"Wrestling is an amazing thing bubble-wrapped in an appalling industry where people hurt themselves for such little money, and there's such a level of bitchiness and childishness. I was a part of this for a long time. I was one of those people he was getting tired of. And Dino was a grown up. He used to say to me: 'I'm getting too old for this s__t.'

"And when Dino said he would do something, he *meant* it."

Steve Corino *did* make it to Hotwired though, although the tight flight schedule, and my mistake of initially sending his driver to collect him at the wrong airport terminal, meant he nearly missed his Friday night booking in Scotland. As 'The King of Old School' was driven at breakneck speed from London all the way up to Kilmarnock, I paced up and down on my mobile in Morecambe all night getting regular updates. Eventually Corino—who got changed into his wrestling gear in the car en route—arrived for his main event match (which had been pushed back to around midnight to allow him time to get there) with just minutes to spare.

The following afternoon, I had the surreal experience of bumping into Steve, looking fresh as a daisy in a white shirt and tie, as he casually strolled down Morecambe promenade having arrived in plenty of time for his match with Hade Vansen that night at The Dome. What a pro!

Also wrestling that night was Colt Cabana, a replacement for fellow American Brian 'Spanky' Kendrick who'd pulled out of coming to the UK soon after being advertised. Colt was pinned by James Tighe, who was increasingly breaking the rules to win matches, so desperate was he not to fall back into his losing rut of earlier in the year.

Former WWE superstar Joe Legend, a tall, handsome and swarthy Canadian with a Tom Selleck moustache, also made his first appearance for FWA on this show, facing Doug Williams. But the highlight of the Morecambe event was a superb angle where Alex Shane booted Doug in the head, busted him open and stole the FWA Title belt. My hometown fans, always some of the loudest anywhere in the country, did me proud on this occasion as they booed Alex with a vengeance.

The next day, I had the dubious pleasure of travelling down to Broxbourne in the ring van. It was the only way of getting me there! Driving the van, as always, was the FWA's head of ring crew, Jon Dobkin. The string vest-wearing Jon was another unsung hero of the FWA operation who regularly drove up and down the country to transport the ring from his home in Southampton, set it up in the venue, take it down again after the show, then drive all the way back. He used to like saying: "I am the most important person on the show . . . until I get to the show!" Jon Farrer would certainly have agreed.

Dobkin was a cantankerous sort, but a hard worker and a straight talker who liked putting the world to rights, and I enjoyed his company. On the way down to Broxbourne that Sunday morning, Jon gave me his opinions on everything that was wrong with the FWA organisationally. One problem, he said, was the amount they were paying him for his services. For example, for a Morecambe show, Jon received £450, which was mainly to cover his fuel costs from the south coast. Why couldn't the FWA find a ring provider nearer to Lancashire, he argued? It would be far cheaper. Instead, they (or rather Mark Kay and myself, the promoters) were paying way over the odds by using Dobkin's services for every single event.

Jon, a haulier by trade, wasn't risking doing himself out of work by pointing this out. Instead, he explained he was actually *losing* work by helping the FWA. Jon was being forced to turn down other more lucrative non-wrestling haulage jobs because he'd agreed to store the ring (which actually belonged to Mark Sloan) on his van in between shows. He felt he was actually doing FWA a favour by working for them and he wasn't prepared to allow this arrangement to go on.

Indeed, at the start of 2005, Jon quit the FWA and told Sloan to come and collect his ring. Sloan was unable (or unwilling) to transport the ring around the country himself, which left the FWA—supposedly British Wrestling's number one promotion—without a wrestling ring, until we found another ring hire provider in the Midlands who was, just as Dobkin had predicted, far cheaper. Why weren't the FWA using these people from the beginning?

One thing's for sure, hiring a ring is one of the biggest costs and stresses for a promoter. When our training school opened in 2009 and we finally had a wrestling ring in Morecambe, it was a massive weight off my shoulders.

So while the organisational structure of the FWA was slowly being exposed as a shambles, fans were none the wiser because the live shows were still bang on the money. So on to FWA Hotwired '04, and the results from this classic event:

Joe Legend beat FWA Champion Doug Williams by DQ, Jack Xavier, Aviv Maayan and Ross Jordan beat Hade Vansen, Stixx and Martin Stone, Mark Sloan beat Simmonz, Steve Grey beat Johnny Kidd, Jonny Storm pinned Colt Cabana, James Tighe downed Spud by submission and Steve Corino pinned Alex Shane.

I was glad to see young Spud make the step up to the main FWA roster. Known to us all as Jay, James Curtin was about 5ft 4 and around 10 stone—small, even by British Wrestling standards. But the blond-haired Brummie was a fiery performer and played the underdog babyface role to perfection.

Spud is one of my favourite people in wrestling. He's a genuine lad, fun to be around and a phenomenal talent with a sharp wrestling brain who is never in a bad match. His bout with Tighe at Hotwired was par for the course. It was quality stuff.

I'd first seen Spud wrestle on a GPW show in November 2003. The pint-sized firebrand was in a wild six-way match with a group of fellow newcomers including future UK stand-outs El Ligero and Kris Travis. But back then, it was painfully obvious they were still learning their trade.

Mark Kay and I had gone to the British Legion in Leigh, near Manchester, that night to review the show for WrestlingX, and ended up sitting in the crowd with Dirk Feelgood, Mike Bishop, Johnny Phere and two big bruising wrestlers we knew called Sabotage and Ruffneck.

Sabotage, real name Alex Grimshaw, was the absolute double of The Undertaker. Seriously, he was the spits of The Phenom. He was a similar height, had the same long dark hair and even wore coloured contact lenses to make his eyes more piercing, just like The Dead Man. Sabo would have been a fantastic Undertaker tribute act, as long as he didn't talk. Once he opened his mouth, the broad Mancunian accent would have been a *dead* giveaway.

His tag team partner Ruffneck, aka Keith Colwill, is a guy whose company I always enjoy; a burly straight-talker from the North East who went on to become a regular with 1PW and later with the hottest new UK promotion of the past two years, Preston City Wrestling. I remember our strange little band of seven had a great laugh watching that GPW show, but we didn't half cringe as we watched Spud and company recklessly drop each other on their heads over and over again in a match where it was a miracle nobody was seriously hurt.

"I was s__t back then," Jay recalled.

"There was nobody around back then to teach us so we were all learning off each other, or from watching tapes of Jonny Storm and Jody Fleisch doing big spectacular moves.

"Then one day at a show, this big burly guy who looked like he'd just walked in off the street came up to me at a show. He looked at me and said: 'I want to help you'."

This was Barry Charalambous—hotelier, FWA TV production editor, video tape trader and future wrestling promoter, commentator and heel manager. Barry was one strange-looking dude, with masses of black hair, an unkempt beard, a long black coat and a mumbling drawl when he spoke. But this Gothic Gandalf possessed a wizard-like understanding of the art of professional wrestling.

"Barry sat me down and told me stuff about wrestling I hadn't really thought about before," continued Jay.

"Sometimes he would phone me at two in the morning to test me on wrestling psychology. He'd ask me why Hulk Hogan and Andre the Giant did certain things in their match at WrestleMania III. He'd also call me to tell me off for doing certain things wrong in the ring. In fact, he f___ed me off to the point that I ended up listening to him!

"Barry told me my height was the most important part of my gimmick. He taught me to make my lack of size into a massive positive, rather than a negative. I'm the same height as Andy Simmonz, but he's always wanted to be a big guy. But why try to be something you're not? Barry told me to embrace my smallness.

"Soon after I met Barry, I sent a tape to Mark Sloan and ended up in a match against Paul Burchill on an FWA Academy show. I hit a splash from the top rope, landed and broke my arm. Then I carried on wrestling for two minutes afterwards. Alex Shane then called me, said he was impressed, and told me to phone him when I was healed."

Spud debuted for the FWA at Bolton on the Crunch weekend the following April, then turned heads when he stepped in as Jake Roberts' replacement at Stevie Knight's event in Hull in

August and had an entertaining match being tossed around like a beach ball by The UK Pitbulls.

Curtin's reinvention in the latter part of the decade as the outrageously charismatic Johnny Rotten of wrestling, The Rock Star, would propel him right into the upper echelons of the UK scene. The Rock Star character, complete with peroxide blonde hair, leather jacket, aviator shades, preposterous in-ring strut and overblown ring entrance to Bon Jovi's Living on a Prayer, has been the *making* of Jay as a performer.

"Nowadays I manage to get the audience to forget how small I am," said Jay.

"I get them so engrossed in stuff that back when I started, I didn't even know mattered, like my ring entrance, facial expressions, the timing of when and why to do things. The stuff that *sells tickets*."

Spud is the perfect example of a young wrestler who realised that being an entertainer was more lucrative and safer for his long-term health than flying about all over the ring taking ridiculous bumps. At time of writing, my good pal is set to debut on TV with TNA in December 2012 in a show called British Boot Camp. Jay will compete for a TNA contract against fellow British wrestlers 'Party' Marty Scurll and pretty Stockport twins Lucy and Kelly Knott, aka The Blossoms. Spud will gain worldwide television exposure from the programme and the chance to work with his idol Hulk Hogan. I really, really hope he does well and proves that when you've got the talent, the brains, the character and the charisma, size really *doesn't* matter in wrestling after all.

Steve Lynskey, though, remains sceptical about his chances.

"I love Spud to death and he'll win that British Boot Camp because he's got 10 times the charisma Marty Scurll has," said Steve.

"But Spud in his street clothes is just another guy. Marty Scurll isn't going to pull any fans in the US because there are 1,000 guys in America who are exactly like him and some are better.

"There will be interest there but as soon as the series ends in January, then what?

"It's the same in WWE unless you are like Barrie Griffiths (Mason Ryan) who looks like Batista, who has the kind of physique Vince McMahon likes, who looks like a *wrestler*."

But The Rock Star has proven people wrong before. So we will see.

Stevie Knight himself was at Hotwired, where his 'odd couple' duo with the straight-laced Mark Sloan was beginning to resonate with the FWA fans. Mark was extremely serious in *and* out of the ring, yet underneath the permanent frown he possessed a hidden deadpan wit and had become a surprisingly effective straight man to play off Stevie's self-deprecating slapstick. So Knight and Sloan formed an unlikely tag team.

"To start with, Mark and I genuinely didn't get on," Stevie told me in 2009.

"Mark and I are complete and utter opposites in everything—in real life and in wrestling. When I was doing UWA, I slagged him off. But we actually started talking when we were doing a tour for the FWA. I remember thinking, actually, he's a nice guy and really funny.

"When they put us together, I was the comedy guy and he was the straight man. But the funny thing is, all the funny stuff we did was *his* idea."

Some of their comedy skits on The Wrestling Channel TV show were an absolute scream. I recall with particular fondness one segment where the long-suffering Sloan was encouraging lazy Stevie to work out using a chest expander. But then the hapless Shining Light lost control of the stretchy piece of equipment, which in true Laurel and Hardy style then flew across the dressing room and smacked one of Sloan's young trainees in the face. I cried with laughter when I saw that!

Anyway, I ran into Stevie backstage that night as he was chatting away with Richard Young and another bloke. I didn't recognise this hefty, stern-faced individual . . . not at first.

"I'd like to introduce you to a good friend of mine Gregor," said Stevie (he always calls me Gregor.) "He's come down from Doncaster to watch the show. I don't know if you've heard of him. He used to be a wrestler and he's thinking of making a comeback. His name is Johnny Angel."

JOHNNY ANGEL! Good Lord, it *was* him!

The same Johnny Angel my mates and I used to take great delight in provoking during those Thursday night shows at The Morecambe Dome all those years ago. The same Johnny Angel who'd called us out for a real fight. Only 14 years later, this Johnny Angel had grown much bigger, much wider, and looked much, much meaner! I exchanged pleasantries, hoped he wouldn't recognise me, and gulped!

In the years to come, when Angel did indeed make his comeback and became a regular for the FWA, I eventually reminded him of that incident at The Dome when he'd challenged us lads to meet him outside . . . and he remembered! But he laughed it off. Johnny Angel turned out to be another one of my favourite people in wrestling, a class act and behind his hard man exterior, one heck of a nice fella.

"Johnny Angel bullied me when I first got into wrestling," Stevie told me in 2009.

"When I first met him, he was not a nice person at all. I think he admits that. He gave me a slapping on quite a few occasions. He broke my nose in Blackpool and it was not an accident. He really beat me up one time in Holbech as well.

"Then I never saw him for 10 years and I always said: 'When I see that Johnny Angel, I'm gonna really hammer him.' Then I saw him and I thought, perhaps not!

"I actually got him back involved in the FWA and it was marvellous to work with him again. It was nice to actually work with him on an even keel this time! And when you wrestle Johnny Angel, he doesn't play about. You know you've had a good hard match. You take some lumps and bumps. And that's how wrestling should be, in my opinion.

"I have a lot of respect for Johnny Angel. He's a man's man, he takes no s__t from anybody and you know where you stand with him at all times. We're best buddies now. I really like Johnny Angel."

The real-life Jonny Adams retired again in 2007 to run a tattoo shop in Doncaster and I haven't seen him since then. Hey Mr Angel, if you're reading this, we'll have to hook up some time soon!

Jonny Storm's return at Hotwired was not without controversy. Back from Thailand earlier than expected, Jonny had changed his image for the better, snipping off his trademark long hair in favour of a crew cut, a Fedora hat and multi-coloured ring wear. Storm was still supposedly 'fired' from the FWA and was in the midst of a desperate attempt to be reinstated.

Days earlier The Wonderkid had held The Bagpipe Report host Blake Norton hostage in a hilarious segment on TWC in an attempt to get the FWA's attention . . . and now here he was campaigning outside the Broxbourne Civic Hall, asking the fans to sign a petition while they queued to get in!

But despite being officially out of a job, cheeky Jonny was somehow allowed to wrestle Colt Cabana at Hotwired. This made no sense at all, in fact it made a joke of the 'Loser Leaves FWA' stipulation. The return of The Wonderkid could, and should, have been a much more spectacular happening than it turned out to be.

Danny Williams' presence that day *was* as big a deal as expected though. Accompanied by his brother-in-law and also by Boxing Monthly and Power Slam writer Anthony Evans, Williams was a gentleman backstage, respectful of the wrestling business and willing to co-operate.

His angle with Alex was basic but effective. Danny and his entourage were sitting in the front row when The Showstealer came out and hurled a tirade of abuse at the boxer. Alex even called the Tyson-Killer "gay-boy" (there really is no political correctness in wrestling whatsoever) before he spat a jet stream of water right in the face of Williams's brother-in-law. This caused Danny to lunge over the crowd control barrier in an attempt to get his hands on Shane.

Bedlam ensued as dozens of stewards swarmed to ringside and hurled their bodies in between the two to stop a fight from breaking out. The TV cameras followed the boxer as he was forcefully dragged out through the front door by security while Shane was restrained at ringside, still screaming insults at Williams. And the Broxbourne fans lapped it up. The atmosphere in the hall was absolutely buzzing! Afterwards Power Slam praised the execution of the angle, saying it was delivered with "realism and restraint".

Danny was originally scheduled to return to the FWA after Hotwired, as the special referee for Alex's championship match with Doug at British Uprising 3. The Brit was originally scheduled to fight the Russian Oleg Maskaev in London in October, meaning he would be free to perform at Coventry Skydome for us the following month. But just days after Hotwired, it was announced that Danny would instead box Vitali Klitschko for the WBC World Heavyweight Title in Las Vegas in December. This meant the November 13 date now clashed with his training.

Williams understandably didn't want to risk injury and jeopardise the biggest opportunity of his life by participating in a wrestling match. And due to the fickle nature of fame in today's society, Danny became yesterday's news when he lost his match with Klitschko and never achieved the same heights as his Tyson victory ever again. So there was no advantage to be gained by bringing him back to the FWA.

Danny did, however, appear at a specially staged 'press conference' at London's Hornsea Tavern in early October 2004, to hype up Uprising and the Shane-Doug bout. Here, the hulking heavyweight gained a measure of revenge on The Showstealer by spitting water in his face! This incident gained FWA another half-page of national press publicity, this time in The Daily Star.

But despite the interest from the 'red top' tabloids, the Danny Williams episode taught me that even a 'star rub' from a world-famous name and resulting stories in the nationals were no guarantee of attracting new fans to British Wrestling or helping us create any kind of lasting impression on the mainstream. After all, today's news is tomorrow's fish and chip paper. So it wasn't the breakthrough moment we'd hoped for—and it would take a lot more than just Danny Williams for the FWA to claim that elusive Holy Grail.

So instead, it was onwards and upwards to our next project. Maybe this would be the one to help us crack the mainstream. After all, British Uprising 3 marked a huge step up. Instead of having to sell 400-500 tickets to fill the Broxbourne Civic Hall or The Morecambe Dome, we had to try to sell 3,500 tickets to fill Coventry Skydome. I really had my doubts about this. How the hell were we going to do that?

The Coventry Skydome was basically an ice rink on a ring road surrounding a Midlands industrial city. It seemed like an unlikely mecca for a British Wrestling promoter hell-bent on revolution. Then again, the leafy Hertfordshire suburb of Broxbourne and the windswept seaside resort of Morecambe were unlikely choices of battlegrounds too. But Alex Shane saw Coventry Skydome as his zenith, the ultimate dominion for another attempt at a literal and figurative British Uprising.

Sadly, it ended up becoming the place where the FWA met its Waterloo.

It had all started so promisingly. A few weeks after Hotwired, Alex called myself and Mark Kay to a meeting in Finsbury Park. Doug Williams was also there. Here, Alex outlined his plans for mission improbable.

At this meeting he told us he was almost certain of getting Mick Foley to headline Uprising 3 and he was sure 'The Hardcore Legend', who was smoking hot following a blistering feud with Randy Orton in WWE earlier that year, would prove enough of a drawing card with smarts and casual fans alike to pack out the Skydome. We also had the TV show on The Wrestling Channel as a promotional tool. He really believed we could pull it off, and he instilled that belief in all of us.

Alex was in full-on Icarus mode at that meeting. Like the character from Greek mythology, our aspirational leader was flying too close to the sun, biting off more than he could chew even for someone of his positive mindset and astonishing ability to achieve the extraordinary. But as always, The Showstealer convinced us all it could be done. Like in the films Field of Dreams and Wayne's World 2, we hoped if we built it, they would come!

Shane gave me the job of bombarding the regional and national newspapers with press releases to promote the show and the FWA wrestlers. I felt so inspired by Alex's positivity and so, motivated beyond belief, I immediately set to work on an unprecedented media offensive. It definitely achieved the desired results. I managed to convince the Birmingham papers to run articles about local boys Spud and Jack Xavier, and did the same for 'Dangerous' Damon Leigh in Wigan.

But that was nothing compared to the success I had with Dirk Feelgood. The media loved the fact that in real life, Dirk was Dr Andrew Dickinson—a doctor in a children's hospital. By day, he treated those in pain . . . but by night, he dished it out! Dirk was all over the press in the run-up to Uprising, not only in his local papers the Liverpool Echo and Ormskirk Advertiser, but in the Sunday People too. Granada Reports, the north-west's regional TV news show, even visited Southport and Ormskirk General Hospital to interview Dr Feelgood!

Alex was also banking on the Coventry Evening Telegraph to give British Uprising 3 some serious column inches, so much so that FWA spent thousands on advertising with them. But he'd also brought a Coventry wrestler into the FWA fold to aid the local publicity drive.

Darren Walsh was the son of ex-wrestler Tony 'Banger' Walsh, who'd been a regular bad guy opponent of Big Daddy in the World of Sport days. A man mountain at 20 stones of solid muscle, this second generation star cut an imposing figure as Thunder, a thuggish brute whose look was made even more intimidating by Road Warriors-style shoulder pads and a metal face mask.

Thunder had made an impressive FWA debut at Hotwired as my hired assassin and Drew McDonald's new partner-in-crime. Drew and Thunder had looked utterly devastating as they brutalised Paul Travell in a one-sided beating while I egged them on, cackling, revelling in my storyline revenge for Travell's treachery. At Uprising, Drew and Thunder would team up with Raj Ghosh not as The Family, which I had officially disbanded after 'The Righteous One's departure, but as The Triad, my new triple threat of trouble-causers.

Their opponents in a six-man war would be Travell, Paul Burchill and . . . . Terry Funk! Sadly, Alex's hopes of getting Mick Foley for the November date had fallen through but I nearly fell off my chair in delighted disbelief when Shane gave me news of his replacement. Foley's great mate, the former NWA World Champion, the 60-year-old four-decade veteran, the absolute living legend that was Terry Funk would be flying in from his home of the Double Cross Ranch in Texas to be at Uprising . . . and I would be managing against him!

I was overwhelmed by the thought of working opposite the iconic Funk. So much so, that all rational thought went out of the window.

So when Alex asked me if I could lend the FWA some cash to help finance the show, I agreed. He promised me faithfully that I would get the money back after the event.

I spent a total of £2,300 of my marital savings on an advert in Power Slam and AJ Styles' flight and work permit. Styles would be main eventing the show in a 30-minute Iron Man match with budding heel James Tighe. I must have been off my head, swept away on a tidal wave of belief that British Uprising 3 would draw big and make a packet, leading the FWA and British Wrestling to that blasted Holy Grail.

But I had been encouraged by news that Doug Williams, who worked as a chartered surveyor as his day job, had been recruited to the FWA's expanding management team with responsibility for looking after the company bank account. I liked Doug, he was level-headed and trustworthy. Surely with him in charge of the FWA coffers, my investment was safe.

"I didn't really want to get involved with the management side of FWA, I was kind of talked into it by Alex and Dino," said Doug, reflecting back on that period.

"I did it somewhat reluctantly because I already had a full-time job and was wrestling too, and I was stretching myself very thin. But they needed someone to run the business side of things, because it didn't actually exist. There were lots of different factions behind-the-scenes . . . a merchandise guy taking money, a little group doing the filming taking money . . . it was very badly run."

By this time, I was becoming Alex's closest confidant and I almost felt like it was my own personal responsibility to make this event a runaway success. I had somehow found myself on the management team preparing for the biggest independent British Wrestling show in nearly 20 years.

With Dino gone, I had suddenly evolved into Alex's right-hand man. He phoned me almost daily to go through booking plans, bounce creative ideas off me and flatter me by saying how much he relied on my help. These intense conversations about nothing but wrestling would routinely last an hour, sometimes even two hours, with Alex usually doing 95% of the talking. I often came off the phone with my head spinning.

But I felt like a drug addict. I knew being part of this highly-pressurised situation wasn't good for me financially, nor was it an easy task juggling my FWA duties with my full-time job and family life. But I just couldn't bring myself to pull away. I felt so close to The Holy Grail I could almost taste it.

Then with just weeks to go before the big night, Alex added another American wrestling legend to the line-up. For me, this was the icing on the cake. Alex had managed to entice Jimmy 'Mouth of the South' Hart to be the special guest referee for our six man tag team match. That's Jimmy Hart, WWE Hall of Famer. Jimmy Hart, manager of The Honky Tonk Man throughout his record-breaking reign as the greatest WWF Intercontinental Champion of all time. Jimmy Hart, who'd guided the career of arguably the most famous wrestler *ever*—Hulk Hogan. When I heard this news, I almost felt like telling Alex to keep my money. It just couldn't get any better than this.

I was also looking forward to finally working with Dean Ayass, who would be managing the opposing team. In the weeks leading up to Uprising 3 we cut promos on each other on the FWA TV show, both claiming we were the best manager in Britain and vowing that our team would win at Uprising. With Jimmy Hart, a legitimate all-time great antagonist, set to be the man in the middle, Dean and I were so excited we were like giddy kids waiting for Christmas.

With a few weeks to go before Uprising, Alex dropped the bombshell news on me that he'd also convinced Jody Fleisch to make a one-off appearance at the Skydome. Not to wrestle, but just to come out and say an official goodbye to the fans.

Jody, if you recall, had all but disappeared into thin air after announcing his shock 'retirement' 15 months earlier. The FWA fans had been speculating ever since over what had happened to their prodigal son, and if he would ever return.

Alex felt that Fleisch's promised presence at Uprising would shift tickets. So he paid Jody £400—nearly three times his usual fee and a massive wage for a British wrestler—just to entice him back to do a non-wrestling segment. This didn't seem like good business to me but it was typical of Alex at the time. He always wanted the show to be the best it could possibly be, whatever the cost.

As one of FWA's biggest names was all set to return, another was on his way out. Paul Burchill's unique talents and superstar look had earned him a WWE developmental contract and once his visa came through, he was off to pursue fame and fortune in the States. Paul told me his good news at Stevie Knight's show in Hull the week before Uprising, where I managed the future WWE superstar as he lost the IWP Title to D'Lo Brown.

Burchill asked me to send him some old Power Slam articles describing his career achievements so he could acquire his work visa. I was happy to help Paul and pleased for him personally, although disappointed for the FWA that potentially its hottest commodity was leaving. Alex had big plans for Paul, starting with a feud with Hade Vansen over the All-England Title in 2005, which would have eventually propelled The Monster to the FWA Title and status as the main guy in the company. Instead, he was heading for America—the land of opportunity.

"The first time I saw Paul was on an FWA Academy show in Portsmouth and he stood out from the crowd from the very beginning because he was bigger than everyone else and had amazing agility," said Dean Ayass.

"I always said at the time, the two FWA people most likely to make it in America were Paul and Kat.

"Paul made it clear from the very start to me that he wanted to get to the WWE. I told him he had to be extra special, because not being from America the WWE would have to pay to fly him over, and sort out all the paperwork and visas; it would be a lot of work for them. So he did all the high-flying moves a person of his size shouldn't be doing to stand out.

"He was also always pushing the WWE, contacting them and sending them tapes of him in action, which was a lot easier for him because of the FWA's professionally-produced footage. He would also come with me to Premier Promotions shows in Worthing and sit at the back of the hall, watching Doug Williams, Flash Barker, Mal Sanders and Steve Grey, always learning and picking things up. Paul used to be a county level rugby player for Surrey before he became a wrestler and he had that athlete-level determination to be a success.

"We kept in touch by email when he went to America, until the day he emailed me to say himself and Jimmy Snuka Jnr, who went on to be Deuce in the Deuce and Domino tag team, were getting a match on a Smackdown TV taping. I never heard from him again after that."

Long-term, the loss of Burchill would turn out to be another blow, a contributing reason why fans lost faith in the FWA because they perceived the promotion was going backwards instead of forwards. But none of us were worrying too much about the future at that point. All that mattered was British Uprising 3.

After months of incessant hype and expectation, finally the weekend rolled around. Mark Kay and I set off for Coventry in his trusty Corsa and after a night in a cheap hotel, arrived at the Skydome bright and early.

I don't think the size of the task we had in front of us really dawned on me, at least until we turned up that chilly November 13 morning and saw the FWA ring being set up. The ring was a tiny dot in the middle of this vast ice rink, surrounded by rows upon rows, thousands upon thousands, of tiered seating stretching all the way up to the bleachers.

My heart sank. I immediately realised there was no way, *no way* on earth we would come anywhere close to selling out.

And sure enough, despite shelling out big wages to put Funk, Styles, Hart and Brown on the marquee, despite the unprecedented level of newspaper coverage and advertising, despite the weekly Sky TV show pushing British Uprising 3 like there was no tomorrow, by the time the show began that evening, the 3,500-capacity Skydome was less than half-full. The 1,500 audience was FWA's biggest ever crowd for sure, but it surely wasn't enough for the big budget show to make money.

We had to cordon off entire levels of empty seats, creating great gaping holes in the arena. And being an ice rink, the Skydome was freezing cold and its cavernous hulk didn't create the kind of in-your-face crowd fervour we were used to enjoying at Broxbourne or the York Hall. It just didn't feel like an FWA show.

"There was a lot of tension hanging in the air and I'm not quite sure why," said Dean Ayass, reflecting on that night.

"It just didn't seem like the usual comfortable FWA backstage atmosphere. There used to be a lot of camaraderie on FWA shows. But I don't know if it was because we'd brought in too many outsiders, or because we were running a bigger venue, it just wasn't enjoyable backstage. It was the first time I actually questioned my involvement in the wrestling industry."

I felt exactly the same way. While I should have fond memories of November 13 2004, the day I had the privilege of working with Terry Funk and Jimmy Hart in front of the FWA's all-time record crowd, I don't. The day, while not quite a disaster, was a major disappointment. So much went wrong, both in and out of the ring.

For starters, there were countless behind-the-scenes problems that day, many of which were landed on muggins here to sort out. My role at Uprising 3 was supposed to be stage manager, in charge of looking after the wrestlers behind the curtain and making sure the show itself ran smoothly. Instead, I found myself dealing with all kinds of unrelated issues, mainly from angry sponsors, merchandise stallholders, VIP guests . . . people who had been promised things by Alex which they felt hadn't been delivered. It started at the pre-show fan gathering in Jumpin' Jaks nightclub near the Skydome, and continued throughout the night.

Mark Kay usually ended up being roped in to run these meet-and-greets. It's safe to say, it's not a job he relished . . . and that's putting it mildly.

"I f___ing hate Fan Fests," said Mark.

"It was all the hanging around. Why did we need to do them? They were just painful. They were just an endless stream of fans standing around in queues just to get to meet wrestlers for a few seconds . . . wrestlers who more often than not didn't even want to be there and were only there because they were being *paid* to be there.

"It wasn't so bad when they had something specific going on . . . someone like a Mick Foley or CM Punk doing a Q&A or an interview. That was quite interesting. But the meet-and-greets, they were a ball-ache because the number of fans and the amount of time it would take each of them to shake a wrestler's hand or get an autograph or a photo was always underestimated . . . and we never seemed to learn from the mistakes.

"This meant that all these afternoon Fan Fests ever did was delay the main show, especially at Broxbourne. You see, the Fan Fests never finished on time, because none of the wrestlers were ever ready for them, so by the time the actual show was supposed to start we always got that familiar call from Alex to 'Hold the doors!'

"For those reasons, I would actually have Fan Fests *banned*."

I couldn't help feeling, as the day passed by in a blur of headaches, that the FWA was out of its depth. This was the big time, by British Wrestling standards, and we didn't step up to the mark, organisationally. I hated not being in control of the situation and having to fob people off as they came at me incessantly throughout the day, firing their questions. And more often than not, Alex wasn't around to provide the answers.

Pinning the boss down that day was like trying to swat an evasive giant fly. Alex was always too busy doing something else. The demands on his time were immense. He was wrestling in the title match and also the man in charge, with no Dino Scarlo to share the load. Had Dino been there, things may have been different.

We needed strong leadership and precise preparation to cope with the massive leap from small halls to an arena. We also needed to have big money behind us, but it simply wasn't there. At one point Alex sent Mark Kay cap-in-hand to the Skydome manager's office to beg for ticket revenue because there wasn't enough cash to pay the wrestlers. The venue manager was incredulous. He was used to working with professionals with years of live event experience, not a bunch of rank amateurs.

It's fair to say that my first experience of helping to run an FWA show was not a positive one.

As for the action itself, it felt like nothing clicked. Although I felt the TV airing of British Uprising 3 on The Wrestling Channel a week later came across rather well, this was one time when live, the FWA simply didn't live up to the hype.

Results from FWA British Uprising 3 were:

(Pre-show matches) Stixx, Martin Stone and Leroy Kincaide beat Stevie Lynn, Damon Leigh and Jack Storm, Colt Cabana beat Dirk Feelgood.

(Main show) Spud defeated Aviv Maayan and Ross Jordan in a three-way, Hade Vansen beat Jack Xavier to retain the All-England Title in a Last Man Standing match, Mark Belton upset D'Lo Brown, Paul Travell, Paul Burchill and Terry Funk downed The Triad, Hampton Court defeated Stevie Knight and Mark Sloan to retain the FWA Tag Team Titles, Alex Shane pinned Doug Williams to win the FWA Title, AJ Styles beat James Tighe in a 30-minute Iron Man Match.

Take the opening match between Spud, Ross Jordan and Aviv Maayan. We'd made a rod for our own back by billing it as the 'Next Generation Three-Way'; the natural successor to the acclaimed Uprising 1 triple threat. This invited comparisons with the 2002 classic featuring James Tighe, Jack Xavier and Raj Ghosh. And while Spud, Aviv and Ross tried hard and assembled one of the best matches on the show, the action was a level below the super-smooth exchanges in front of the rabid York Hall crowd two years earlier. At least the fans seemed to enjoy it, responding with a warm ovation for the three young combatants after local boy Spud notched the win.

Hade Vansen's victory over Jack Xavier in a Last Man Standing match also suffered from comparisons, as the brilliant build-up videos on the FWA TV show rammed it down viewers' throats that the last time Xavier was in such a match, it was his epic Crunch 2004 war with Alex Shane. So I really felt for Hade and Jack, who were desperate to live up to the original. I remember both guys panicking backstage before the match, trying to come up with a finish that would satisfy the FWA fans' craving for violence.

In the end, they opted to use a metal crowd control barrier. The ever-willing Xavier plunged head-first into the springy steel mesh from a top rope South City Driller DDT, allowing Hade to beat referee Mike Bishop's 10 count and retain his title. But, remember, the spoiled FWA fans had been brought up on a diet of balcony dives and flaming tables. A top rope DDT into a steel mesh crash mat, while undoubtedly a dangerous move, was tame in comparison. The fans' lukewarm chants of "Holy S__t!" couldn't hide their disappointment. Good grief, what did they want Hade to do . . . kill the guy?

Mark Belton's match with D'Lo Brown also failed to spark, although no blame can be attached to either man.

My old pal Five Star had come such a long way to earn his place on the big show against an international star like D'Lo. The mouthy troublemaker who was a pariah after Telford 2002 had earned the respect of his peers and developed into a solid mid-card heel. He'd worked hard in the gym to pile muscle onto his slender frame, adapted his ring style to cut out the flashy high spots and adopt a more ground-based approach, and developed an obnoxious aura making him a man fans loved to hate.

Alex took notice, and wanted to align Belton with James Tighe in a villainous stable of moody technical wrestlers who were bitter at playing second fiddle to the flamboyant Jonny Storm and Jody Fleisch. So Shane had big plans for Mark, starting with a win over D'Lo Brown at the Skydome.

I wasn't sure this was the right move. Like when Jack Xavier beat Homicide at Uprising 2, I didn't think the FWA fans would buy that the relatively unheralded Five Star was capable of beating someone of D'Lo's size and stature on the big stage. But Alex stuck to his guns. So Belton took a beating for most of the match, then faked a knee injury. Brown turned his back and Mark rolled him up for the three count. This benefited neither man. It made D'Lo look foolish and Five Star like a chump who wasn't in the American's league. The fans saw through it. They *hated* the finish.

Earlier, the task of telling D'Lo we wanted him to lose to Mark Belton had fallen to yours Truth-fully. It was not a task I relished. I thought D'Lo might feel disrespected at being asked to lose to a mid-card Brit on the FWA's biggest ever show. And indeed, The Rock's former tag team partner eyed me coldly when I delivered the news backstage, just before the show began.

"Lose? Absolutely not," frowned the Brown.

Then he broke into a big cuddly teddy bear grin and said: "Just kidding, man. I'll do whatever you want."

D'Lo had been winding me up. But what a pro, he didn't care whether he won or lost, he just wanted to have a good match and entertain the fans.

Pity I couldn't say the same for Drew McDonald and Thunder.

The six-man tag was on immediately before the interval. I'd been rushing around like a lunatic all day long, fire-fighting, and had hardly any time to plan what I'd be doing in my own match. I wasn't even sure what the finish was meant to be. By the time I crammed into the pokey Skydome changing room with Drew, Thunder, Raj, Burchill, Travell, Ayass, Hart and Funk, I felt stressed out and low in energy. And suddenly, as I looked around the room, it hit me there was going to be nine of us involved in this match. Each of these very different individuals had their own ideas of what should happen. And some had bigger egos, and were more determined to get their own way, than others.

The match was supposed to showcase Paul Travell. Paul had half-killed himself over the past two years for the FWA cause. He deserved his moment in the spotlight. Alex wanted him to score the pinfall and then have a poignant moment in the ring afterwards with Terry Funk. It would be an emotional passing of the torch, or rather the barbed wire baseball bat, between the two hardcore generations.

But Drew scoffed at this idea. He didn't respect Travell's abilities and didn't care that he'd set himself on fire and bled bucketfuls to earn his big moment. All The Highlander from Hell could see was a smaller guy in a vest and pleather trousers, and he *hated* the notion of losing to him, especially in a match that would be televised on The Wrestling Channel. The gruff Scotsman also told me he'd been similarly unhappy at Revival, when asked to lose on Bravo to Jody Fleisch.

The thing was, both Drew and Darren took their image as hard men extremely seriously. I'd found this out personally prior to Uprising. Walsh had phoned me, angry about the local press coverage of him I'd organised in the weeks prior to the show. He was furious that a Coventry paper had published a photo of him in his Thunder costume, but used the name 'Darren Walsh' on the caption. He explained that he was a doorman at some of Coventry's roughest pubs and clubs, and he didn't want any of the ruffians he had to deal with to know he was a wrestler. He said they would make fun of him now I had revealed his 'secret identity'.

So Travell stood there in the Skydome dressing room, trying to suggest spots to make the match entertaining and give it some structure, but Drew and Darren weren't interested. They weren't bothered about making Travell look good, of working with him to plan a dramatic story for the fans. They just wanted to know the finish and they'd make the rest up as they went along. Drew was a veteran and wanted things done his way.

"I got on well with everybody in wrestling, but that was sad," said Paul, recalling what happened.

"I suggested a spot where I would splash one of them through a table at ringside. It wasn't the hardest, most dangerous thing in the world. But they didn't want to do it, and I got the old school attitude of either 'you're smaller than me' or 'you're less experienced than me, so basically, you can shut up'.

"They put me in my place, giving it the 'Big I Am' in front of Terry Funk. It was more Thunder than Drew, as I recall it. Thunder had nothing but contempt for me. A lot of the big guys looked down on the smaller guys, like me, Jody and Jonny. Yet Ulf Herman, another big guy, he always gave me nothing but respect."

Jimmy and Funk, our visitors from another country, were just sitting there, looking bewildered by this bizarre backstage power struggle over a scripted fight. And Raj didn't care one way or the other. Never a big fan of hardcore matches, he seemed to have fallen out of love with the business completely by this point. This would be his final FWA outing.

I had absolutely no experience of dealing with 'old schoolers' like McDonald on a management level. Up until that point, my main knowledge of how to plan a match came from observing Alex Shane. Incidentally, the Denis Norden of Wrestling who usually improvised everything he did in life was a completely different animal when it came to working out his matches. Alex always displayed an obsessive perfectionism for running through absolutely everything he wanted to do in the ring in advance with his opponents . . . and he'd do it over and over and *over* again until he was satisfied.

I should have stayed out of it. Instead, because I was now management and had some degree of responsibility for how the show turned out, I felt obliged to try to take control of the chaotic situation.

"I cringed as Greg said to Funk: 'Is there anything you'd like to do in the match, Terry?'" recalled Dean Ayass.

"I knew Terry just went out there and called everything on the fly. He never planned *anything*. But he was really polite with Greg and just said: 'No, no, don't worry.'

"Then Greg said the same thing to Drew. 'What would you like to do?'

"Drew just laughed and said: 'Why don't you go and ask The Internet?'"

Virtually nothing had been planned by the time we got the call to go to the ring. By that time, the atmosphere in the Skydome was sizzling, because of the star power involved in our match. Burchill got a huge ovation and chants of "PLEASE DON'T GO!" because his imminent departure to America had leaked out, as expected. But it was clear the person most fans had come to see was Terry Funk. His arrival received the biggest pop of the night.

The match started promisingly. McDonald was happy to sell (pretend to be hurt) for Burchill, because he respected him as a future WWE superstar with size and strength. The bulky Scotsman allowed Paul to suplex him and then in the best moment of the match, Burchill hauled The Highlander from Hell onto his shoulders and delivered an athletic rolling slam, followed by his patented pair of standing shooting star presses.

But every time Travell got into the ring, Drew and Thunder cut him off. They wouldn't give the FWA's Hardcore Icon a thing. And it soon became clear that the 60-year-old Terry Funk, the man everyone had come to see, was so shopworn he was no longer physically capable of doing much in the ring. The battle-weary Funk was reduced to throwing left hand punches as Drew and Thunder beat him mercilessly, allowing the legend virtually no comeback. It was a sad sight.

With no forward planning to fall back on, the match soon degenerated into chaos. Jimmy Hart, bless him, turned out to be the world's worst referee. The Mouth looked on, waving his arms helplessly, as a bar-room brawl erupted all around the Skydome. I watched at ringside, frustrated, as the six-way fight went on, and on, and on, and on, with no peaks and troughs, no drama and virtually no entertainment value. Thunder never left his feet the entire time, it was like he believed he was indestructible. The masked man just wouldn't sell at all, even for Burchill. I *did* take a bump though, an ungainly one for Dean Ayass, who I allowed to shove me on my backside at ringside as tensions rose.

Still, it was a mercy when, completely out of nowhere, Travell blasted Ghosh with his Sacrificial Slam and pinned him to end this disjointed mess. Even then, McDonald couldn't allow the bloody Paul his moment of triumph without attacking him after the finish.

Afterwards, Alex was livid at the behaviour of McDonald and Walsh. Neither man wrestled for the FWA ever again . . . not that they were all that bothered. They didn't have the same kind of love for the FWA as many of us did, as both had regular work with other promotions.

"For a lot of us, it was the biggest show we'd ever done," said Dean.

"But for Drew and Darren, it was just another booking."

Later, Drew went on to earn a significant job as the European talent scout for WWE. The Scot was responsible for recruiting many of the Brits who followed the example set by Burchill to ply their trade in America over the past few years. I met Drew again in that capacity in 2010 at a show in Nottingham, and everything was fine . . . there were no hard feelings on either side.

Looking back, I kind of realise why Drew acted like he did at Uprising. The Highlander from Hell learned the trade in a different era, when wrestlers had an entirely different mentality. That night was simply a clash of cultures, a perfect example of the divide between British Wrestling's old and new schools of thought.

Today, when I look back on the Uprising six-man tag, it's with a mixture of regret and pride. But at least I got to manage in a match with Terry Funk and Jimmy Hart. No-one can take that away from me.

And I have to say, both Terry and Jimmy were really cool guys to be around. The ageing 'Funker' was like a kindly granddad outside the ring, speaking gently in that famous raspy voice with a teasing sense of humour. As for Jimmy, he was as tiny as he'd always looked on the telly and a boundless ball of energy, enthusiasm, encouragement and advice. We had breakfast together at the hotel on the Sunday morning and I loved his company.

Both legends seemed impressed with the FWA set-up and it was a shot of confidence to hear them compliment the British talent and especially the big-time appearance of the event. Production values were one thing we did get right at Uprising. The taciturn Mark Sloan and the animated Ralph Cardall rarely got along, but at Uprising 3 they worked together to ensure the set-up looked and sounded sensational.

As a former musician himself, Jimmy was particularly taken with our music videos which blared out on big screens as each wrestler entered the ring. But this lavish production didn't come cheap. It must have contributed to overstretching the FWA's finances.

After the interval, came Jody Fleisch's big return. Jody had put on a little weight since his absence but seemed genuinely pleased to be back and was willing to get physically involved. So we'd constructed an angle where he'd come out to support the reinstatement of his old buddy Jonny Storm, only to be jumped by Tighe and Belton. The Phoenix was warmly received by the audience and the beatdown got great heat, but I felt the segment dragged on too long. Perhaps we erred by giving Commissioner Flash Barker, Tighe and Fleisch too much microphone time. They weren't three of the FWA's most dynamic speakers. I take responsibility, because the angle was mainly my idea.

This was followed by a lacklustre FWA Tag Team Title match. Simmonz pinned Sloan to win it after Stevie Knight was lured backstage by the charms of Buttercup. The fans barely mustered a cheer. What a contrast to the overwhelming reaction to Simmonz at Vendetta. Perhaps Hampton Court's act had peaked already.

Then came the title bout, Alex v Doug. Shane won the title, ending The Anarchist's 19-month reign after Ulf Herman returned looking for revenge, but accidentally nailed Williams. I felt the match came across better on The Wrestling Channel than it did live, mainly thanks to commentary team Tony Giles and Nick London. Giles seemed genuinely devastated that the evil Showstealer had become FWA's champion. And the camera close-up on Alex's devilish facial expression was a picture as he cradled the belt in his arms.

Finally, came AJ Styles v James Tighe. The post-match brawl where Jonny Storm returned and Jody Fleisch rolled back the years to deliver a springboard shooting star press to Tighe and Belton, brought the house down. It did at least ensure that British Uprising 3 ended on a high note.

Well, at least the wrestling part ended on a high note. My evening certainly didn't, as organisational lapses continued to haunt me. I found myself having to smuggle Jody Fleisch, his girlfriend and a bottle of vodka into a hotel room, without paying, because his lift back to London hadn't been arranged. I also had to pacify a disgruntled D'Lo Brown who wasn't allowed in to the after-party at Jumpin' Jaks. Security turned the former WWF superstar away, because his tracksuit bottoms and trainers didn't adhere to their dress code and his name had been omitted from the VIP guest list.

D'Lo had been an absolute professional on the show, a delight to be around, only to be treated like this. Meanwhile Alex and Doug were inside the club partying, almost without a care in the world. Mark Kay and I couldn't be bothered to party. We felt too dejected and exhausted. We also felt terrible for D'Lo, who just kind of skulked back to the hotel with Steve Lynskey, who had his ever-present bum bag around his waist. I noticed that Lynskey always spent a lot of time with the American wrestlers.

"I bet if you ask 95% of the boys, they will tell you I'm an arse-kisser, but I'm not," explained Lynskey in 2012.

"It's a simple premise for me. When the Americans come over, nine out of 10 of the British wrestlers *will* kiss their arse. But I treat everybody the same. I'll take the piss out of Raven just as much as I would a British wrestler. The boys are the boys the world over, whether it's Sting or Kevin Nash or whoever. They all do the same job.

"When they're over here, the Americans don't want wrestlers coming up to them saying how great they are, they can get that from the fans. They just want to chill and hang out.

"That's why I get on with so many people in wrestling the world over. I treat everybody on the same level. The only difference between the Brits and the Americans, is their cheques are bigger than ours."

Steve's analogy wasn't quite true at British Uprising 3.

The next day at breakfast, Jimmy Hart asked me in his famous high-pitched Memphis squeak: "Who should I talk to about getting paid, baby?" Mark and I pointed at the man in charge of the cheque book, Doug Williams. Doug told the unusually morose 'Mouth of the South' he'd sort it out later.

A few weeks later, Alex phoned me and broke some bad, but not entirely unexpected news. Uprising had made a massive loss and the FWA couldn't afford to repay my loan. Alex blamed the venue for charging more than had originally been agreed. He muttered something to do with unexpected music licence fees.

However, knowing the haphazard way FWA shows were budgeted at the time, I knew there had also been a gross miscalculation about how much money the show would make. To achieve his dream of running a show at the Coventry Skydome, Alex had taken his biggest gamble . . . and lost. But it wasn't just his own cash he'd gambled with.

"We bit off more than we could chew," said Doug in 2012.

"We thought we could draw enough to make a profit, but in the end, I didn't have full control of how much money was being spent—I only had control of about half of it.

"The cost of the TV and British Uprising 3 were the two things that contributed the most to FWA's downfall. We were getting £300 a week from TWC and spending £2-3,000 making the show. That money had to come from somewhere.

"I ended up covering costs with my own money and not seeing a return. But it was my own choice. If I hadn't wanted to use my credit card to pay for things, I wouldn't have.

"I really thought there would be a turning point when the company would start making money again. I could see in maybe another year or so it might be possible . . . maybe if we licensed the TV show overseas like TNA does. They were struggling for years until they sold their TV shows to other countries. But somebody would have had to cover the losses until then. And there was nobody left.

"In total, the loss the FWA made on British Uprising 3 was £24,000."

£24,000 may not seem like a devastating amount for a business to lose, at least not when compared to the $15million WCW frittered away in 1999 in America, a sum which eventually sunk that company two years later. But for a small British Wrestling organisation with limited income and no assets, and which had now alienated its few sponsors and investors, the loss was crippling.

I personally was really upset. I was £2,300 out of pocket, close to Christmas time when I needed money for presents. And Sharon wasn't impressed at all. She already hated my involvement in wrestling and felt Alex was taking advantage of me, and this only reinforced her belief.

But at the end of the day, it was my own stupid fault. I was so wrapped up in the FWA and the dream of The Holy Grail that I shelled out an obscene amount of money in the false hope that Uprising 3 would sell out, lead to a terrestrial TV deal and make us all rich. How dumb.

Then again, I wasn't the only one who'd loaned the FWA cash to help make British Uprising 3 a reality. Doug, Barry, Mark Sloan, even Mark Kay put £700 into the pot that month towards advertising . . . and there were plenty of others who had been coaxed into parting with their money, and who would never see a penny ever again.

And I don't know if Jimmy Hart ever got paid either.

CHAPTER 13

UPS, DOWNS AND
INTERNATIONAL SHOWDOWN

My illusions about the chances of the FWA ever achieving The Holy Grail were badly dented after Uprising 3. For the FWA, it was now less a case of revival, and more about survival.

The company had no money, the TV show was on its last legs, and those who had invested in getting Uprising 3 off the ground would never be so naïve as to pump their own finances into an FWA venture again—and that included myself.

But although some people walked away from the FWA after Uprising, I stayed loyal to the cause. I think this was partly because I still held out hope of getting my money back, and partly because I didn't actually *want* to quit . . . I still loved being part of British Wrestling and was determined to keep fighting for the FWA's future.

It's a commonly held myth that FWA started to go downhill immediately after British Uprising 3. That's not strictly true. Just two weeks after the Skydome, the first annual FWA Goldrush at Broxbourne Civic Hall was a cracking little show. The FWA was right back on form that night and most importantly, made money at the box office to ensure we could keep going into 2005.

I wasn't sure what the future held for me as a wrestling manager in the FWA, as it was pretty clear The Triad was finished already. So at Goldrush I remained behind the cameras, so to speak, and focussed solely on my new job as stage manager. Back at Broxbourne, and without having to worry about the dual responsibility of being a performer and organiser, it was amazing how less stressful things were. The show drew a big crowd and received strong reviews. It felt like business as usual for the FWA. Results were:

Leroy Kincaide beat Mark Belton, Damon Leigh and Paul Travell in a four way, James Tighe beat Aviv Maayan, Stixx and Joe Legend beat Ulf Herman and Doug Williams, All-England Champion Hade Vansen beat Low Ki by disqualification, Jonny Storm pinned Chad Collyer, FWA Champion Alex Shane beat Paul Burchill, Jonny Storm won the first ever Goldrush rumble.

Alex booked the show but I pitched a few ideas in my new role as assistant FWA booker. Highlights included Hade Vansen's title match with the returning Low Ki. The Brooklyn martial arts master gave Vansen a real beating in that match, delivering stinging chops until the champ's chest was red raw. Still, it was a fine bout, arguably Hade's best to date.

Meanwhile Alex defended his newly-won title for the first time against the departing Burchill. This was a really good match, both men were bang on form, and afterwards The Monster received a guard of honour from his fellow wrestlers as he left an FWA venue for the last time.

Some experts predicted that Burchill would go on to WWE and become the next big British wrestling superstar, a Davey Boy Smith for the 21st century. But after displaying so much potential in the FWA, Paul's five year career in the States never caught fire.

Burchill was just an average-sized guy in WWE's land of the giants. He didn't stand out physically like he had in Britain. And instead of allowing him to display his athleticism and array of spectacular moves, they dressed him up like Johnny Depp in Pirates of the Carribean and made him swing to the ring on a rope. This comical pirate gimmick lasted only a matter of months. Then Paul got injured and the rest of his WWE career was spent in virtual anonymity. After WWE terminated his contract in 2010, Paul got a job as a fireman and remained in the US, having settled down with his wife and two sons.

The highlight of Paul's final FWA show was the main event, our answer to WWE's Royal Rumble. A 15-man over the top rope battle royal, the Gold Rush was meant to be Andy Simmonz's finest hour. Alex wanted to elevate Simmonz into the main event picture by having him win the Gold Rush in a major upset. He then wanted to feud with Simmonz over the FWA Title and eventually, lose the championship to the butler.

I had real misgivings about this. I didn't feel the manservant was a credible 'face of the company'. I thought the fans would support the plucky underdog while he chased the title, but once he won it I didn't think they would accept him as the Heavyweight Champion of the World. This had been shown by the crazy reaction to Simmonz winning the tag team titles, compared to the tepid response to his first successful defence.

I also felt Andy was starting to believe his own hype. He was developing a big-headed attitude, turning up to one show wearing a T-Shirt emblazoned with the word ICON in big letters. Alex always used to tell me that Simmonz would one day be a really effective heel, because in real-life he was hard to like. I was starting to see what he meant by that.

Perhaps the wrestling gods didn't want Simmonz to be FWA Champion either. Andy never made it to Gold Rush, missing out on his big moment, because he was hospitalised days before the show. Simmonz had a condition called Cystic Fibrosis, an inflammation of the lungs. He suffered sporadically with breathing problems and they flared up again at the worst possible time for his career.

Simmonz's loss was a gain for Jonny Storm, whom I suggested should take the Hampton Court member's place in the first ever Goldrush. The returning Wonderkid became the number one contender to The Showstealer's title in a beautifully executed surprise finish.

Storm had been attacked in the aisleway by James Tighe and helped backstage. But towards the end of the rumble, the plucky Essex boy managed to drag himself back to the ring, just as Doug Williams and Ulf Herman were fighting by the ropes with their backs turned. With his last ounce of energy, Storm sneaked up behind Williams and Herman and managed to eliminate both. I certainly felt a lot happier with Alex Shane v Jonny Storm as a main event calibre feud to take us into 2005.

But the FWA still had plenty of problems. We had lost Dino Scarlo, the rudder of the ship. We had lost Paul Burchill. Ulf Herman never wrestled for FWA again after Goldrush, as you know. They were two of our most popular wrestlers. We had also lost Kieran Lefort, producer of the TV show. He quit, because he was owed money. He was replaced by Barry Charalambous, who soon followed him out of the door. Barry, a true company man who once would have walked over hot coals if Alex Shane had asked him to, was owed a ton of cash for hours and hours and *hours* of painstaking video editing work. Without Kieran and Barry, there was nobody to make the television show.

"The last match Barry ever edited for FWA was me against Hade at New Frontiers, which never aired on TV because the show was cancelled," said James Curtin.

"He'd left the hotel business at that point and was trying to make a full-time living in wrestling, but he wasn't getting paid. The bailiffs ended up turning up at his house to repossess a load of money."

Barry's another guy I really admired; a multi-talented asset to the FWA whose loss was deeply felt.

"He used to do loads of driving for the FWA," continued Spud.

"He'd drive the Americans like Steve Corino, Terry Funk and Raven everywhere. He learned a lot of stuff off them.

"One time Raven said to Barry. 'Do I offend you?' and Barry said: 'Yes. I think you're a bit of a cock.' Raven just looked at him and then smiled and said: 'Eeehhh, I like you. You don't just nod your head and agree with me like everyone else'.

"Barry is so generous too. He used to take some of the boys out to restaurants and pay for their lunches.

"Some of the boys would get pissed off with him because he wasn't a wrestler but he would tell them straight if their matches were crap. Yet he had more knowledge of wrestling in his little finger than most wrestlers have in their entire bodies.

"As a performer, Barry used the name 'Charming Don Charles'. This was ironic, because he was probably the least charming man alive. He was a great panto baddie though. He was great, ahead of his time.

"He also ran a promotion called SAS, which was like WWE only in front of crowds of about 60 people. Myself, Jack Storm, Bubblegum, Ligero and others learned so much from doing those shows. We worked for next to nothing, but in return we got filmed, learned how to work for TV cameras, got a full critique of our performance and as a result, we got more work with other promotions.

"Barry is still living in Harrow and back running the hotel. But he doesn't promote wrestling anymore."

Alex wasn't overly concerned about the loss of TV. He had achieved the two goals he had mentioned after Uprising 2 and as he would often say: "Without goals, you end up just kicking the ball around until you get bored and go home". So he sank his teeth into a new project called The Supershow.

Backed by The Wrestling Channel, The Showstealer was planning to return to the Skydome on March 19 2005, looking for redemption. Instead of being chastened and cautious after his unhappy Uprising 3 experience, the irrepressible Shane was about to risk more money than ever before on an all-star night of wrestling featuring the best talent from around the globe.

The line-up was simply mouthwatering. Mick Foley, CM Punk, Samoa Joe, Petey Williams, 2 Cold Scorpio, Chris Sabin, Raven and even a contingent from Japanese organisation Pro Wrestling NOAH, led by the legendary Oriental star Mitsuharu Misawa, *all on the same bill.*

I hoped to god that Alex knew what he was doing here. If this show didn't sell out, then surely someone was going to end up bankrupt. I had to admire his ambition though.

However, there were two problems with this Supershow. The star-studded extravaganza was bound to make the FWA events look second-rate in comparison, especially now we had to make drastic cutbacks on overseas talent in an attempt to pay off the debts. And with Shane devoting most of his time to planning International Showdown in early 2005, the first FWA event of the new year was bound to suffer.

Alex knew he couldn't organise New Frontiers 2005 on his own, and no longer had the desire to. So he relied on me more than ever before. He also recruited a large booking team to come up with ideas for new FWA characters and storylines for the New Year. I didn't feel comfortable with this at all. Around 10 of us assembled at Finsbury Park in January and sat around a table, all pitching creative ideas. There were wrestlers Stixx, Andy Simmonz and Paul Travell, Alex, myself, John Atkins, Dean Ayass, even a pair of wide-eyed FWA fans called Sean and Jody who couldn't believe their luck.

Looking back on this now, it was bloody ridiculous. We weren't like the team of WWE scriptwriters. None of us were getting paid, so in my mind it was just an excuse for a load of us to sit around a table and play booker for a day. I could just imagine what Dino Scarlo would have said about this indulgence.

Too many cooks, as they say, and with hindsight, some of the ideas we flung into the broth that day were downright stupid.

After all the national media attention on Dirk Feelgood prior to Uprising, we decided to take advantage of his real-life job and transform him into *Doctor* Dirk Feelgood, the wrestling physician. He would wear a long white doctor's coat and a stethoscope, and be accompanied to the ring by a buxom nurse called Stephanie Scope, who in real life was Stixx's then-girlfriend Amanda. Stixx, who is one of the nicest guys and hardest workers in British Wrestling, had pushed hard for her to be brought into the FWA.

At the booking meeting, Alex also explained his idea to play off Simmonz's real-life condition with a dramatic storyline where Alex would beat up Buttercup, then batter Simmonz until he coughed up blood, but then Andy would fight back and beat Alex for the FWA Title. Aside from my misgivings about Simmonz as a main event babyface, I also had reservations about taking advantage of his real-life health issues so graphically. It seemed crass to me.

Then there was the awful 'Mystery Attacker' storyline. Someone had pitched an idea for a long-running 'whodunnit' style saga where a mystery individual would be attacking wrestlers at random backstage. This would eventually be revealed as Paul Travell, who would be suffering from schizophrenia. He would have a split personality and wouldn't actually realise what he was doing. Again, I thought the fact that we were going to weave a wrestling angle around mental illness was tasteless and over complicated.

Needing fresh stars after the departure of Burchill, we also came up with the idea of the Open Invitational, a brand new concept that would give 12 new wrestlers from smaller promotions all over the country the chance to wrestle on an FWA show. I was massively in favour of this, because it gave me the perfect platform to get Johnny Phere another FWA opportunity!

The concept of the Open Invitational was to give each newcomer a 30-second promo to endear themselves to the live crowd, who would then cheer to decide which two rookies they liked best. They would then meet each other in a wrestling match later in the evening to decide who got an 'FWA contract'.

Twelve inexperienced wrestlers talking consecutively for 30 seconds each? That was surely microphone overkill.

Perhaps I didn't push Alex hard enough to have a rethink. But at the time, I was still inexperienced myself, learning the tricks of the booking trade, and still in awe of Alex to a certain extent. Despite my nagging feelings of worry, I either didn't speak up or didn't have the courage of my convictions to make my voice heard. I bowed to Alex's superior experience and knowledge and allowed The Denis Norden of Wrestling to convince me that everything would be all right on the night. So all of these storylines were approved and we decided to launch them at New Frontiers. And I take 50% of the responsibility for the disaster that ensued.

The show, at Broxbourne Civic Hall on February 26 2005, received scathing reviews. It was probably the worst show in FWA history to that point. We crammed far too much into it, sacrificing the high quality of matches FWA was famous for in favour of short bouts and naff soap opera aimed at our flagging TV product. And the fans loathed most of the new characters and storylines. The results were:

Stevie Knight beat Damon Leigh, James Tighe and Mark Belton beat Aviv Maayan and Ross Jordan, Stevie Lynn downed Mark Sloan, Zebra Kid defeated Chris Hero, FWA All-England Champion Hade Vansen beat Spud, Stixx and Martin Stone crushed The Manchester Massive, Leroy Kincade beat Paul Travell, Jack Storm beat Max Voltage, FWA British Heavyweight Champion Alex Shane beat Jonny Storm in a 2/3 falls match.

Dr Dirk Feelgood debuted at New Frontiers, cutting a promo to tell everyone that Jack Xavier had been attacked backstage (by the Mystery Attacker) and wasn't medically cleared to compete. His speech didn't get over at all.

I don't think the idea of a wrestling doctor was a bad one, but the execution was terrible. Feelgood was all about fun. But we booked his new medical character in a serious situation where it was impossible to raise a laugh. Besides, Andrew himself was really uncomfortable playing the role. He felt playing a medical baddie might reflect badly on his real-life profession. I empathised completely, although from my own experience playing a heel news reporter I knew it wouldn't adversely affect his true vocation at all.

The Open Invitational segment was as I'd feared. It went on forever, there was far too much talking from newcomers the fans didn't know, and the crowd found it deathly boring. Johnny Phere delivered one of the better speeches but being a heel, he was booed out of the building so had no chance of winning. So once again, Operation Get Johnny Phere into the FWA was sabotaged!

Instead, the fans cheered loudest for Jack Storm and Max Voltage. Because we were overrunning, we could only allocate a few minutes to their match. The bout between the two inexperienced newcomers was unexciting, and fans basically sat on their hands throughout. They couldn't have cared less about poor Max and Jack.

At least there were *some* positives to come out of this car wreck of a show. The ever-improving Hade Vansen had the match of the night against the talented Spud. Stixx and Martin Stone also looked the business as a hard man tag team under the management of Dean Ayass.

They decimated another new team—a pair of scruffy young chavs called The Manchester Massive.

Capitalising on 21st Century culture, we'd thrown together two talented teenagers from Manchester who had impressed at FWA Unsigned the year before. Declan O'Connor and Joey Hayes dressed in Burberry and acted with the cocky swagger of the youths you see hanging around on street corners in Broken Britain. Ralph Cardall created the perfect Oasis-themed entrance music for the chirpy Mancunians and they got over as an instant smash. The Massive would go onto become one of the most popular acts in the promotion, really big favourites in Morecambe in particular, and just about the only good idea the FWA booking team came up with.

The only international talent we could afford to book for New Frontiers was Chris Hero, who now wrestles for WWE's developmental group under the name of Kassius Ohno. Hero faced The Zebra Kid, Roy Bevis. Roy had just been released from prison and the FWA fans had missed him. We thought the Knight prodigal son could fill the void left by Burchill and Ulf, so we planned a long-term storyline where Roy would face, and defeat, different American opponents. We hoped his match with Hero would be a classic. But for whatever reason, it didn't quite live up to expectations. Hero v Zebra was good, but just 'good' was never good enough for the FWA's demanding fan base.

Neither was the main event. Alex beat Jonny Storm, but only after the referee restarted the match after everyone thought The Wonderkid had pinned The Showstealer and won the title. When the hated Shane came back to win in three falls, the crowd was livid. We sent the fans home with a sour taste in their mouths, and with no cliffhanger to make them desperate to come back next time.

Despite the cutbacks we'd made, New Frontiers turned in a loss because the attendance was poor by Broxbourne standards. After the show Alex, Mark Kay and I sat around in the dressing room counting out the cash, and soon realised we didn't have enough to cover the wage bill. We were forced to try to convince many wrestlers to either wait for payment until the next show, or take a post-dated cheque. And I knew those cheques were bound to bounce because there was no money in the account. It was one of the most embarrassing and unprofessional situations of my life. I hated it. I felt like I'd been kicked in the gut. And I think it was at this point that the FWA talent began to realise the company was in trouble and slowly began to lose faith.

Soon after New Frontiers, I suggested to Alex that we disband the booking team. He agreed. I don't think he really minded either way at that point. His mind was focussed on his return to Coventry Skydome and his latest gamble.

This was one gamble that paid off, and spectacularly so. International Showdown was like the chalk to New Frontiers' cheese. Saturday, March 19 2005 was one of those beautiful occasions during my wrestling career when the stars seemed to align. And whenever I reflect on my decade in the business, this show always springs immediately to mind.

Alex had learned from the mistakes of British Uprising 3. For one thing, the organisation backstage at International Showdown was light years better, partly thanks to Sean Herbert and his team from TWC, who did a lot of the donkey work, assisted by myself, Mark Kay, Dann Read, Dean Ayass and his then-wife Lisa Gifford, aka FWA's ring announcer-turned-manager Jane Childs.

I got on really well with Dean and Lisa, and was sad when their marriage broke down a year or so later. Lisa has since married again, to FWA's storyline owner Elisar Cabrera. The Cabreras are now no longer involved in the wrestling business and instead run their own successful film and theatre production company in London.

International Showdown's marquee attractions of Foley and Misawa definitely did the business at the box office. The attendance was 3,400, a near sell out, well over double that of four months earlier and to my knowledge, the biggest paying audience for a non-WWE or TNA wrestling show on British soil during the past 10 years.

Power Slam quoted the cost of the event as a mindblowing £75,000. Even so, International Showdown made money. And yes, Mark Kay and I actually got paid well for once!

The results of International Showdown were:

Petey Williams defeated Chris Sabin, Jonny Storm and Spud in a four-way, Steve Grey beat Mal Sanders in a World of Sport Rules match, Samoa Joe pinned CM Punk, Doug Williams, James Tighe and Scorpio downed Mitsuharu Misawa, Yoshinari Ogawa and Kotaro Suzuki, Raven pinned Alex Shane in a streetfight with help from Mick Foley, and TNA X Division Champion Christopher Daniels pinned AJ Styles.

Just read and digest that line-up of worldwide wrestling talent for a second. Just absorb for a moment the fact that a British Wrestling promoter was able to bring Punk, Joe, Raven, Foley, Daniels, Scorpio, Styles and Misawa all together under one roof on one night. Impressive, to say the least.

Alex Shane deserves all the credit in the world not only for this groundbreaking achievement, not only for showing the balls to rebound so spectacularly from the disappointment of Uprising 3, but also for pulling off the in-ring highlight of his wrestling career on the very same night. Raven v Alex Shane was a classic. And I am bursting with pride to say that I had a significant role in the build-up to that match.

When I arrived at the Skydome that day, I had no idea if I would be given any kind of performing role on the show. So when Alex told me I'd be working an angle alongside himself and my old hero Bill Apter, who had flown in to make a special guest appearance, it was a complete surprise. Then when he told me the segment would also include Mick Foley, I almost died and went to wrestling heaven. I knew that working with the former Cactus Jack would be the highlight of my career, and I can never thank Alex enough for giving me the opportunity. I almost had to pinch myself as I stood with Bill, Mick, Alex and Raven backstage to work things out.

It was great to get to know Bill properly. He called me his 'Evil Enemy' and we got on famously. Foley is much wider and taller in person than you'd imagine from the telly, just this hairy, cuddly slab of a man; like Honey Monster in a checked flannel shirt.

Raven was a difficult guy to get to know at first. But think we bonded when he came to Morecambe a few days later. That week, I interviewed him for Power Slam over tea in a pub on the seafront, took him shopping for tracksuit bottoms in a promenade discount store, then let him crash in my bed. The things us promoters do for our talent! Just for the record, Sharon and I weren't in the bed at the time . . .

The Showdown angle worked like a dream. Apter came out first to a respectful ovation and explained he was there to collect a Lifetime Achievement Award on behalf of his good friend Foley. This brought out The Truth to the loudest chants of "HARRY POTTER!" this side of a Hogwarts convention. I spewed insults at my diminutive idol, proclaimed myself not just Britain's but now the *World*'s number one wrestling journalist and informed my ageing American foe that Alex Shane was coming out to accept the award instead. But like a true babyface, 'Wonderful Willie' stood his ground and warned me he'd "Power Slam my butt!" . . . a line Mr Apter remains proud of to this day!

The Showstealer then emerged to back me up but was quickly followed by Foley, who received Skydome-shaking chants of "FOLEY! FOLEY!" as he squared up to Alex. The two microphone maestros tore into each other verbally, as I cowered in the corner of the ring, hiding behind my friend and mentor, but in reality hardly believing that I was actually in the same ring as Mick Foley. Eventually Mick departed, but this gave Alex and me the chance to attack poor Apter from behind, infuriating The Hardcore Legend and the near-capacity crowd as we fled the scene of our crime.

I stayed in the back for Shane's match with Raven later on and watched goggle-eyed as it evolved into a manic arena-wide brawl, but unlike the sloppy six-man at Uprising 3, this fight had story and structure. The drama built and built as the two men warred all around the ice rink, surrounded by an ecstatic hubbub of fans and stewards. Power Slam's glowing four-page report on International Showdown takes up the story:

"The height of this tour de violence came when a bloody Raven dragged Shane halfway up the stands and hurled him off the 15-foot balcony into the crowd below. That section consisted of planted FWA trainees. Unfortunately, some holes appeared in Shane's human crash mat and he nearly suffered a serious injury when he struck the concrete floor."

Alex thought he'd broken a bone in his foot from this epic plunge, which was even more risky than his balcony dive at Revival or Nikita's leap from the bleachers at Frontiers of Honor. But he picked himself up and dragged his aching body back to the ring for the finish—a finish which saw Foley run in for revenge.

The Skydome erupted as The Hardcore Legend pounded the FWA Champ with his trademark running knee and then stuffed his hand, gloved in his famous sock puppet Mr Socko, right into Shane's mush! Alex freed himself from the smelly sock torture only to spin around into The Raven Effect DDT for a one-two-three that almost blew the dome off the Skydome.

What a performance by Alex Shane. No other British wrestler could have been so credible going toe-to-toe on the stick with the legendary Foley and pulled off such a pulsating scrap with Raven. Alex has never wanted to go to America and become a worldwide superstar—his determination to revive British Wrestling has always been first and foremost for him. But his performance at International Showdown showed what I'd known from the day I first clapped eyes on him, that on his game, Alex Shane is a world class wrestling performer. International Showdown was surely the pinnacle of his career, the night he unleashed all the potential I'd first seen at Revival three years earlier.

I felt light-headed with pride afterwards, as I sat around the dressing room watching Foley and Raven count their money while they bantered back and forth. Alex was in a fantastic mood, the best I'd ever seen him at a wrestling show where he'd normally pace the floors and climb the walls from the tension. Mark, Dann, Dean, Lisa and I joined him for a night out at Jumpin' Jaks afterwards and we partied like there was no tomorrow. And *everyone* was allowed in this time!

The other Brits on the show also rose to the occasion marvellously. I was especially proud of James Tighe, who came backstage after the six-man tag with blood pouring from his ear after taking a pounding in the NOAH six-man tag. In the time-honoured tradition of wrestling, he quickly sought out Misawa, Ogawa and Suzuki to shake their hands and bow, thanking the stoic Japanese trio sincerely for the beating they'd just given him!

The rugged Misawa had such an aura surrounding him. I just wish I'd managed to get him better streamers. It was traditional for NOAH fans to shower Misawa with large rolls of green crepe paper streamers whenever he entered the ring, as a mark of respect. Before the show, Alex suddenly told me to buy some streamers. At such short notice, the best Mark Kay and I could do was to rush down to the Coventry branch of Birthdays. We sheepishly turned up at the Skydome with a handful of flimsy thin streamers, the kind you might chuck around at kids' birthday parties.

British Wrestling, eh?

Like the rest of the wrestling world, I was saddened when four years later, Misawa died in the ring during a match in Japan. He landed badly on a back suplex, damaged his spinal cord and suffered a heart attack. This much-loved icon of Japanese culture was taken from us aged just 46, a stark reminder of the dangers pro wrestlers face whenever they set foot inside the squared circle.

But International Showdown was a great night for Misawa and indeed for everyone connected with it. "Independent events don't come much bigger—or better—than International Showdown," gushed Power Slam in its review.

The title of the article was 'As Good As It Gets'. That proved prophetic, as Universal Uproar—the sequel to International Showdown at the Skydome nine months later—would fail to live up to its predecessor. To be honest, I don't think *any* British Wrestling event has matched it since.

I was a bit taken aback by comments made by Alex in the PS article though. He said: "Even though we had the FWA set-up, personnel and referees, the strength of the show was such that it cannot be called an FWA event."

I didn't understand this. It almost felt like Alex didn't want the FWA to get any credit for its major part in the success of The Supershow and that he was distancing himself from his own company. As far as I'm concerned, we had FWA referees, the FWA ring announcer, FWA wrestlers, the FWA production team, the FWA's creative leader running the show—International Showdown *was* chiefly an FWA event.

A week later, we returned to The Morecambe Dome for the first annual War on the Shore, headlined by a rematch between Raven and Shane. Alex gained revenge, retaining the FWA Title after interference from Stixx, in front of our first ever sell-out crowd in Morecambe. The entire show was aired on The Wrestling Channel, the first and only time a full Morecambe event would be shown on the telly, which was a proud moment for me.

Raven was a class act that night. The former WWE superstar seemed to really appreciate our northern hospitality and was a pleasure to be around. Like I said earlier, I'd even allowed him some pre-show shut-eye in the Lambert marital bed (the things my poor wife had to put up with!) This was also the first show I ever booked on my own from start to finish and I went home from with a prized souvenir—the running order sheet signed by Raven with the message: "Good show, old bean!"

"Raven was great when he came to Morecambe, and he even apologised to me for being a grumpy bastard at the post-show Fan Fest at International Showdown," said Mark Kay.

"I'd been stood there at the end of the Coventry show, getting ready for *yet another* meet-and-greet, muttering to myself 'This is going to be a debacle. This is going to be a debacle.' And sure enough, it *was* a debacle.

"Yet again, they had underestimated how long it would take. Alex had organised this complex ticketing system, so we had to let the people with a special meet-and-greet ticket get to meet the wrestlers first, then we had to let in the people who had complained because they hadn't been *given* a special meet-and-greet ticket, even though they'd paid for one, meet the wrestlers next. I was trying to move people through as quickly as I could, but it was just taking *forever*.

"In the midst of all this chaos, Raven was sitting there looking totally pissed off. Eventually, even though people were still waiting to see him, he just got up and left.

"When he came to Morecambe, we put him and Alex up in a cheap B&B just off the promenade. I'd driven them there, driven back home, and was settling down for the night.

"The next thing, Alex rings. 'Can you come and pick us up mate? Me and Raven want to use your internet. We'll only be 10 minutes.'

"Well, you know what Alex's '10 minutes' was like. Midnight came and went, and Alex was still on the PC while Raven was on the lap top. And I was thinking: 'I've got work tomorrow . . .'

"I'll say this for Raven though, we did have a fascinating conversation about how to equalise the temperatures inside and outside of your car to stop the windows steaming up. And he complimented me on my parallel parking too, so he's all right by me."

After the triumphs of International Showdown and War on the Shore, I believed that the FWA had weathered the storm and I felt re-energised with confidence for the future. But then four days after WOTS, on March 30, Alex put a message out on the internet, saying he was no longer in charge of the FWA.

"When I first took over the day to day running of FWA, I had no other full time hobby or occupation, no full time relationship and was far less jaded towards the wrestling business than I am now," he wrote.

"It was always my dream to run a promotion more so than actually wrestle. My goal was to give people on this side of the Atlantic a company they could follow and be proud of without flying overseas.

"My passion enabled me to talk my way in or out of anything because I believed so much in what the FWA was doing. FWA was my entire life. I cared about it more than my various partners, family, friends and even myself. I was so tunnel vision-ed that I could not see further than my own ideals and it led me to see and do some things that I am not too proud of.

"On November 13 2004 I promoted my first show at the Coventry Skydome. I also achieved a career highlight by beating Doug Williams for the British Heavyweight Title. Right there, the FWA had reached its peak for me personally and from that point there is only one way to go.

"March 19 2005 marked my single biggest career highlight as both a wrestler and promoter with TWC International Showdown. Not only was it the biggest crowd at an event I have organised but without a doubt the best all round show to boot. I now know that this is where my future lies and even though the show was an amazing success and we only had 150 empty seats I cannot rest until we sell the Skydome out with a turn away crowd. That's why I am going to continue to promote these events and maybe even build into three-day International Showdown tours by next year.

"So where does this leave FWA? In truth in a better position than it has been in over a year. The company has badly needed fresh ideas and new blood driving it and that's exactly what it will get. I will still wrestle for the FWA and represent the company wherever I go.

"I want to ask the fans one thing. Please give the new guys a chance. The FWA only ever has had ONE full time employee. Everybody else did it part time or as a hobby. Yet the expectation levels from fans were always so high and the criticism sometimes so unfair.

"FWA has made me friends and enemies. It has given me my highest points and my lowest moments. It has bought out the best side of me and my worst. Above all else though it has proven to me that anything is achievable by anyone if you willing to work for it and believe in it enough.

"My favourite motto is 'Do not go where the path leads, go where there is no path and leave a trail'. That's how I view the FWA and its how I'd like it to go on.

"I am always going to be FWA to the core. I am just no longer able to be the core of FWA."

At face value, this appeared to be an emotional resignation speech from Alex. The reality was slightly different.

When Alex said "I will sit on the booking team from time to time" what he *meant* was "I will still have the final say over all the booking". Although Alex told me privately that he no longer had any interest in running the business side of the FWA, he insisted on remaining the head of the creative process and duly continued as head booker until January 2006. Why did he tell the rest of the wrestling world something different? Alex told me it was because he'd made enemies and he felt it would be best if people thought he wasn't in charge any more.

After Alex 'stepped aside', the "new guys" in charge of the FWA, at least publicly, were a four-man team of myself, Mark Kay, Doug Williams and Mark Sloan. Williams and Kay were in charge of the finances and I was in charge of booking the talent and scripting the shows, subject to Alex's final approval. Sloan would run production and merchandising.

I always found the introvert Sloan difficult to get along with. I'm very much a 'glass half-full' person but he was full of 'glass half-empty' cynicism. By nature, I'm enthusiastic, positive, talkative and passionate about my beliefs. But Mark was my polar opposite. He was cautious, quiet and often grouchy, so we sometimes rubbed each other up the wrong way. Mark Kay never really got on with Sloan either, which I found strange as they are very similar characters.

But to be fair to The Specialist, if it wasn't for him, there wouldn't even *be* an FWA. I also respect Mark's skills as a trainer who churned out standout grapplers like Burchill, Tighe, Maayan and many others. He had a keen eye for talent and, like Alex says, is indeed a very good businessman who would later also promote successful tours of the UK by Japanese promotions Pro Wrestling NOAH and Dragon Gate. And he was also a tireless production workhorse behind-the-scenes whose toil got many an FWA event off the ground. So we felt keeping him involved was the right thing to do.

Plus, as Sloan was very fond of reminding us, he owned the FWA Title. The FWA was only being allowed the use of it on loan. So if we'd decided to cut Mark loose, we would have had to buy a new championship belt.

I soon discovered that having too many chiefs turned the FWA's creative process into a living nightmare. Not only was I hamstrung by an ever-decreasing wages budget, but having to check everything with Alex, who at the time was turning into the Scarlet Pimpernel and rarely returned phone calls or emails, made it virtually impossible to come up with, and stick to, any long-term creative plan.

It would be easy to say that if Alex was indeed jaded with the FWA, he should have just severed ties completely, giving myself, Doug and Mark Kay a fairer chance of turning things around. But the FWA at that point was like the Titanic. The iceberg of British Uprising 3 had hit, there was a gaping hole in its underbelly, and the water was rushing in. Whatever we did, the promotion was doomed.

At the next FWA event, Alex went through the motions of being there just as a wrestler. When The Showstealer turned up to Crunch on April 16 2005, for the first time he didn't have any involvement in running the show. He seemed more relaxed, but at a loose end, like he couldn't get used to not needing to worry about the usual things a wrestling promoter has to worry about. Mark Kay and I did all the organising and made sure everything ran smoothly and professionally. The show started on time for once (there was no Fan Fest, you see). Plus everyone got paid, and quickly, because we scrapped the FWA wages queue too!

I look back at the results of FWA Crunch 2005 and I remember it was a solid all-round show, with no overseas imports on the card. But it's the fact that I *have* to look back at all that's the problem. I can barely remember what happened that night without checking. Crunch 2005 was entirely forgettable. For those of you, like me, who can't recall it, here are the results:

Tony Sefton pinned Jack Storm, Spud pinned Max Voltage, Ricky Knight pinned The Zebra Kid after Sweet Saraya turned on her stepson, Aviv Maayan and James Tighe fought to a 20-minute draw, Leroy Kincaide pinned Hade Vansen in a non-title match, FWA Champion Alex Shane beat Doug Williams and Jonny Storm in a three-way, Mark Belton pinned Jody Fleisch.

Like New Frontiers, Crunch suffered from the disjointed booking process, especially the finishing angle.

Jody Fleisch had rediscovered the taste for wrestling after his cameo at Uprising 3, and had decided to return to action. His comeback match against Mark Belton was the Crunch 2005 main event. I believed The Phoenix had to win and pushed strongly for this feel good ending. Our plan was then for a masked man to gatecrash the ring, beat down Fleisch and Jonny Storm, then reveal himself to be Doug Williams!

We hoped this shocking heel turn for The Anarchist, forming an alliance with fellow disgruntled ring mechanics Tighe and Five Star, would be a huge FWA moment on a par with Hampton Court winning the tag titles at Vendetta '04 and Jody's balcony moonsault at Uprising 1. But first, surely Jody *had* to win his comeback match.

Alex disagreed. He wanted the angle to draw such mega heat that the FWA fans would almost want to lynch Doug, James and Five Star. So he said Jody should lose, in fact he insisted on it, and as always, the most persuasive man in wrestling got his wish. So Belton pinned the 'ring-rusty' Phoenix's shoulders to the mat for a three count, then the trio of villains kicked the holy hell out of him and Jonny. The Broxbourne crowd was livid, but not in a good way. We'd basically just buried our top babyface.

The huge moment we'd hoped for was executed well, but didn't have the desired effect. The fans went home, got on their keyboards and gave the show a New Frontiers-style slating. "Why did Jody lose?" "Why turn Doug heel?" "Where are the Americans?" The new low-budget FWA didn't impress them at all. Europe's most revolutionary and exciting wrestling company was in decline, and the fans were starting to notice.

And if they were bemused by Crunch 2005, they absolutely despised the next show at Enfield on May 7. It was a nightmare from start to finish.

Sanjay Bagga was now the FWA's regional promoter for Enfield. Bagga is a really hard worker when it comes to marketing and did an effective job getting bums on seats into his local venue the Southbury Leisure Centre. But because Bagga was putting in the finance and taking the risk, he insisted on the tightest budget ever for an FWA event.

Sanjay is a businessman first and foremost. For him, making money always came before the quality of the show, hence why this shrewd young man was an even bigger skinflint than Mark Kay. There was even a story going around the dressing rooms once that Sanjay was such a tightwad he paid one of his wrestlers not in cash, but in *sandwiches*.

"It's not true," laughed Bagga, when I asked him about it.

"I think a wrestler started that rumour because I wouldn't book him!"

So I arranged a frugal five-match card for the Enfield event, drafting in the fast-improving Bubblegum, the former Symon Phoenix from AIWF-GB. Doug and Alex were there to wrestle, as were Spud, Jack Xavier, Aviv, Hade Vansen and Paul Travell, so at least we had some established names. But otherwise, we'd scaled back financially to the point that it was hardly worth bothering doing the show at all.

Things began in chaotic fashion. The acoustics in sports halls are always appalling and Bagga's sound system wasn't much better. So when young Sloan trainee Dan Head emerged for the first match, Jody Fleisch's theme tune came crackling over the leisure centre PA by mistake. Something had gone wrong with the CD, the fans booed when they realised Fleisch wasn't actually there, and it started the show on the most amateurish footing imaginable.

It went from bad to worse when Dr Dirk Feelgood and Nurse Stephanie Scope arrived for their new in-ring interview show The Clinic, featuring special guest Andy Simmonz. I'd hoped The Clinic would become FWA's answer to Chris Jericho's Highlight Reel, The Brother Love Show or maybe even Piper's Pit. But while WWE would have the luxury of thousands of dollars to spend on an expensive background set, we just had a tatty wooden desk and sofa in the Southbury Leisure Centre ring. It looked stupid.

I'd come up with this segment as a way of developing the Simmonz Cystic Fibrosis angle. Accompanied by Nurse Stephanie, Doctor Dirk gave Andy a good ticking off, telling him it was irresponsible to be wrestling with such a condition, leading to a match between them which Simmonz won. With the doctor, the butler and the nurse in the ring at the same time, it was like a bedroom farce with The Village People. Plus Bagga's microphone kept cutting out. It didn't go well.

Once again, using the Carry On-style Feelgood character to get across such a serious issue was a major blunder. The trio looked like they wanted the ring to open up and swallow them whole as the fans chanted "BORING!" In short, the segment was an absolute stinker. I hold my hands up. The Clinic was my idea, a rotten one, and we never did it again. At least, not in the FWA . . .

Following the Enfield disaster, Bagga promoted one more show for the FWA in July 2005. Then he quit to concentrate on his own promotion, LDN (London) Wrestling.

"I soon realised that being a promoter for another company just wasn't beneficial," said Sanjay.

"Nowadays, I run up to 150 shows a year all over the south, the Midlands and Wales, and promote them all myself with a team to help me. I would never employ another promoter because before too long, they would realise there's more money to be made on their own, like I did.

"I was also getting disillusioned with the FWA having seen how disorganised it was from the inside. I kind of hoped things would get better, but I could see it was on a downward spiral."

Today, that brash young lad in the leather jacket who sold programmes in the Broxbourne Civic Hall foyer is giving Brian Dixon a real run for his money as the most prolific promoter on these Isles. And he's doing it the British way.

LDN promotes British Wrestling with British wrestlers. They don't fly in any foreigners and many of their matches apply the traditional Mountevans rules of two falls, two submissions or a knockout to decide the winner.

"If I was to bring over someone like AJ Styles, it would be for only two or three shows a year out of the 150 I do," said Sanjay.

"Why would I do that when I can build up my own British wrestlers who are always going to be there? Why spend a couple of hundred pounds on a flight and sorting out a visa, when I could put that money into marketing?

"I have a group of my own guys who don't work anywhere else. I run venues several different times a year, and when the people come back for the next show, they remember my guys."

Bagga also has strong links with the old school and believes the veterans still have a place as active competitors.

"Whenever I used to go out and put posters up in shops, shopkeepers would always talk to me about Mick McManus and the World of Sport days. They would never mention Hulk Hogan and the WWF.

"If these shopkeepers then come to my shows, because they remember the older guys, they might bring along their kids and their grandkids.

"Mal Sanders still wrestles for me. Jon Ritchie was a big help to me, with his knowledge of the history of British Wrestling. Johnny Kidd is not only a tremendous wrestler, but conducts himself like all British wrestlers should. Johnny helped me get the legendary Johnny Saint out of retirement in 2007, asking him to do one more match. Johnny Saint is going to retire again in February 2013 at a show in Croydon. He's amazing . . . still wrestling at 73 years old."

Bagga has a clear and admirable vision for his product and I applaud how he has marketed LDN as a distinct brand within a marketplace where many British Wrestling promotions are very similar to each other. I also 100% agree with his stance on only using wrestlers from the UK. I've enjoyed working with American wrestlers and admire their skills, but he's right, they don't need the exposure as much as the Brits do and UK promoters should get behind our own talent.

So over the past five years as promoter of the XWA, I have successfully followed an exclusively British path. Although if I'm being honest, my patriotic outlook was also influenced by the fact that British talent is much cheaper . . . as I'm sure Bagga's was too.

Where I differ from Sanjay is I believe you can't fight the fact that pro wrestling has moved with the times. While I have great respect for the traditions of British Wrestling, I believe the omnipresent WWE has become so ingrained in our culture that when most British grapple fans pay for a ticket these days, they prefer to see the over-the-top, crash-bang-wallop American style of wrestling rather than the slow pace, intricate chain submissions and rounds system of British folklore.

Granted, there are some masterful exponents of the traditional style still around today, like the evergreen Saint, Kidd and young Jack Gallagher from Manchester. I appreciate their silky technical skills, but couldn't sit through an entire show of that type of wrestling. It's just not to my personal taste. And I doubt the Morecambe fans would stand for it either. These days, people don't have the patience. They expect lots of action, aggression and pizazz. It's the way the world has evolved.

But that's the beauty of pro wrestling. There are lots of different styles all over the world, and not necessarily a right or a wrong way of doing things. And while I may not agree with Bagga's personal vision, it clearly works for him. LDN has turned out to be a sustainable project.

Bagga can be ruthless and outspoken, and has annoyed a lot of people in British Wrestling over the years, including myself at times. But I've always respected him. To me he'll always be that entrepreneurial kid selling FWA fanzines and writing self-promotional columns for WrestlingX. I'm impressed with how far he's come.

Now back to the Enfield dressing room after the May 7 debacle, where the atmosphere was tense. Doug and Alex muttered their displeasure with how things were developing in the new FWA. They were angry about the error-ridden show, frustrated at the skin-tight budget we were being forced to work to, and hinted that I was to blame, undermining me in front of all the other wrestlers.

I felt like I was being made a scapegoat for matters that were mainly beyond my control. How the hell had I got myself into this situation? I'd had some unbelievable experiences over the previous three years. I'd followed my dreams and met my heroes. I should have been feeling on top of the world.

But instead, there were days, to quote the great Kenny Dalglish when he resigned as Liverpool manager in 1991, when I felt like my head was going to explode. I was working so hard, holding down my full-time newspaper job, writing articles in my spare time for Power Slam, and now I was effectively in charge of the UK's most celebrated wrestling promotion.

I was on my mobile phone and computer constantly. I barely had time for my wife and two kids. I look back now and wonder how the hell I kept going for as long as I did, especially as it felt like everything was spiralling downhill for the FWA, and I was powerless to stop it.

But no matter how big a debacle Enfield turned out to be, it paled in comparison to an even bigger calamity that month.

And no, I'm not talking about how AC Milan threw away a three goal lead as my beloved Liverpool FC made the most thrilling comeback in football history to win their fifth European Champions League title.

I just *had* to get that in the book somewhere

CHAPTER 14

REALITY BITES

It was Alex Shane (who else?) who first let me know about ITV's plans to launch a Saturday night prime time reality show based around British Wrestling.

In late 2004, Alex told me he had been employed as a consultant on the new show. Details were sketchy about its exact format, but Alex certainly seemed excited about its prospects . . . at least at first. He told me other FWA wrestlers such as Hade Vansen, Jonny Storm and Andy Simmonz would be involved in filming the pilot episode, and that he'd recruited D'Lo Brown and Joe Legend too. Celebrity Wrestling, as it was likely to be called, would be shot in London in front of a live studio audience and would loosely resemble the smash hit 1990s game show Gladiators, except with celebrities in the role of contestants and the theme of professional wrestling.

In January 2005, ITV went public with its plans for the new show. Amidst much ballyhoo, they revealed that Celebrity Wrestling would be shown on Saturday night in the prime time slot for family viewing, at around 7pm. The celebrities would be split into two teams called The Crusaders and The Warriors, and would be coached by two professional wrestlers.

ITV also unveiled their celebrity contestants, a who's who of Z-listers, many of whom had the word 'former' before their job descriptions. There was former tennis star Annabel Croft, former Big Brother winner Kate Lawler, former EastEnders actor Marc Bannerman and Princess Diana's former lover James Hewitt, as well as page three model Leilani Dowding, Liberty X singer Michelle Heaton, model Victoria Silvstedt, TV presenters Mark Speight, Jenny Powell and Jeff Brazier, showjumper Oliver Skeete and athlete Iwan Thomas.

"This is wrestling as it's never been seen before!" roared an ITV press release.

"The celebrities will be taught real skills to win real bouts!

"The celebrities are not just competing for fun. There are points and pride at stake and ultimately there can be only one king and queen of the ring!"

Apparently some of the bouts would also be fought inside a cage. I must admit, the thought of seeing the annoying Jeff Brazier rammed head-first into steel bars kind of appealed to the sadist inside me.

At the time, Celebrity Wrestling sounded like a can't-miss prospect and there was a high level of anticipation for the programme. Sure, it was bound to be dumbed-down, lowest common denominator, bottom of the barrel entertainment. But that's the era we're living in. In 2005, reality TV was at its peak. We were slap-bang in the middle of the decade where Big Brother, Strictly Come Dancing and The X Factor were amongst the highest-rated programmes on television. The British viewing public, fuelled by the tabloid press and trashy magazines, seemed more obsessed with famous people than ever before. And they particularly seemed to enjoy watching them suffer, as demonstrated by the ratings winner I'm A Celebrity . . . Get Me Out Of Here. The concept of celebrities being filmed enduring the rigours of pro wrestling training, then beating each other to a pulp inside the ring, sounded like potential TV gold.

With ITV pumping untold amounts of cash into promoting their new baby in the national newspapers, on TV adverts and billboards all over the country, how could Celebrity Wrestling fail?

Even more importantly, the FWA was going to be on prime time Saturday night television, watched by millions of people.

British Wrestling was returning to ITV at last! The Holy Grail, people! The Holy Grail!

You don't have to be a rocket scientist to work out what happened next.

Weeks before Celebrity Wrestling hit the screens, Alex quit his role as consultant. Brown and Legend were retained as coaches of the two teams, and WWF all-time great 'Rowdy' Roddy Piper was drafted in as co-host alongside Kate Thornton, a presenter so wooden she could have passed for a coffee table.

It was clear that when it came to the crunch, ITV had absolutely no faith whatsoever in British Wrestling or in even attempting to turn our relative unknowns into household names. Instead, they plumped for the tried and trusted (and physically bigger) North Americans who were already known to the mainstream wrestling audience. What a crushing blow.

Alex warned me that ITV executives had meddled with the original format and the finished article wasn't likely to be anywhere near what we'd hoped for. He wasn't kidding. Cage matches? The show didn't even have any wrestling matches!

ITV Celebrity Wrestling was launched on Saturday, April 23 2005. To say it flopped would be a gross understatement.

When ratings came in for the first episode, they were a paltry 3.8million, way below the predicted number. That same night, cult sci-fi show Dr Who was re-launched on BBC1 after an absence of 16 years and attracted a whopping 10.5 million viewers. Few predicted the incredible success of the Dr Who comeback, but that doesn't deflect any blame away from ITV for the failure of their heavily-hyped 'next big thing'.

You see, Celebrity Wrestling was pants. It was the pits. It was one of the most dismal television programmes I've ever had the misfortune to clap eyes on.

I only managed to drag myself through the first episode then switched off, quickly erasing Celebrity Wrestling from my brain. So my memories of it are almost non-existent. But Christ on a bike, it was bad. The show was based around a tame series of games loosely themed on wrestling, which took place not inside a ring but on a raised circular platform surrounded by crash mats, involving minimal physical contact. Celebrity Wrestling turned out to be a poor man's Gladiators rip-off, but this was 13 years after Gladiators was cool.

The show lost viewers week on week. By the third episode, only 2.6million were bothering to tune in. Celebrity Wrestling was immediately moved to a Sunday morning death slot then put out of its misery, cancelled after one series.

So much for The Holy Grail . . . again.

There are few better placed than Joe Legend to tell the inside story of Celebrity Wrestling.

"It was Alex who contacted me to tell me about the concept initially," said Joe.

"I remember one of the guys from the production team turned up at a Brian Dixon show and half sold me on the idea. Then they invited me over for a try-out. Wrestling being such a small community, by that point I'd heard they also had D'Lo. So I didn't understand why they wanted *me*, at first. Surely they'd want Alex on TV, him being British, and D'Lo who was a lot more famous than me? I felt like an alternate.

"But then Alex said he didn't want the part. Jonny, Hade and Andy were only ever intended as 'games testers'. They wanted guys who were known.

"So I did the audition at a judo gym in London. I put this office guy and a fitness trainer through a gruelling 45-minute workout. The office guy quit after three minutes and so I picked him up by his coat and dragged him back. The fitness guy lasted the 10 minutes and then collapsed. I think this won them over, so they hired me.

"At first I loved Celebrity Wrestling. I can't complain about the money, it was great. Hanging out near Piccadilly was great too. London is a great city and there's always something to do. And the celebrities worked so hard. Kate Lawler was a machine. James Hewitt, who I thought would be a pushover, was an animal. The only one who drove me mental was Victoria Silvstedt, who would be sat there doing her nails and being hot, which she undoubtedly is, while everyone else was busting their ass.

"The show flopped because it was completely misrepresented from day one. We all warned ITV as soon as they showed us the set-up. I said: 'But that's just like Gladiators!' You could hear a pin drop. I could tell they weren't happy.

"It just wasn't *wrestling*. We told them to call is Celebrity Combat or Celebrity Challenge. Don't call it Celebrity Wrestling because the wrestling fans who tune in will get pissed off because it's not wrestling, and the non-wrestling fans won't tune in at all because they think that it *is* wrestling!

"But they already had Roddy, myself and D'Lo involved, so it was too late. It kind of already implied it would be wrestling."

Could Celebrity Wrestling have worked with a less cheesy format? Could it have been more entertaining with my mates from the British circuit involved alongside D'Lo, Joe and Roddy? Would it have pulled higher ratings if the celebrities had engaged in actual wrestling instead of stupid games? To use one of Mark Kay's favourite sayings—maybe it would, maybe it wouldn't. We'll never know. Surely anything would have been an improvement.

But Celebrity Wrestling proved once again that terrestrial TV executives don't seem to want to touch British Wrestling with a bargepole. So what's their problem?

I always felt there was scope for a major TV network to commission a behind-the-scenes documentary series about the lives of British wrestlers. And I've had my own experiences of this.

During my years as a wrestling promoter I was approached by numerous production companies. At first, they all seem enthusiastic about making a British Wrestling documentary. But once they approach their paymasters, the big telly networks, the entire project goes dead. In 2011 one camera crew even travelled all the way up from London to Morecambe to film both myself and the trainees at my wrestling school for a pilot programme. They took it to Sky One. They told me Sky One quite liked the pilot . . . but not enough to actually make the show.

So what on earth was mainstream TV's problem with British Wrestling? Alex Shane's theory is that pro wrestling is what he calls "the bastard child of entertainment". What he means is, wrestling isn't easily definable. It can't be categorised into a neat compartment because it's a hybrid of so many different sports and entertainment forms. Wrestling is martial arts, athletics, pantomime, soap opera, theatre, comedy, stunt work, all rolled into one. It's all things to all men, and that's its appeal as well as its downfall. Unless you're a fan of wrestling, you either don't understand it or don't want to, because you think it's a joke. TV execs obviously fall into one or both of those categories. Either that or they look down their noses at British Wrestling because it's not the WWE or TNA. So they'd rather fund the kind of brain-dead dirge they do understand, like The Only Way Is Essex and Geordie Shore. Oh, and Celebrity Wrestling.

For years, I wished that TV executives would take a chance on actually making a programme about the lives of modern-day British wrestlers, like the BBC did so successfully with Robbie Brookside's Video Diaries way back in 1993. We have so many talented characters with interesting life stories to tell, who are ready-made to come out of the shadows and become TV stars, especially in this era of reality shows.

We have RJ Singh (formerly Ross Jordan)—primary school head teacher by day, wrestling's outrageous Bollywood film star by night. We have Leroy Kincaide, a handsome, eloquent Adonis who also happens to write and perform rap music, while also finding time to front his own paranormal investigation team. We have Simon Musk, an ordinary lad from Leeds who dons a horned mask to become the masked 'Mexican' hero El Ligero. We even have a wrestler called David Deville, whose day job is working inside Buckingham Palace as a royal footman for the Queen. For crying out loud, you can't *have* a better basis for a TV show than that!

Then there's the fascinating and complex life of Alex Shane. I reckon you could just follow Alex around with a camera for 24 hours and obtain more material for a hit TV show than you'd find on most channels in a month.

But then finally, in July 2012, a TV channel finally took a punt on a documentary about British wrestlers, and chose as their subjects the Knight family—Ricky, Saraya, Zebra, Zak and Saraya-Jade. The Knights were the stars of their own Channel 4 fly-on-the-wall documentary called The Wrestlers: Fighting with my Family, which focussed on Zak and Saraya-Jade's attempts to make it to the big-time of WWE. It followed the family's fortunes as they coped with Saraya-Jade's departure to America and how Zak reacted to WWE's rejection of him.

"I felt bad for Zak watching that programme, because WWE said he didn't have the body to get signed by them," said James Curtin.

"But he's not a failure just because he didn't go to WWE and I hope he doesn't think that. There are more places to earn a living. I remember Zak when he started out as this little masked kid, and where he's got to now is phenomenal. He and Roy tag now as The Hooligans and they draw big crowds for their dad in WAW and in IPW:UK."

The one-hour expose received rave reviews from TV critics and national newspapers, giving British Wrestling some positive mainstream attention . . . and not before time.

Ricky Knight is certainly delighted with how the programme turned out.

"The response has been brilliant and now we're looking at doing a series," he said.

161

"The director Max from Lambent Productions in Brighton is a big wrestling fan and originally the programme was going to be about WAW and the whole of British Wrestling . . . but then in the middle of filming, 'Raya (Saraya-Jade) got the phone call from WWE and that turned into a better story for them.

"It's amazing really because 'Raya never wanted to be in the business. She still got into the ring and trained with Zak, but until she was 14 she wanted to be a vet. Then one night we were one girl short, 'Raya wrestled and that was it. It's all she wants to do now.

"But a series would not only follow Zak on what happens to him in future, it would cover other promotions and wrestlers across the whole spectrum of British Wrestling."

A series on Channel 4 would be great, especially if Lambent continues to present the UK wrestling business as respectfully as they did in Fighting with my Family. Too often whenever British wrestlers make it onto mainstream telly, they are portrayed as buffoons or the butt of the age-old 'it's all fixed' jibes. But that didn't happen in the Knights' documentary.

And when wrestling husband-and-wife duo 'Loco' Mike Mason and Becky James were the subjects of a one-hour episode of Don't Tell the Bride on BBC3 a few months later, it was a similar story. Both programmes showed that wrestlers aren't always larger-than-life superheroes; they are real people with interesting and sometimes gritty real lives, and while British Wrestling may be low budget compared to the Americans, our grapplers are plucky underdogs working hard to make a living while always striving towards a better day. It's a story everyone can relate to.

The Knights and the Masons' forays onto national TV may not be The Holy Grail but they certainly haven't done our industry any harm. Maybe some viewers will have watched these programmes and thought to themselves: "Hey, British Wrestling looks kind of cool, I'll go and watch a live event." Here's hoping.

Back in the spring of 2005, as the Celebrity Wrestling affair unfolded, another British wrestler with the surname Knight was even more horrified than most. That man was Stevie Knight.

Steve is one of my favourite people in wrestling. As two northern lads in an FWA dressing room dominated by southerners, we hit it off from the start. And when we talk about how British Wrestling attracts some fascinating characters, well, they don't come much more intriguing than Stevie Knight—wrestler, promoter, radio presenter, nightclub DJ, professional dog trainer, and £10,000-winning television quiz show contestant.

I first saw Stevie wrestle on one of Chris Curtis' shows in Stoke in the summer of 2003. Stevie was like Robbie Brookside, he was old school, and he didn't have to do much in the ring to get a reaction. And his match that night, against Johnny Phere's younger brother Simon (aka Kid Chaos) was hilarious. Some of the pompous Knight's over-the-top mannerisms, facial expressions and witty aside comments to the crowd made me laugh until I cried.

"I was watching my first ever match from 18 years ago the other day and it's hilarious . . . you wouldn't think it was the same Steve Knight—back then I took bumps!" Stevie told me in 2009.

"When I came back after injury, I couldn't do that anymore, but I'd learned how to talk, slow things down and make everything mean something, rather than all the moves I used to do. But I was once that young guy who everyone thought was really good! I started at the back end of the World of Sport era. I was lucky to work with Skull Murphy, Giant Haystacks and Big Daddy."

The mid-2000s version of Stevie was always the first to admit that he was no athlete. Although he was still the right side of 30 during his FWA years, he'd been a pro since he was 14 and revelled in his image as an 'old man of the ring'. 'The Grimsby Gob' loved to complain about his various injuries and always adamantly claim he was about to quit smoking—yet always mysteriously find a reason to start again. And he loved to take the mickey out of himself for being so unfit.

One of the few highlights of New Frontiers 2005 came when Stevie announced he was entering the tournament to crown the first ever FWA Flyweight Champion. This was comedy at its finest, because Stevie was to high-flying what Johnny Phere is to anger management.

Knight came striding out with a purpose during Mark Sloan's match with Stevie Lynn and vowed to do a top rope moonsault to prove his Flyweight worthiness. As the podgy Shining Light tottered to the top rope, exaggerating attempts to get his balance, the Broxbourne crowd mocked him with a chant of "YOU CAN'T DO IT!" Sure enough, Stevie took a world-class pratfall, toppling on his face as the fans laughed not with derision, but with genuine affection for the loveable Knight's comic genius. He was the Santino Marella of the FWA at the time.

"All that ever bothered me, was that when I left an arena after a show, I wanted the fans to remember who I was," explained Stevie.

"I didn't want them to remember my match because it was the best. I wanted them to remember *me*. And I wanted the promoters to know, that when they booked me on a show, whether as a good guy or a bad guy or whatever, I would get a reaction off the crowd.

"Nobody ever went to the toilet when I was in the wrestling ring. And that's all I want to be remembered for."

There are so many Stevie Knight stories I could tell. We used to take the mickey out of Stevie's ring tights because he'd had the slogan 'It's Knight Time' stitched on the back, but the words were mixed up so it actually read 'Knight It's Time'. There were also his quirky little turns of phrase. If a wrestler was in good shape with a tan, Stevie would say "he looks well". And if he thought a particular grappler wasn't very good, he'd call him "rotten".

Another great Stevie Knight story happened the night before International Showdown, when the FWA's comic turn got the chance to wrestle the great Mitsuharu Misawa in a tag match in Scotland alongside his great mate Doug Williams. Steve once told me he'd deliberately not had a fag that day, not wanting to offend the great Misawa by smoking in front of him. But then the Japanese warrior produced a bottle of Jack Daniels in the dressing room, then began to puff away on a pack of Marlboro Lights! Stevie needn't have worried. Misawa was clearly one of the lads.

My peak years as a promoter in Morecambe were 2007-9, when The Dome was sold out for virtually every show and we built our company around Jonny Storm, Johnny Phere, Spud, The Manchester Massive, RJ Singh, Stixx, El Ligero, a super-popular strongman called Sam 'Slam' Nayler, and Stevie Knight. Some of my favourite moments from that era involved Stevie; like the night when he strutted around the ring wearing a preposterously pristine white all-in-one dinner suit which made him look like The Man From Del Monte, and the time when the Morecambe crowd was so incensed by Knight's cheating that they began pelting him with plastic cups and other rubbish as he stood celebrating a tainted victory in the middle of the ring.

As far as I'm concerned, Stevie was wrestling's 'Mr Morecambe' and I love him to bits.

Back in early 2005 Stevie Knight was on an absolute roll both personally and professionally. His two IWP shows in Hull had done a roaring trade. Big-hearted Stevie then earned the undying respect of the British Wrestling fraternity by organising a major charity show in aid of those whose lives were destroyed by the Tsunami in South East Asia. (He'd coaxed Johnny Angel out of retirement for that one.) He'd got married to a pretty teacher called Emma, and was planning to give up wrestling before his body completely fell apart, and move to sunny Spain to start a new life.

Full of confidence, Stevie heard about the plans for Celebrity Wrestling, thought it was bound to make household names out of D'Lo Brown and Joe Legend, and saw a fabulous opportunity. So he decided to promote a series of wrestling shows to capitalise on ITV's newest Saturday night prime time programme. Knight booked a week-long tour of Yorkshire and Humberside for May and June 2005, when he believed Celebrity Wrestling would be at its peak, with D'Lo Brown and Joe Legend as headline attractions. Stevie called it the Celebrity Carnage Tour. He even asked if he could put the FWA name to it.

By the time Celebrity Wrestling hit the screens, Stevie had already booked his venues and paid deposits. As it became clear the show was a turkey, there was no going back. By the time the Carnage Tour began at Bridlington on May 28, the name of Celebrity Wrestling was mud. So the shows barely drew flies. Knight's calculated risk backfired spectacularly. By the time the tour ended at Sheffield on June 3, Stevie had made a loss of £12,000. It kind of put my Uprising 3 problems into perspective.

"I didn't think it could fail," Stevie said in 2009.

"It was a bit like doing an X Factor touring show with Simon Cowell and Louis Walsh as the judges—because Celebrity Wrestling was on ITV, at the same time as The X Factor is, and D-Lo Brown and Joe Legend were the two stars of the show. Anybody would have thought, my God, this could be massive.

"It all went tits up because Celebrity Wrestling was crap. The name actually tarnished the shows. I booked some very big venues like Leeds Town Hall. It seats about 3,000 people. We drew 300 . . ."

I'd turned up on the afternoon of the Leeds show, just to say hello to the guys and lend moral support, to meet with Alex to discuss booking for Vendetta '05, and to once again try to persuade The Showstealer that Johnny Phere was the new commodity the FWA desperately needed. Even the latest hot young girl who was following Alex around that day was a Johnny Phere fan and joined in the conversation . . . on my side! But The Showstealer *still* didn't see the potential we saw in The Psychotic Warrior.

Stevie Knight was down in the dumps that day, for sure, but he was still out with The UK Pitbulls and Alex, giving out promotional leaflets in Leeds city centre, trying desperately to make the best of a bad situation. That's because Stevie is a survivor. Many weaker characters (like me) would have curled up under a rock and died. Instead, The Shining Light put a brave face on his personal financial meltdown.

Two years later, Stevie earned most of the money back when he won £10,000 on Noel Edmonds' TV quiz show Deal or No Deal. I couldn't have been more delighted for him.

Alex recognised the same qualities in Stevie as I did. That's why he made him FWA Tag Team Champion in his first match back in 2003. And that's why The Showstealer personally requested to wrestle Steve on our second Morecambe event of 2005, which turned out to be the FWA's best show of the year.

For every depressing low we had in 2005, there was an ecstatic high and they didn't come much higher than FWA NOAH Limits. The night of June 18 2005 was probably when I realised that while Broxbourne seemed to be falling out of love with the FWA, my beautiful Lancashire home was as passionate for our product as ever. Perhaps that's because the FWA's northern fans still turned up solely to enjoy a night of entertainment, and not to criticise our every move like some of the southern smart marks did.

Doug Williams deserves a ton of credit for making NOAH Limits such a memorable happening. The Anarchist had become the first Englishman since The British Bulldogs to carve out a lucrative career for himself in Japan. Such was his growing status in Pro Wrestling NOAH, the FWA mainstay and his partner 2 Cold Scorpio had been rewarded with a run as the company's GHC World Tag Team Champions.

"I was on a show in California a few years before where some of the Japanese wrestlers were there, and they were already aware of who I was," said Doug.

"Pro Wrestling NOAH had just been formed, having split from All-Japan Pro Wrestling. They'd had British guys before, like The British Bulldogs, 'Super Destroyer' Pete Roberts and Johnny Smith, and they were looking for someone else to fill that role.

"I eventually became their booking agent for the UK. I arranged all their tours in Europe and found them accommodation. They were very keen to come over to Britain to get their young guys experience. Mitsuharu Misawa himself, the head man at NOAH, wanted to come over because he'd never wrestled outside of Japan before, other than in Mexico, and wanted to see what it was like.

"The Japanese saw the best and the worst of British Wrestling at the time, because I got them bookings on any show I could. They did shows for All-Star and 1PW in front of big crowds. Then they would work for other promotions that only drew 50 people and would put the young Japanese lads on with some British kid who'd only had five or six matches. And the kid would beat them! But the Japanese always found that amusing. They had no egos about winning or losing. They knew they could beat the hell out of these guys if they wanted to.

"It all went very smoothly, working with the Japanese. It was probably my favourite time in wrestling."

At the time, the Japanese promotion wanted to switch the titles back to two of their own, Naomichi Marufuji and Minoru Suzuki, while they were over on a tour of Europe. Our much-loved little venue was the right place at the right time. NOAH bosses were persuaded that the atmospheric Morecambe Dome would be the ideal place for the titles to change hands. And Mark Kay and I were more than happy to welcome our Oriental friends to Lancashire, especially when we learned the match would only cost us a pittance.

Results from FWA NOAH Limits were:

**Ross Jordan beat Aviv Maayan, FWA All-England Champion Hade Vansen pinned
Stevie Lynn, Stixx and Martin Stone beat Hampton Court to capture the FWA British
Tag Team Titles, Damon Leigh beat Joey Hayes, FWA British Heavyweight Champion
Alex Shane beat JC Thunder, FWA British Heavyweight Champion Alex Shane beat
Stevie Knight, Naomichi Marufuji and Minoru Suzuki downed Doug Williams and
Scorpio to win the GHC World Tag Team Titles**

Every match that night was quality. Ross Jordan, a great lad who was on the verge of becoming
a superb bad guy, and Aviv Maayan had a terrific little opener. Hade Vansen and Stevie Lynn
followed suit with their own absorbing battle. Stixx and Stone then ripped the tag team titles
from Simmonz in a virtual handicap match. Alex had lost faith in the abilities of The Duke of
Danger and wanted him written out in a pre-match injury angle, so Andy was forced to battle
the two bruisers on his own in vain. This would mark Dane Hardie's last appearance for the
FWA. I'll always have fond memories of working with Dane, another sound bloke who I'd
first met on a Showstealer Night Out three years earlier.

Although most of the packed-out Morecambe Dome had come for the once-in-a-lifetime
experience of watching a prestigious Japanese championship defended on UK soil, the
undisputed highlight of the show turned out not to be Williams and Scorpio versus Marufuji
and Suzuki. The best match at FWA NOAH Limits was Stevie Knight versus Alex Shane.

The greatest wrestling angles are always based on reality, so we had Stevie come out and
inform the fans he was moving abroad and retiring from the ring. The arrogant champion
then arrived, mocked Knight and challenged him. What followed was professional wrestling
at its very best.

Although Steve had previously been a bad guy, the Morecambe fans' feelings for him had
always been of amusement rather than real hate. But they *loathed* Alex Shane, who was a
tremendous heel champion. So the people got right behind the underdog Knight, as a super
match erupted full of big moves, wild brawling and false finishes. Most importantly, it was
a match built on pure emotion, as the great Dusty Rhodes would say, because unlike in the
NOAH main event, the fans really cared who won and who lost.

It was Stevie who ultimately lost. Afterwards, as The Shining Light lurched to his feet, with
a look of pure disappointment etched across his face, he slowly turned around in a full circle.
Time stood still, as Knight seemed to make eye contact and a heartfelt connection with every
single fan in that building. The Morecambe Dome crowd rose to its feet as one, and gave the
tearful Stevie a standing ovation.

Knight did move to Spain after one more Morecambe show where he beat Alex in a rematch.
But three months later, he returned home to Grimsby. In an interview with me in 2009, he
explained what happened.

"While we were there, my wife attracted a stalker.

"He was following her about everywhere . . . sitting outside our house. Obviously I wasn't
too impressed with him so I went and had a little word. The next thing we know, there's about
seven Spanish men sitting outside the house, following me about, threatening to kill us . . . so
we thought it was prudent to return home."

From then on, until he retired from wrestling again a few years later (for something like the
276th time) The Shining Light became a *bona fide* main eventer in Morecambe. Stevie always

used to joke to me about the number of times the phrase 'bona fide' was used in Power Slam, so I'm sure he'll appreciate it being used to describe him!

In 2009 Stevie would once again follow his dream to live in sunnier climes when he settled in Cyprus, where he still lives with his wife and baby daughter. I haven't seen him since then, and I don't half miss the old scoundrel!

NOAH Limits climaxed with the historic main event as Mark Kay and I watched from backstage. While Suzuki, Marufuji, Williams and Scorpio were tearing the house down, we caught each other's glance. And we both smiled. No words were needed. We both knew it was a magical night, and we might never see the like in Morecambe again.

While Morecambe ticked along nicely with superlative shows, strong attendances and positive reviews, matters at Broxbourne were never that straightforward. Living 200 miles away, I always found it tough to promote Broxbourne effectively, especially with no money for advertising and a dwindling number of volunteers willing to put posters up. Still, when we returned to Herts for Vendetta on July 10 2005, we delivered what I felt was a first-class evening's entertainment. Results were:

Dave Moralez pinned Dragon Phoenix, Ross Jordan defeated Spud, Aviv Maayan and Bubblegum in a four-way, Paul Travell won a Battle Royal to earn an FWA Title shot, James Tighe beat Jack Storm by submission in a Clown Suit Match, The Zebra Kid defeated 'American Dragon' Bryan Danielson, Joe Legend pinned Jack Xavier, Doug Williams and Robbie Brookside fought to a 20-minute draw in a World of Sport Rules Match, Alex Shane pinned Paul Travell to retain the FWA Title after interference from Iceman, Jody Fleisch and Jonny Storm beat James Tighe and Mark Belton.

When scripting Vendetta '05, Alex and I went back to basics. We pulled the plug on the Paul Travell schizophrenia angle and scrapped the Andy Simmonz Cystic Fibrosis fiasco, and instead booked a no-frills show focussed on great wrestling, logical storylines and plenty of fun. Alex and Dino always used to say that a wrestling show should be like a buffet, with something to cater for all tastes. Vendetta '05 was a perfect example.

There was a blinding Flyweight four-way full of jaw-dropping dives and innovative spots, an action-packed Battle Royal, a violent hardcore brawl (Shane v Travell), a textboot 20-minute exchange of old school British style holds (Williams v Brookside), a dream match between two of wrestling's hardest hitters (Zebra v Danielson), a tag team main event with a feel good conclusion (Fleisch/Storm v Tighe/Belton) and lashings and lashings of comedy.

The Clown Suit match was a particularly inspired piece of hilarity. James Tighe had failed to make good on a pre-match boast that he would make Aviv Maayan tap out at Crunch. According to the stipulation, he now had to perform a forfeit. So Commissioner Flash Barker forced the straight-laced Tighe to wrestle a match while dressed as a clown.

Backstage, James really didn't want to don the curly wig, red nose and silly costume at all; he complained non-stop that it was a ridiculous idea. That is, until the Clown Suit Match got the loudest reaction of the show.

The fans loved every minute of James' embarrassment, mocking the reluctant clown with a derisive chorus of the famous circus theme Entrance of the Gladiators. Tighe, who wasn't exactly known for his sense of humour, was a revelation in feigning his fury at the fans' taunts, and his sidekick Belton was equally hysterical in laughing at James behind his back! Afterwards, Tighe came backstage and conceded: "I really enjoyed that!"

167

But not everything at Vendetta got over quite so well. Zebra Kid and the future Daniel Bryan's supposed 'dream match' failed to sparkle. The FWA fans were expecting a lengthy, intense and realistic-looking fight from Danielson, who specialised in such matches for Ring of Honor in the States. But The American Dragon, who was over in the UK on a family-friendly tour for Brian Dixon, wasn't keen on performing at his ROH level that day at Broxbourne. When I suggested beforehand that he and Zebra go all-out for 30 minutes, Bryan raised his eyebrows. The ensuing 15-minute, slow-paced, mat wrestling clinic was not what I, nor the Civic Hall faithful, had envisaged.

But Bryan's a good guy. I interviewed him for Power Slam a few years ago, he worked for me again in Morecambe in 2008 and I'm delighted that today he's one of the biggest superstars in WWE. His skits with Kane in 2012 were some of the funniest wrestling television segments I've ever seen. YES! YES! YES indeed, they were.

Meanwhile, Alex Shane and Paul Travell pulled out all the stops and still didn't get the appreciation they deserved from the cynical FWA followers who'd seen it all before. Blood, chair shots, Mr Pointy, fighting in the aisles and in the bleachers . . . Shane and Travell reprised every dangerous tactic from their classic brawls of two years previously, but the sporadic cheers for the mayhem were far less enthusiastic than they had been in 2003.

The chaos concluded when I made my return as an actual performer, running in to break up the referee's count when The Righteous One seemed on the verge of winning the championship. My new hired assassin Iceman, who I'd first seen at the No Ring Circus in Blackburn two years earlier, then made his debut, sending both himself and Travell through a ringside table with a crushing power bomb. Even after such a spectacular stunt, the Broxbourne fans' chants of "Holy s__t!" seemed almost indifferent.

Even so, I felt really satisfied with Vendetta '05. That is, until I went home and read the online reviews.

The ultra-critical smarts picked holes in everything; from the cost-cutting removal of the wrestlers' entranceway to the choice of young Jack Storm as James Tighe's opponent. This was really unfair because Jack was doing a tremendous job playing a new character I'd developed; a loveable but slightly deranged obsessive wrestling fan who idolised his namesake Jonny Storm. Sadly we had to drop the younger Storm's 'stalker' gimmick in 2006 due to wage cutbacks, but Jack by then was already making his name with another UK promotion called IPW:UK. More on them later.

The internet community also complained Vendetta contained too much talking and not enough wrestling. Sure, there were a few promo segments on the show, but they were all relevant to furthering our plotlines and most of them were very entertaining. Ricky Knight's speech was especially dynamic, ending with the gravel-voiced veteran challenging his 'estranged son' The Zebra Kid to a final showdown at Hotwired. Zebra accepted, then turned around and superkicked his wicked stepmum Sweet Saraya square in the jaw!

Danielson v Zebra may have been a disappointment, but the post-match furthering of the Knight family feud was a compelling angle deserving of more acclaim than it received. It's a real shame the father v son rivalry never culminated with the decisive final showdown we'd planned for. But sadly, due to further brushes with the law, Zebra was unavailable for FWA shows during the rest of 2005 and 2006.

Roy had a long history of outside-the-ring violence, which I've always found hard to believe knowing the placid fellow he is backstage at shows. But he used to get into fights in pubs and found himself up in court several times during that period. A keen footballer away from the ring, he even got into scrapes on the pitch, including on one notorious occasion when he angrily knocked a referee unconscious after being sent off.

But I'm pleased to say that today, Roy seems to have left those dark days behind him and the Knight family is closer and more successful than ever.

"Roy had his demons over the years but he has always admitted what he's done," said his dad Ricky.

"It's been a monkey on his back and people who don't really know Roy have always said things about him. Maybe he felt he had to be the hard man. That's why being with Zak in The Hooligans has helped him . . . he's being that character in the ring now instead.

"Roy has got over his demons now. He's married with children, he's settled down and he's got a mortgage. He's back on his feet.

"My kids are all great, loyal kids. I see people of Zak's age standing on street corners, drinking and smoking the ganja, but Zak doesn't do that and look how far he has come. 'Raya too, and then there's my wife Jools . . . she's off doing a three-week tour of America at the moment.

"I'm 60 this year and I'm going to do my retirement show next September. I'll have been in the business 28 years and it's time to pack in the actual wrestling because I don't want other people saying that I'm too old and not taking me seriously.

"I'll just concentrate on the promoting and training because I know the wrestling side of my family is in good hands."

As 2005 developed, the North-South divide between FWA's fan base continued to bamboozle me. The bulk of the Morecambe fans were kids and families who didn't comment on the shows on the internet; they just went to the wrestling for a fun night out. The southerners were mainly young adult males, who seemed less concerned with enjoying themselves, and more with trying to outdo each other for attention-seeking chants and online nastiness. I've always had a deep affinity with my hometown fans and understood exactly what they wanted from a wrestling show. But it was a source of deep frustration to me that I couldn't seem to get it right down south.

In contrast, even the most surreal of ideas went down a storm 'oop north', thanks to our magnificent Morecambe Dome crowd.

We'd started doing a raffle before the main event at Morecambe shows, to raise extra cash. One night, a fan named Ben Corrigan—who travelled all over the country watching the FWA—started a "MORECAMBE RAFFLE!" chant. The chant spread quickly throughout The Dome and soon every man, woman and child were chanting "MORECAMBE RAFFLE!" It became a bizarre cult craze, to the point that other wrestling promotions later tried to duplicate it in their own towns. Years later, Morecambe fans still chanted for The Morecambe Raffle, sometimes even louder than for the wrestling itself!

"I still remember one night when Stevie Knight drew The Morecambe Raffle . . . and he was such an entertaining *cock*, wasn't he?" said James Curtin, who modelled many of his over-the-top 'Rock Star' mannerisms on Steve.

"He pulled out a ticket and said: 'Ticket number 212? 212? Come on down, you've won yourself a PlayStation3!'

"This kid came up to the ring, all eager and excited as hell, with what he thought was the winning ticket.

"Stevie just looked at him.

"'Sorry son. My mistake. I meant ticket number 213'."

Our July 30 2005 Morecambe show had its fair share of such surrealism. At the pre-show fan gathering in the Waterfront Bar, I somehow found myself playing the contortionist board game Twister with Colt Cabana (I let him win, of course). Then when the show began, referee Richard Young managed to rip a gaping hole in the back of his trousers during a match, which had the audience (if not the pants) in stitches.

That night also saw the triumphant return to Morecambe for Johnny Angel. My old adversary's comeback was made all the more special because he had the most inappropriate theme tune in wrestling history. The grizzled hard man entered to a 1962 Shelley Fabares ballad, conveniently named Johnny Angel, which had the sloppiest romantic lyrics imaginable. Altogether now . . .

"Johnny Angel, how I love him, he's got something that I can't resist, but he doesn't even know that I exist . . .

"Johnny Angel, how I love him, and I pray that someday he'll love me. And together we will see how lovely heaven can be!"

Johnny Angel, the ultimate ring bully, coming out to a cheesy '60s love song? It just shouldn't have worked. But everything worked in Morecambe! The crowd lapped it up!

I must tell you a quick anecdote about Johnny Angel's scathing sense of humour. Before the last ever FWA show at The Winter Gardens in Cleethorpes on September 23 2006, we had a last-minute withdrawal. We decided to add a trainee wrestler to the show as a replacement, but wanted to put him under a mask because he looked like such a young rabbit in the headlights. But for the life of us, we couldn't come up with a name for the shy youngster's masked character.

There was myself, Mark Kay, Stevie and others all sitting around on the afternoon of the show, throwing ideas for names around and getting nowhere. Nothing seemed to fit and the room eventually fell silent as the ideas dried up. But then out of the silence, Johnny Angel, who was sitting quietly in the corner lacing up his boots, and who had contributed nothing to the discussion, came up with a suggestion.

"Why don't we call him . . . .The Masked *BASTARD*?"

It was so ridiculously out of left-field and sarcastically inappropriate, it had everyone falling about laughing. Needless to say, Cleethorpes was a family audience, so we eventually picked a different name. But you never know. One day, when you least expect it, British Wrestling may yet see the debut of The Masked Bastard!

The Morecambe fans also took Dr Dirk Feelgood to their hearts, once we turned him babyface and gave him a tag team partner, a charismatic GPW wrestler named JC Thunder. The Young

Doctors debuted on our August 27 2005 show at The Dome and proved straight away that laughter is indeed the best medicine.

We re-named Dirk's new sidekick Dr Jason Allbetter, who emerged for their match with The Manchester Massive dressed in surgeon's scrubs. The only problem was, when he got to the ring, he couldn't get them off! His trousers were stretched so tight over his wrestling boots that Dirk needed to give him a helping hand. It was one of the funniest sights I've ever seen as Allbetter lay shame-faced on the canvas while Feelgood yanked away at his pants, until they finally peeled off to a deafening cheer. Dr Jason then took a bow and milked the applause by parading around the ring holding his trousers as a trophy! Dirk and JC played the doctor gimmick for laughs, exactly as it should have been done from the very beginning.

Further wage cutbacks meant we had to drop Jason Allbetter in 2006, so The Young Doctors team sadly didn't last. But Dirk and JC's paths would cross again . . . just one more time. More on that later.

The August 27 2005 show was also the night when Andy Simmonz dropped his butler gimmick. By then, I'd managed to persuade Alex that Andy wasn't yet Heavyweight Championship material. To keep Simmonz happy, we complied with his wishes to kill off his manservant alter-ego, which he believed was the albatross around his neck keeping him from being a serious main event singles competitor. Andy didn't want to wear the waistcoat and bow tie any more. A huge admirer of 'The British Bulldog' Davey Boy Smith, he wanted to be Andy 'Boy' Simmonz, complete with running powerslam finishing move.

To introduce the new stripped-down Simmonz, we tried the exact same scenario that worked with Stevie Knight two months earlier. Andy came out at Morecambe in his butler garb. Then Alex came out, in full beard and Aviator shades (I called this look his 'George Michael' phase) to mock his outfit and challenge him to a match. But when Simmonz returned for their main event later that evening in more traditional ring wear, his make-under didn't resonate. Simmonz the butler had been the ultimate downtrodden underdog, a working class hero the fans rallied behind in droves. But plain old Andy Simmonz didn't attract anywhere near the same support. Behind the butler outfit, the real Andy lacked Stevie's natural likeability.

Perhaps we should have just turned him heel. Simmonz certainly proved a revelation when he turned bad the following year. But I'll admit, at the time I didn't really know what to do with him and from a personal standpoint, I wasn't his biggest fan. From the heights of Simmonzamania, Andy's FWA career would eventually peter out. I hardly booked him at all in 2006.

We also ran a couple of shows at a leisure centre just outside Blackpool in 2005, which drew quite well—especially the second one on October 23 headlined by a fantastic match between Alex and Joe Legend. The first had taken place on August 28, which happened to coincide with Paul Burchill's WWE television debut across The Pond.

"I was in my hotel room watching TV with Martin Stone and my friend Rich Leaney, who used to help out at FWA shows, and we saw Paul do a run-in on a match between William Regal and Scotty 2 Hotty," said Dean Ayass.

"We decided to pull a rib (play a joke) on James Tighe, who was always good for winding up because he'd always react.

"James hadn't seen Burchill's debut. So before the Blackpool show, we told James that Paul had used his finishing move the Tighe-tanic on WWE television, and this meant he wouldn't be allowed to use it any more.

"James was really proud of the Tighe-tanic so his face fell. The thing was, we'd let everybody else on the show that night in on the joke. So everybody was telling James the same thing and eventually James believed it was true. So he wrestled his match (against El Ligero) and didn't use the Tighe-tanic, he won it with some other move. It was only when we were leaving the venue that we told him we were winding him up. His face was a picture!"

It may have been all smiles amongst the boys, but continuing financial problems meant tensions were running high within the FWA management team in summer 2005. After the July 31 Enfield show, I finally lost patience with Alex and we had a huge row on the phone. This came about after I'd had a bit of a moan in front of The Showstealer about Sanjay Bagga's stingy nature. Alex then told Bagga I didn't want him as an FWA regional promoter any more, which simply wasn't true, I just wanted him to spend a bit more money. I went mad when I found out and rang Alex to have a right go at him. Shane hung up on me as I yelled down the receiver, then texted me later, saying I'd "lost my speaking privileges" with him. He then refused to talk to me for days.

We eventually talked it out and smoothed things over. Alex explained that he had only stretched the truth in an attempt to squeeze a better deal out of Bagga. I accepted his explanation, I hate falling out with anyone, but this spat was a definite turning point in our relationship.

I'd moved on from being in awe of Alex Shane, of being something of a 'yes man' around him, to someone who wasn't afraid to speak up when I didn't agree with his actions or ideas. Like me, Alex is sensitive and hates being criticised, and he can really lose his rag when he's upset. But although we've had several other heated discussions over the years since our Bagga blow-up, I think he actually respects me more now I'm honest with him.

I had numerous other frustrations in summer 2005 and at times I felt like I was banging my head against a brick wall.

We'd scheduled Hotwired for September 3, but decided to delay it until October due to poor advance ticket sales. We also had to keep delaying a long-term plan to put Doug Williams, Robbie Brookside, James Tighe and Mark Belton together as a heel stable, because Doug's Japanese tours were increasing in frequency and he wasn't available for FWA dates. Not that I felt bitter about this, far from it. A hard-working and humble ambassador for the British Wrestling scene, Doug truly deserved his success. In a business full of egotists, nobody ever has a bad work to say about Doug.

"I've always tried to be professional and know my job," said Doug.

"Like with any job, you don't have to be a dick. I wasn't in the business for making friends, but I wasn't trying to alienate people either. I was just being myself, not trying to impress anyone or backstab or take anyone down. I think far too many of the guys are worried about what everyone else thinks of them. You've got to get over that."

'The Anarchist's career would go from strength to strength in 2008 when he signed for TNA. Later, he would become their X Division Champion and tag team champion alongside former Gladiator and fellow Brit, Nick 'Magnus' Aldis. Today, Williams is a weekly television star known all over the globe, and works as a coach for the next generation of TNA stars at their training promotion OVW in Kentucky.

Another setback for the FWA in 2005 came when Jack Xavier quit. I don't know why, he just stopped returning my calls. It was nothing personal. Like so many others, he'd just fallen out of love with the business and never returned. I next saw Jack in Wolverhampton when he popped in to say hello at an event where I was commentating in 2010. Renzo looked trim, tanned and content with life. Be warned kids—getting out of professional wrestling can seriously *improve* your health.

Attendances also temporarily dropped at the usually impregnable fortress of The Morecambe Dome, but that was our own fault for getting greedy. Shows in June, July, August *and* October were just too many in a short space of time. So we took five months off after the October show—headlined by an Alex Shane and Johnny Angel v Jonny Storm and Joe Legend tag match—then came back to The Dome in March 2006. Absence made our adoring Morecambe fans' hearts grow fonder, and we duly sold out.

But Morecambe's temporary blip at the box office was nothing compared to what happened in Broxbourne. FWA Hotwired on October 16 2005 was the worst-attended Civic Hall show in history. There were blocks of empty seats everywhere. The cumulative effect of shoddy advertising and disillusionment with the perceived decline of our southern shows combined to keep the fans away in droves.

The show saw the fast-rising Leroy Kincaide beat Hade Vansen for the All-England Title, the return of The New Breed and an Alex Shane-Joe Legend main event. Other than that, it was too depressing a night for me to want to recall it in too much detail. It also forced us to make the heartbreaking decision of cancelling FWA Goldrush, which was scheduled for late November. We simply couldn't afford the crippling financial loss that show was bound to make.

And so instead, we closed 2005 with the bittersweet experience that was Universal Uproar.

Alex put a huge amount of effort into promoting his second Supershow but met obstacles at every turn. In an attempt to meet or even exceed the expectations created by International Showdown, he secured the services of not only Mick Foley, AJ Styles, Rhino and Austin Aries, but the Japanese icon Kenta Kobashi and Matt Hardy, who at the time was the hottest free agent in wrestling following an acrimonious departure from WWE.

Hardy had signed a contract with Alex that spring, confirming he would be at Coventry Skydome on November 12 2005. But then in July, he shockingly returned to WWE and Vince McMahon insisted Hardy withdraw from Universal Uproar. Unable to afford the costs of a legal battle, Alex was forced to grit his teeth and accept defeat. He maintains to this day that McMahon deliberately tried to sabotage the Supershow. Alex's claim does seem to be borne out by the fact that WWE decided to run their own event at the Skydome, *seven days* after Uproar, which *must* have had an adverse effect on ticket sales. In a perverse way, though, Alex must have found it flattering to be thought of as competition for the great Vincent Kennedy McMahon.

TNA also caused problems for Alex by suddenly arranging their own pay-per-view event in Florida for November 13. The world's second biggest wrestling company then pulled Styles, Rhino and Aries from Uproar, concerned they wouldn't get back from England in time. Undeterred, Alex added Low Ki, Homicide, Shannon Moore, Sonjay Dutt, D'Lo Brown and Joe Legend to a line-up which also included Colt Cabana, Nigel McGuinness, Kobashi, Amazing Red, NOAH's Go Shiozaki and Jun Akiyama, The Sandman and Foley's first match on British soil in years.

Despite the star-studded bill at Universal Uproar, the show drew 2,400, a drop of 1,000 people on International Showdown.

Alex suddenly had other competition closer to home as well. A fan called Steven Gauntley, who ran a wrestling merchandise shop in Doncaster, had set up a promotion in his hometown called One Pro Wrestling (1PW). Copying the successful formula of International Showdown, Gauntley had begun his own series of Supershows a month before Uproar. Name Americans like Low Ki, Steve Corino, Austin Aries and AJ Styles dominated the card as 1PW's debut event drew a sizeable crowd of 1,400 to The Doncaster Dome. His next big event was two months after Uproar, featuring all-time great Bret Hart and future WWE World Champion Christian. Many wrestling fans couldn't afford to attend every single one of these exciting cards so close to Christmas and were forced to choose between them. This definitely affected the gate on November 12.

Alex quickly recognised that the Supershow market was becoming saturated and going forward, he would struggle to draw the size of crowd he needed to make money. So Universal Uproar would be the second and final Alex Shane Supershow of its kind. But as always, The Showstealer had been the pioneer for others to follow. He went where there was no path, and left a trail.

As for the show itself, it was very, very good indeed. Not quite on a par with the near-perfection of Showdown but then again, that was "As Good As It Gets", remember? Results were:

Jonny Storm, Spud and The Amazing Red defeated Jody Fleisch, James Tighe and Aviv Maayan, Joe Legend defeated D'Lo Brown, Colt Cabana beat Nigel McGuinness in a World of Sport match, Low Ki beat Homicide, Shannon Moore pinned Sonjay Dutt, Mick Foley, The Sandman, Steve Corino and Paul Travell (with Bill Apter) beat Alex Shane, Stixx, Martin Stone and Iceman (with Greg 'The Truth' Lambert) in an elimination match, Doug Williams and Jun Akiyama beat Kenta Kobashi and Go Shiozaki.

It was another immense thrill for me to be managing at ringside against Mick Foley. The Hardcore Legend was a joy to work with again, even though he must have been exhausted from his hectic travel schedule that week. Mick landed at Heathrow on the Wednesday then ended up criss-crossing up and down the country for the next six days, starting with a show in Newcastle-upon-Tyne on the Thursday, then Newport on Friday, the big show in Coventry on Saturday, Kilmarnock in Scotland on Sunday, then he travelled all the way back down to Essex on Monday, before flying back to New York from Heathrow on the Tuesday.

It was also a spine-tingling moment to be in the ring when The Sandman came out. When the beer-drinking ECW veteran's iconic music Enter Sandman hit and the crowd roared, the hairs on the back of my neck stood up.

At one point earlier in the day, it had been touch and go whether Sandman would even be part of the show at all. Alex nearly sent him home, furious that he'd partaken of too many alcoholic beverages at a show in Newport the night before, where the unpredictable drinker got into an argument with Foley.

"Sandman was completely blotto during that show," recalled Dann Read.

"He staggered out onto stage during Alex's match, where Foley was the special guest referee. He wasn't supposed to be there and he had his shirt off, acting like a drunken punter, and started laughing at what was happening in the ring.

"Sandman then came backstage and was in a mood, for some reason. Then he went outside and was trying to get naked in the street, was annoying police officers and random women, and was being a right pain.

"Then he wanted to go, but he had to wait because there was a minibus hired to take him, Alex, me, Foley, Shannon Moore, Sonjay Dutt and Bill Apter to Coventry. So Sandman started walking into the street, cars were having to swerve to miss him, and he even tried to rope in fans to help him tip the bus over!

"At this point, Cactus (Mick) came out and got into a verbal with Sandman, because he was being such a t__t. Sandman started challenging Cactus to a fight, and Cactus was fuming over his behaviour, He ended up trying to book a taxi from Newport to Coventry. The show had gone long, it was now after midnight, and everyone was trying to talk Mick out of it because of how much it would cost.

"When we finally got on the bus, we had to sit Cactus and Sandman well apart from each other. Everyone else was really quiet because they didn't want to set Sandman off, because we didn't know what on earth he was going to do next. But for the entire journey Sandman was just ranting and raving, having a go at everyone, until he started to sober up and began saying: 'Cactus, I'm sorry . . . I get like this sometimes . . . I'm so sorry'."

The next day Sandman apologised again, stayed sober, and behaved himself at Uproar.

Before the match, Alex gathered his new American valet and latest girlfriend 'Simply Luscious' Veronica Stevens, myself, Iceman, Stixx and Stone together into a huddle at ringside, and whispered to us all.

You may have often wondered exactly what wrestling team-mates utter under their breaths to each other before or during matches. So what were Shane's words of wisdom? What inspired plan of action had the most cerebral mind in British Wrestling devised? What Churchillian speech of motivation was he sharing with his team? Well, I'll tell you.

"Mary had a little lamb

She tied it to a pylon

Ten thousand volts went up its arse

And turned its wool to nylon

NOW LET'S GO GET 'EM !"

The ensuing ding-dong eight-man elimination match ended when Alex was pinned by his old rival Corino, but not until the FWA Champ had himself eliminated Foley. The selfless Mick had insisted beforehand that Alex pin him, and Shane was overwhelmed by the kind gesture. The chaotic bout was also notable for not one . . . but two balcony dives. One by Paul Travell, and one by referee Lance Lenahan who was sent plummeting on his merry 15 foot way by a stray Travell elbow!

It was a thrill to meet the great Kenta Kobashi at Universal Uproar. The Japanese veteran was past his best, with two knackered knees, but the fans ate up every single thing he did during the pulsating main event. I also loved interacting with the ringside Japanese photographers, whose enthusiastic presence really added to the legitimacy of Uproar as a major event.

I'd also love to say it was an honour to meet the World of Sport legend Kendo Nagasaki, who was up there with Big Daddy and Giant Haystacks for notoriety during the '70s and '80s. But I can't, because Kendo has never been one for exchanging pleasantries, or even for mixing with the other performers full stop! The ultimate bastion of Kayfabe, the permanently-masked Samurai warrior insisted on a private dressing room, where he remained with his manager Lloyd Ryan until it was time to go to the Skydome ring. Nagasaki then got into the ring, twirled his Samurai sword, accepted a Lifetime Achievement Award, left the ring, then immediately got into his car and drove back home. Even years after retiring as a full-time wrestler, Kendo was determined to maintain his mystique. What a guy!

There were two disappointments for me at Universal Uproar. First, Bill Apter didn't get to put me in his figure-four leglock. We wanted to do the spot during the eight-man, but Alex wasn't keen because we hadn't practiced the move beforehand. Shame, I would have loved to have been figure-foured by Bill, although Alex was probably right. Having my lanky legs wrapped like a pretzel by a much-shorter middle-aged man surely wouldn't have looked pretty!

My second disappointment was that Universal Uproar made a loss, so I didn't get paid again. I found this particularly galling after the amount of work I'd put in helping to organise the event, particularly in booking all the flights for Foley, Cabana, Low Ki, Dutt, McGuinness, D'Lo, Red, Apter, Sandman, Moore and Homicide and applying for all of their work permits too, a painstakingly lengthy and high-pressure task which I absolutely hated.

Feeling skint, I didn't join the nightclub after-party this time. Instead, Mark Kay and I drove back to the hotel, accompanied by Colt Cabana and a young female admirer he'd picked up. It turned out that Colt hadn't been allocated a room, so he had nowhere to go for privacy with his lady friend.

So he asked me a question Austin Powers would have been proud of. It was a question I politely said no to, but one I'll never forget.

"Hey Greg . . . can we *shag* in your bathroom?"

As a promoter, I do like to look after my wrestlers. But that would have been going much too far . . .

176

CHAPTER 15

IT'S REAL IN MORECAMBE

At the start of 2006, the FWA had a £3,500 public liability insurance bill to pay. There wasn't enough money in the company account and Doug Williams, Mark Sloan and Alex Shane no longer wanted to invest in the FWA. So Mark Kay and I said we would stump up our own cash, on condition that we took full control of the FWA under a new limited company name, meaning no debts.

The others agreed. None of them were interested in running FWA anymore, the ghost-town attendance at Hotwired and cancellation of Goldrush had been the final straw for them. At a meeting in early January, Alex finally stepped aside from any involvement in running the company. The Showstealer was suffering with a bad neck again, so he decided to retire from in-ring competition, step away completely from the FWA and focus on his next project, as promoter of Ring of Honor's first ever UK tour that summer. As for Mark Sloan, he actually advised me to let the FWA go out of business. Sloan didn't believe the promotion he'd created could recapture its former glories. With hindsight, he was right.

But I didn't want the FWA to die. I was passionate about those three letters, because of all the amazing experiences they had given me over the previous four years. And I was bullish about my chances of turning things around, given a fair crack of the whip with no restrictions, no overly-complicated processes and no outside interference getting in the way. It was a challenge for sure. But at first, I was determined to meet it head on.

With hindsight, I wish I hadn't.

But in the first week of January 2006, I became the managing director of the Frontier Wrestling Alliance. The fan who had turned up at Crystal Palace four years earlier was now running Britain's best known wrestling company. Yes, little old me. Who would have thought it possible?

Most importantly, that meant I could finally bring in Johnny Phere. RESULT!

I had a very clear vision for the FWA's future. For starters, I had no intention of shelling out thousands on the kind of stressful, risky and costly extravaganzas FWA was renowned for. There is only one Alex Shane, and I don't have his gambler instinct and insatiable self-belief.

Instead, I wanted my FWA to adopt a more conservative approach. I wanted to stabilise the FWA and turn it into a well-organised, professionally-run, profitable and sustainable business, one capable of running entertaining and well-attended events in towns all over the UK for years to come. But the days of frittering money away willy-nilly were well and truly over. I just had to re-educate the fans, and the wrestlers, that the gravy train had come to a screeching halt.

This, as I was about to find out, was an impossible task.

As new FWA head booker and the man in charge, I immediately had a number of issues to deal with. Mark Kay insisted that from now on, FWA shows should be run to the strictest budget imaginable. He analysed the wage bill and told me to trim costs even more than the previous year. So I reluctantly asked our three highest-paid stars, Doug Williams, Jody Fleisch and Jonny Storm, to take a pay cut. They agreed, but I could tell they weren't happy.

Morale amongst the other wrestlers had also nosedived. At Universal Uproar, the buzz amongst the wrestlers backstage had been all about other wrestling companies like IPW:UK and 1PW, not FWA. They didn't see coming to work for FWA as anything special any more. So I felt there were times in 2006 where some wrestlers weren't trying as hard as they had in the past, causing the shows to suffer a dip in quality.

The wrestlers were losing interest, the fans (outside of Morecambe) were losing faith, but the biggest problem I had to cope with in early 2006 was the infighting between those two unsung heroes of the FWA, Ralph Cardall and Mark Sloan.

Ralph and Mark had never really seen eye to eye, but their professional rivalry had now exploded into a personal antipathy which gave me a serious headache in the run-up to New Frontiers 2006. The outspoken Cardall had joined forces with long-serving FWA cameraman Ian Dewhirst to form a production company called Redchurch. Ralph felt his unique contribution to the FWA had never been rewarded financially. The sardonic music maestro often complained that despite producing all the FWA themes, build-up videos and T-shirt designs, he was taken for granted; an afterthought when it came to actually being paid.

With a new regime at the helm, the feisty Ralph saw an opportunity to get what he felt he deserved. So he told me that he wanted the exclusive rights to continue to make branded T-shirts and other merchandise, film our shows and produce DVDs, and in return he'd get the FWA TV show off the ground again. But Redchurch also wanted all the money from merchandise sales. They also wanted Mark Sloan, the reason why the FWA existed in the first place, gone from the company altogether.

Mark Kay and I then travelled to Sloan's training centre in a Portsmouth warehouse to meet with him. The Specialist also wanted exclusivity, but said he'd split sales profits with us 50-50. His offer definitely seemed more reasonable. We mulled both offers over, then decided we wanted to work with *both* Mark and Ralph because their skills complemented each other. Cardall was the more creative, but Sloan had a proven retail business. So we came up with a compromise deal offering for Redchurch to film and edit the shows for DVD and design T-shirts, but everything would be sold through Sloan's company A-Merchandise and everyone would get a fair cut.

Sloan had no problem with my compromise deal. The Specialist and I didn't always see eye to eye, but I always found him to be fair. But to my surprise, Ralph went ballistic. He immediately quit the FWA and sent me an angry email, withdrawing his permission for me to use any of the wrestler entrance themes he'd created. Cardall threatened that if we played any of his music at live shows in future, he'd demand considerable licensing fees and take legal action if necessary.

I was completely taken aback. Up until then, Ralph and I had always got on like a house on fire. But we have never spoken since that day. Falling out with Ralph is one of my biggest regrets in wrestling and I have no idea why he over-reacted in that way. Cardall ended up defecting to Bagga's LDN, leaving Sloan to take sole charge of FWA production and merchandising.

But Cardall's hissy-fit left us with a serious problem just days before our return to Broxbourne on February 5 2006. The laid-back Mark Kay wasn't bothered by Ralph's ultimatum at all, he just went online and bought rights to a load of generic rock music to use for wrestler entrances. My hard-headed best mate didn't want to be held over a barrel by anyone. But I knew just how important Ralph's distinctive theme tunes had been in setting the mood at a live show. The new music was awful, it didn't fit any of our characters, and the FWA fans and wrestlers hated it. It wrecked the crowd atmosphere at New Frontiers and contributed to further damaging dressing room morale.

New Frontiers was to be Alex Shane's wrestling swansong, so he had to drop the FWA Title. I wanted a new face to replace him, someone new who would symbolise the fresh start. So I plumped for Hade Vansen as the man to take Alex's crown.

I believed The South City Thriller had the presence, the poise and the promo skills for the job. Hade's ability to have entertaining matches had steadily improved over the past 12 months too. I also decided to turn Nikita heel and put her at Hade's side. They were both easy on the eye, and they knew it, so were bound to get heat as the FWA's Glamour Couple, the King and Queen of British Wrestling. It turned out to be a good move. Hade and Kat had perfect chemistry as a dastardly duo, and their catwalk good looks would attract interest in the FWA from glossy lads' magazines such as Maxim.

On paper, New Frontiers should have been a blow away show. I booked four singles matches, Doug Williams v Jody Fleisch, Jonny Storm v James Tighe, Joe Legend v Aviv Maayan and Hade v 'The Pukka One' Darren Burridge, all of which looked like sure-fire great bouts on paper. The winners would advance to a five-way title match against Shane. But then the usually reliable Doug, Jody, Jonny, James and Aviv all had an off-night at the same time. Only the visionary Burridge (whose new cheeky chappie Essex gimmick got over a good five years before The Only Way Is Essex exploded into popular culture), Joe and Hade rose to the occasion. A decidedly average show ended with Vansen pinning Legend, after interference from Nikita, to win the FWA Title.

Vansen was a fighting champion and made his first defence against Fleisch in late February 2006 at a Futureshock Wrestling card in Stockport in another rip-roaring contest. Then he pinned Damon Leigh on March 4 at Goldrush, which we'd switched to Morecambe.

That night, as crowds queued down the seafront waiting for The Dome to open, the cocky champion and his gorgeous femme fatale arrived in style—in a stretch limousine donated by one of our sponsors. The boos rained down as the King and Queen got out of the limo right in front of what Hade called the "talking turds of Morecambe". Then Vansen, oozing superstar arrogance, proclaimed himself "The Midnight Sinner, The Lady Killer, the Super, Sexy, South City Thriller!" I was already really impressed with the charisma and confidence of the new Vansen-Nikita combination.

Goldrush 2006 sold out. This was a massive achievement, especially considering 1PW was running a major show in Doncaster that night with TNA stars Rhino, Abyss, AJ Styles and Christian on the bill.

Morecambe may have been smoking hot in 2006, but I was more desperate to solve the Broxbourne conundrum. By the time we returned down south for Crunch Weekend, we'd brought our old buddy Dann Read onto the management team. Dann had already replaced Tony Giles and Nick London as FWA commentator, which was ironic, recalling that he'd hired me for that very job on my first ever show in Ipswich four years earlier. He would now also reprise his role as a local promoter, as April 1 2006 saw FWA's return to Sudbury after an absence of three years. The event, headlined by Vansen and Tighe v Storm and Fleisch, is perhaps best remembered for the debut of a young curly-haired prodigy named Ben Satterley, better known as 'The Man Gravity Forgot', Pac.

It was Mark Sloan, with his keen eye for wrestling talent, who first drew my attention to this new sensation from Newcastle. On Sloan's recommendation, I booked the untested newcomer for the Crunch Weekend, without ever having seen him wrestle. It would turn out to be a far more productive gamble than Sven-Goran Eriksson's on Theo Walcott in the World Cup that year. Pac was a natural, who could do things in the ring I'd never seen anyone do before. The shooting star kneedrop from the top rope, the drop kick into a moonsault, the stupendous 630 rotating senton splash . . . this guy really could defy gravity!

Pac's performance in beating Stevie Lynn at Sudbury had everyone jumping out of their seats in amazement, so I made the snap decision to allow him to win the FWA Flyweight Title the very next night in Broxbourne. Pac duly beat Lynn and champion Ross Jordan to lift his first major championship in a three-way where his kamikaze moves had Alex Shane showering the lad with praise backstage like I've never seen him rave about anyone before or since! Little wonder that Pac went on to phenomenal success in Japan's Dragon Gate promotion, signed for the WWE in 2012 and is now rated as one of the top wrestlers anywhere in the world.

As Pac celebrated with the Flyweight belt in front of the ecstatic fans, I was starting to think I'd finally cracked the Broxbourne enigma. The show was progressing nicely and aside from Pac's triumph, had already seen a super-heated angle where the unstoppable Vansen and Nikita beat up Jonny Storm and a writer from Maxim magazine, an entertaining little scrap between Burridge and Tighe, and a crowd-pleasing tag team duel between Stixx and Stone and The New Breed. We'd also advertised more heavily in the local area than ever before, meaning the show drew the biggest crowd to Hertfordshire since Goldrush '04 . . . this with an all-British line-up.

What I didn't realise from my position backstage, is that our promotional campaign had drawn in a very different type of Broxbourne audience to the norm, with far less smart marks and considerably more families. It was more like a Morecambe crowd. And in front of this audience of mums, dads and young kids, I'd only gone and booked a No Holds Barred match between the two most X-Rated performers in British Wrestling.

Isaac Harrop was an interesting character. In real-life, he was a deeply religious man. But once inside the ring, he was an absolute raving lunatic.

The first time I met Iceman was at that WZW show in Carlisle in 2004. I was sitting down with some of the wrestlers in the venue, talking about the afternoon's show. I remarked that I'd been unimpressed with two skinny young kids from the North East, who'd been doing a blatant rip-off of Trent Acid and Johnny Kashmere's gimmick The Backseat Boyz. "They need to carve their own identity instead of copying someone else," I mused. "I wonder who came up with *that* idea?" Iceman stared a hole right through me. "Actually, it was me." Talk about putting your foot right in it.

But I really liked Isaac when I got to know him and we worked well together. The 'Insane Icon' didn't have the ideal look for a wrestler, in fact his fleshy torso and moustache led FWA fans to chant "DAVID BRENT!" at him, thinking he resembled Ricky Gervais' character from The Office. But he did a lot with his limitations and although primarily known for his crazy, violent stunts, was a decent wrestler too when he wanted to be, going on to have some big matches with the likes of Low Ki and Homicide in 1PW.

He held nothing back in the ring though. *Nothing*. I remember one show at Blackpool where he smashed Stevie Lynn with a full-force somersault flip into the corner, and Stevie cracked the back of his head wide open on an exposed metal turnbuckle. Lynn had to be rushed to hospital, blood gushing from a gaping hole in the back of his head. It was a scary moment.

On the night of Crunch 2006, Iceman and Paul Travell went *much* too far. But I take full responsibility. Beforehand, I naively gave Isaac permission to use scissors as a weapon. But I didn't realise exactly what my protégé was going to do with them.

Soon after their grudge match began, The Insane Icon dug the sharp implement into The Righteous One's forehead, sending blood geysering from a grisly wound as Travell yelped in pain. This was no wrestling illusion, this was real as real could be. The crowd—who had loved the show up until that point—were shocked into silence. One father and his little girl actually got up and walked out in disgust.

As the ultimate four-eyed, stringbean, card-carrying coward manager, I'd hitherto managed to skilfully avoid taking any major bumps during my wrestling career. But at Crunch '06, I felt I needed to earn the wrestlers' respect as the new man in charge and wanted to lead by example. So in the closing moments of the match, I allowed Travell to body slam me on a pile of sharp drawing pins and then he jumped off the top rope, crash-landing hard on my stomach with his flying Bloodshot Splash. Paul handled me like a true pro and I didn't feel a thing. I also had my trusty "Harry Potter" coat to thank for protecting my back from the pins!

Storyline-wise, it was a long-time coming. After 18 months, The Righteous One had at last got his hands on the perpetual thorn in his side and I'd expected the sight of The Truth finally getting his come-uppance to raise the roof in Broxbourne. Instead, the crowd barely mustered a cheer. The sickening scissors incident had completely sucked the wind out of their sails.

The match ended after Iceman powerbombed Travell with gusto back-first onto the barbed wire wrapped around Mr Pointy. Ouch! Somehow, the indestructible Hardcore Icon dragged himself upright and retaliated by delivering a huracanrana on my hired henchman, straight through a ringside table. With both men glassy-eyed and rubber-legged from the inhuman punishment they'd endured, referee Steve Lynskey then waved the match off, calling for a draw as neither man was in a fit state to continue.

This highly unsatisfactory conclusion deflated the fans even further. Iceman-Travell could have been an all-time classic FWA confrontation, a match talked about for years on a par with The Showswearers-Family feud for intensity, creativity and sheer brutality. But it was the wrong place, at the wrong time, in front of the wrong audience, and with an inconclusive ending. My mistake.

At this point, Paul Travell was winding down his wrestling career. His masochistic style was only ever going to give him a short shelf-life in the business before his body gave up on him, and I think he did the right thing for his long-term health by quitting in 2007 while still only 27. My old rival is now retired from wrestling and lives at his home on the south coast with his partner and their children. But he admits that pulling away from the addiction of the ring was one of the hardest things he's ever done.

"When the FWA ended, I ended too," said Paul.

"I loved wrestling, I had the time of my life doing it, I met so many unique and interesting people. When I left, I mourned it. It absolutely devastated me.

181

Holy Grail

"But wrestling is so full of egos and a lack of governing, of fairness and consistency around the world. When the FWA ended, I didn't want to search amongst the scumbags to find somewhere new I could call home.

"I hardly ever speak to anyone from my wrestling days now. The only one I speak to regularly is Jenna (Buttercup) . . . she works as a nurse. I used to be so close to Simmonz, and I haven't spoken to him in such a long time.

"I haven't spoken to Alex properly in about five years. Our friendship used to be so solid. But it damaged me being around him all the time.

"He was such a force of nature. He could get people to do stuff. He'd call me up and say 'Paul, come to London!' for no reason, really, and I'd be like: 'I haven't got the money' but he'd talk me into it. He held too much power over me. He wasn't consciously manipulating me, it's just the way he was.

"Alex is such an intense guy. He would always go into something full on and jump into the deep end without checking first, whether it was with a girlfriend or with wrestling. He came up with so many ideas and launched into them so strongly. But love him or hate him, Alex is a special guy. I've still got all the time in the world for him.

"Wrestling itself took an awful lot out of me. When I wrestled, I had no money. I had no means of supporting myself. If I was still wrestling, I'd probably be working in a factory somewhere earning minimum wage and then spending it all on weekends just to keep my wreck of a car on the road so I could get to shows.

"It took me five years after quitting wrestling to get myself a proper career. Now I've finally got one. I work as an ambulance driver."

Back at Crunch 2006, the atmosphere picked up again at the end of the show when Robbie Brookside arrived out of nowhere, having come straight from wrestling on an All-Star event in Croydon, to cause Jonny Storm to lose to Hade, screwing him out of his chance to become FWA Champion. The fans were outraged. Jonny was the backbone of the FWA; he'd been there since the very first show in 1999. But Storm had never won the title. The fans were right behind his quest but The Wildcat had just shattered his dreams. As the beaten Jonny looked on in fury, Brookside seized the microphone and gave his reasons.

Robbie said the idea of the 5 ft 7in, 12 stone 'Wonderkid' as a *heavyweight* champion made him sick. The scathing Scouser then reprised his rant of four years earlier in Ipswich, cutting loose with a tirade about FWA's smart mark followers (which was ironic, as hardly any of our regulars were in attendance) and extolled the virtues of his home company All-Star, stating the FWA was "For Wannabe Americans". Storm responded with an angry pro-FWA rallying cry, and Crunch 2006 concluded with the Broxbourne crowd chanting "FWA! FWA!" like the old days, as my new top-line feud was born.

Ever since I'd first spotted the real-life tensions between Robbie and Jonny four years earlier in Ipswich, I knew they could have a successful and long-running in-ring rivalry. The two men were polar opposites in style, look and philosophy. Brookside preached that UK wrestlers should be proud of their roots and wrestle a traditional British style. But the 10-years younger Storm was from the new generation, who'd grown up watching WWE and wrestled like an American.

In my opinion, Jonny Storm is the most talented all-round British wrestler and performer of the past decade. The Wonderkid can do it all in the ring and what sets him apart is his burning passion for his art. This deep love for the business is why Jonny eventually surpassed his pal Jody Fleisch. The chilled-out Phoenix always gave the impression he could take or leave wrestling. After his comeback in 2004, I felt Jody lost his spark. Fleisch's career would never again reach those dizzy heights of the King of England tournament and that iconic York Hall balcony moonsault.

"The thing is, Jody is still as talented as the day he first started . . . he can still do it, but he doesn't have the motivation," said Jonny.

"He used to do tours of Japan with Michinoku Pro Wrestling at his peak and had he carried on, he could have been huge over there. He still wrestles, but not very often. Now he works as a personal trainer."

Jonny, though, lives and breathes wrestling. In fact Storm cared so deeply about his performances, I got the impression at first that he wasn't keen on working a programme with Robbie because their styles were so different. Jonny thrived on wrestling at a fast pace with lots of acrobatics, while Brookside stuck firmly to a ground-based submission-style game. But I wasn't going to back down on this one. I knew a properly-booked Brookside-Storm feud over the FWA Title would be one for the ages.

"I actually enjoyed that feud," said Jonny.

"Robbie and I *were* opposites, but there was never anything malicious or nasty between us backstage. I'd known him a long time, because we both worked for many, many years for Brian Dixon and Scott Conway as well as the FWA.

"When he first met me, maybe he didn't like me very much because I was new school and that went against the values he'd been taught. But when we did that feud, all we did was put our real life feelings into it. And it worked. I even remember him pulling a few new school moves of his own on me. Yeah, he definitely used a chair on me once!"

"I have a lot of respect for the FWA," Brookside told me during our interview in 2003.

"I like some of the things that they do. I think there's always going to be room for Jody, Jonny and Doug and the style that they do . . . and also Alex. But when I look at the younger lads some of the matches leave a lot to be desired. I know they are only youngsters but over a year now it's gradually got worse. It seems that the crowd is dictating what is going on in the ring and that shouldn't be the case.

"I try to tell them. I'm proud that I go all over the world and wrestle like an Englishman. With the English lads it should be part of your training and grounding, especially if you have any ambition to wrestle away. You should learn about where you've come from. Has any English guy ever gone into WWE or WCW or ECW and done moonsaults, swan dives and all this? Regal is the most successful and he has wrestled like an Englishman. You've got to offer them something they don't already have.

"I'm happy that Doug Williams is starting to get it together with regards to that now. He's got tremendous raw talent but he still needs to wrap himself up in his English culture of wrestling. And I'm sure when he does, and I'm sure he will because he's an intelligent lad, he's not a div, I think doors will start to open for him.

"I always have a go at Jonny Storm because he has good potential and I try to help him . . . and Jody as well but I seem to have come across Jonny a lot more. I've told him for a long time now to slow down in the ring. And I will say this, Jonny is a lot smaller than I am and you've got to utilise what you know best. But if you blink you're going to miss about two moves and what's the point in doing something if the people are going to miss it? Again, it's pleasing the internet crowd and not the general public. You want to please the people who are actually buying the tickets. So I've told him to take his time and make the moves count. It's like a cook putting two dozen eggs in when you only need four.

"I remember before British Uprising 1, Jonny was getting all hyped up because he was working with . . . . one of those young lads who flies around a lot, AJ Styles, and Jonny was really up for it. So I tried to tell him again, but then whatshisname was there . . . Jerry Lynn. I remember Jerry from WCW and I've worked with him a few times. He's a nice guy but because he's worked for ECW everyone drops their trousers to him and what-not.

"After I'd said the same thing 18 times to Jonny, Jerry Lynn pulled him over and said: 'You're doing far too much.' It was like a scene from Oliver. Jonny had his arms behind his back intently listening. And I said to Jerry: 'You're wasting your time, mind you he might listen to you because you've worked for ECW.' That's the thing. A lot of the new lads are fans of ECW and it's just horrible, it shows."

Jonny did eventually listen. He toned his whirlwind style down a notch, focussed more on the showmanship side of wrestling and allowed his natural likeability to shine through. By 2006, he was the top babyface on the UK scene, the perfect combination of skilled wrestler, acrobat and entertainer.

After the Brookside-Storm confrontation ensured a memorable ending to Crunch 2006, Mark Kay and I were driving back home the following day on a real high. The show had turned a profit, and the online reviews were the best for a Broxbourne event for 18 months. Our methods seemed to be working.

But then I received a phone call from the extremely irate Civic Hall manager. He'd received several complaints from parents about the graphic content of the Iceman-Travell match. He was furious there had been no warning about the potential for blood, guts, gore and bad language. I felt that familiar knot of stress in my stomach. I realised I'd made a serious error of judgement. I apologised profusely and promised it would never happen again.

And it didn't, because that was the last time I ever ran a show at Broxbourne.

Soon afterwards, the local council increased the already extortionate Civic Hall hire charges to well over £1,000, three times as much as The Dome. Mark Kay told me it simply wasn't worth the price to keep financing shows there. So I bid a reluctant goodbye to Broxbourne, which was a shame. I really felt we were on the verge of turning things around in the FWA's southern spiritual home.

We resolved to find a new Broxbourne or Morecambe somewhere else, and sought out new venues and local promoters in other parts of the UK. Stevie Knight came back on board to run shows in Cleethorpes. A Worcester-based wrestler called Richard Price offered to organise an entire tour of the Midlands for us. Richard talked a great game and owned a ring which he offered to hire us cheaply. I was also struck by how much he looked like Tazz, the TNA commentator and former WWE/ECW star.

We accepted Richard's help because we really liked him. To be honest, I can actually count on one hand the number of people I *dislike* in the British Wrestling business.

After Jon Farrer left the scene, he wrote a blog where he slated UK wrestling as being "full of paranoid losers and t__ts, and that's the good ones". Thankfully, I've been lucky enough not to come across many of the lowlifes.

I must have met hundreds of people at wrestling shows over the years. Many of them I just shake hands with and exchange first-name greetings. Real friends are few and far between. But most people I've found to be easy to get along with. It's partly because we all have a shared passion that unites us as a brother and sisterhood. It's also because I have so much respect for wrestling people. Professional wrestlers deserve far more credit than they get for participating in such a multi-skilled art form which is both physically and mentally demanding.

I did once meet a wrestling person who made it absolutely impossible for me to like him, though.

Ryan Parkinson.

When I first came across Parkinson in 2007, he was a teenager with almost zero experience of the wrestling business. He had recently quit the 1PW training school because its head trainer, my old pal Keith Myatt, had quite correctly told him he wasn't ready to wrestle on shows. But Parkinson wanted so desperately to be part of the scene, to rub shoulders with his heroes and look like a big-shot to his friends, that he wouldn't accept the advice of one of British Wrestling's most respected veterans. So he decided to do things his own way. The *wrong* way.

To cut a long and sorry story short, the green-as-grass trainee decided to promote his own wrestling show in Morecambe. Ryan claimed that the star attractions, the big marquee names for his mega-event, would be Bret Hart, Mick Foley, 'Nature Boy' Ric Flair, Kurt Angle and Rob Van Dam. This line up of legends was obviously pure fantasy, yet Parkinson sold tickets for his show with a straight face, adamant these global greats would all be coming to work for him at the North Lancashire seaside. He also billed *himself* on the poster alongside the Hall of Famers, under his wrestling name of AJ Spitfire . . . most definitely *not* to be confused with AJ Styles.

Fearing for the reputation of wrestling in Morecambe and worried that fans were being ripped off due to Parkinson's lies, Mark Kay and I ended up reporting him to Trading Standards. This triggered a nasty turf war lasting most of the summer of 2009. Parkinson evaded punishment from the authorities and continued the dirty tricks campaign in the run-up to his event. He went around Morecambe taking our event posters down (we had a show at The Dome about a month before his), threatened us with legal action and even roped in his *mother* to badmouth me on Facebook.

Parkinson eventually revised his advertised line-up; changing it to The Sandman, Nunzio, Ulf Herman, Ring of Honor's masked star Delirious and former WWE grapplers Eugene, Kid Kash, Tyson Tomko and Rene Dupree. Then his show went ahead at The Carleton club in Morecambe on August 1 2009. It was a colossal disaster. Of the advertised names, only Sandman and Nunzio showed up. Fans complained. The show didn't draw numbers anywhere close to covering its costs. Parkinson lost a ton of money and eventually left town with his tail between his legs.

I'm very grateful to Alex Shane, Dann Read, Damon Leigh, Stixx, Spud and others, who backed me 100% during the whole Ryan Parkinson episode. Although some other established British wrestlers actually agreed to wrestle on Parkinson's show, lured by the high wages he promised them, these guys understood the bigger picture.

"I'm very selective about who I work for," explained Spud in 2012.

"I won't wrestle for promoters who only draw 10 people. If I do, then afterwards my picture is on a poster for a good promoter, someone might think: 'Oh, he was on that s__t show' and they won't go to the *good* show. That's one of the reasons why I backed Greg when that kid was running his show in Morecambe.

"A lot of wrestlers just take as many bookings as they can for the money, and I understand that. But it doesn't do much for your reputation or your ability to draw crowds."

I'm sad to report there are quite a few Parkinsons on the British Wrestling scene, know-nothing kids with more cash than sense, who'll go out and buy a ring, hire a hall, and try to put on a wrestling event just so they can be like their heroes on TV. These people profess to love the wrestling business. Yet their actions are damaging to it.

Parkinson then changed his wrestling name to Drazic Jericho (most definitely not to be confused with *Chris* Jericho . . . can't this kid find his own identity?) and went on to run a number of less ambitious events in Cumbria under the banner of G-Ring Promotions. For a while, reports from his shows weren't too bad and I hoped he'd learned his lesson. But now I'm told he's burned his bridges there too.

AJ Jericho, or whatever he's calling himself this week, was useful for one thing though. He inspired me to create a wrestling character who turned out to be one of my most successful.

Around that time, I'd met a young wrestler from London called Thomas Chamberlain, after he tagged along to a Morecambe Dome show with his friend Ross 'RJ Singh' Jones. A fan pointed out that Tom looked like a younger version of me. This gave me an idea . . . to pretend that Tom and I really were related. So Tom Chamberlain became my real-life cousin, Tom *Lambert*.

Cousin Tom's gimmick was that of a clueless dreamer with ideas above his station, a wannabe pro wrestler who was desperate for the limelight and would do absolutely anything to achieve his dream. Sound familiar?

The hapless character, brilliantly played for laughs and sympathy by Chamberlain, caught on to the point that Tom Lambert became one of the biggest wrestling heroes in Morecambe. The people *loved* him. Tom was so effective in the role, that to this day, many wrestling fans still believe that he really *is* my cousin. It's Real in Morecambe, remember?

My favourite Tom Lambert moment happened at one particular Morecambe show when my mum turned up to watch. Tom walked right up to her, bold as brass, and asked: "How are you Auntie Beryl?" I'll never forget the look of sheer bemusement on Mum's face!

Incidentally, the fan who initially pointed out the resemblance between Tom and me was Matt Whitfield, who British Wrestling followers will today know better as Stallion. The brash and pompous Geordie was a front row regular at our Morecambe shows for years, until I realised his outrageous personality and colourful attire (including his trademark bandana) made him a natural wrestling performer and I plucked him from the crowd to join our roster. I'm delighted to report that Stallion has gone on to become a terrific heel manager and commentator, one of the very best around. Not as good as me, mind, but he's right up there!

Around the time we met Richard Price in 2006, we also entered talks with another would-be promoter called Alan Ravenhill. He wanted to run FWA shows in Wales, but I didn't warm to Ravenhill at all, especially when he boasted on the UKFF that he was in talks with the FWA before we'd even agreed a deal. So we quickly knocked the plans on the head.

To Ravenhill's credit, he has gone on to become the promoter of his own company Welsh Wrestling and is relatively successful at it, most notably in 2012 when he booked celebrity politician Lembit Opik in an angle and gained widespread media attention. Good for him. No hard feelings eh, Alan?

At around the same time, I also had my first contact with Nick Aldis. I'd been having some trouble finding a ring provider for a show in Morecambe. Time was running out before the show so I phoned Brian Dixon for help. Brian kindly referred me to Nick, an up-and-coming grappler who at the time was running his own promotion called Summit Wrestling in Norfolk.

Nick and I had a couple of telephone conversations, and I found him to be well-spoken and courteous. What impressed me most was he was willing to be on standby at short notice to drive the 220 miles to Morecambe to bring his ring and wrestle on my show. In the end, I found a cheaper ring supplier closer to home but made sure to thank Aldis for his kind offer.

Today, Nick Aldis is one of the most successful British wrestlers of the modern era. After taking part in the remake of UK Gladiators on Sky One, the handsome and muscular youngster was snapped up by TNA in 2009 and went on to become one of their most established overseas stars under the name of Magnus.

Sadly I never got the chance to bring Nick to Morecambe before he went off to America . . . although we nearly made it happen just before he signed for TNA. Fresh off his Gladiators notoriety, I'd booked him for the 2009 season of Dome dates but just before I was about to start my advertising campaign, Nick called me to let me know TNA were interested in him. He hadn't yet signed the contract, yet went out of his way to keep me informed there was a possibility he wouldn't be available. I thought this was very professional of him.

Nick is going great guns out in the States where he has twice won the TNA Tag Team Titles, first with Doug Williams and then with Samoa Joe, and also held New Japan's IWGP Tag Titles with Doug. More recently he and Joe went to Japan and captured the Pro Wrestling NOAH tag belts too. Aldis is still only 26 but already has nine years' experience and is improving all the time. With his film star looks, height and speaking skills, I can see him moving on to WWE one day. It's great to see a young Brit doing so well.

In spring 2006, a friend of Dann Read's, the wrestler Paul Tyrrell who I'd watched as a fan in the crowd at the second Morecambe TWA show nearly four years earlier, also offered to put on an FWA event in Colchester. Tyrrell was the 'anti-Bagga', he didn't want to do things on the cheap, and volunteered to invest his own money to put on the kind of event FWA used to be famous for. We were happy to let him take the gamble.

So FWA NOAH Limits 2 at Colchester Hippodrome nightclub on April 30 2006 saw a brief return to the days when international stars lit up the FWA ring. Former WWE Cruiserweight Champion Billy Kidman, and NOAH's Mohammed Yone and Takeshi Morishima were brought in for the night. And Mark Sloan pulled off the biggest coup of all, managing to acquire the services of the almighty Bret 'The Hitman' Hart!

Results from NOAH Limits 2 were:

Darren Burridge pinned Stevie Knight, All-England Champion Leroy Kincaide beat Ricky Hype and Matt Vaughn in a handicap match, Leroy Kincaide beat James Tighe by countout, Max Voltage and Dan Head beat Mark Sloan and Ollie Burns, Charlie Rage defeated Andy Simmonz, Doug Williams and Hade Vansen overcame Mohammed Yone and Takeshi Morishima, and Jonny Storm beat Jody Fleisch and Billy Kidman in a three-way match to become number one contender to the FWA Title.

Tickets had sold slowly at first, but as soon as Bret Hart was announced for the show, they went like the clappers. By bell time, the Hippodrome was full to bursting. And it was great that Power Slam was interested in covering the FWA again thanks to our association with 'The Excellence of Execution'.

As for Mark Sloan, he was more than happy to remind us that he'd saved the show by getting us Hart. This was typical of Sloan. Mark Kay used to call him 'The One-Man Cavalry', because he loved to steam in at the last-minute to the rescue when situations looked lost. Credit where it's due though, Mark because yes . . . at NOAH Limits 2 you *did* indeed save the show!

Hart, who had been forced to retire due to post-concussion syndrome in 2000 and was still recovering from a subsequent mild stroke, was only capable of coming out to soak up the adoration and give a brief speech to the crowd that night in Colchester. I was lucky enough to meet and exchange a few words with Bret backstage at an autograph signing before the show.

But it remains a proud moment for me, and a monumental privilege to have the five-time WWE Champion and Hall of Famer visit the FWA. Dann Read, a huge 'Hitman' fan, was Master of Ceremonies that day and was bursting with pride as he shook Bret's hand.

"That was awesome," said Dann.

"But to be honest, that night I completely forgot that I was on a show with a man who I looked up to my entire childhood, my hero in *life*. I was in too much of a foul mood after the show because it wasn't as good as I'd hoped for.

"For me, putting on a great show for all the fans mattered more than 'marking out' (acting like a fan) in front of my hero. That's just the way I am. So working with Bret didn't actually sink in until afterwards."

Unlike Dann, the ultimate perfectionist, I *do* think NOAH Limits 2 was a great event. It was the first time I'd ever seen a wrestling show in a nightclub and I was impressed with how wrestling fitted snugly into the raucous club environment. And the main event between Storm, Fleisch and Kidman was simply masterful.

Mark Kay didn't have the best of nights though. His Fan Fest-phobia came back with a vengeance.

"The queue to meet Bret Hart before the show was immense . . . literally every single person who had come to that show wanted to meet Bret Hart.

"The show started, and they were still queuing. People were actually missing the show so they could see Bret. Then when Bret went out to do his bit in the ring, they were *still* queuing! They were thinking he was going to come back and sign more autographs afterwards . . . but he didn't.

"So you had this ridiculous situation where some people actually didn't get to meet Bret . . . and didn't get to see the show either because they'd spent all that time queuing to meet Bret.

"I'd said beforehand, there was not a hope in hell that we were going to get through all these people, and nobody listened. It was infuriating.

"It was a perfect example of how Fan Fests, although designed to give the customers a better experience on the day of a show, can actually leave them feeling dissatisfied, and why half the time you shouldn't even bother doing them.

"They should be outlawed."

Aside from the Bret signing debacle, I felt that overall things went swimmingly in Colchester. The FWA was right back on top that night and I think Dann was doing himself a dis-service by beating himself up. He had matured and learned from his own mistakes of the past and alongside Paul Tyrrell, did a good job promoting NOAH Limits 2.

I like Paul and really wanted to work with him again to establish Colchester as the FWA's new southern base. Unfortunately, Paul wasn't keen on running a follow-up show. Despite the large attendance, he hadn't covered his costs. Tyrrell learned, just as we had, that booking expensive foreign imports was a fast-track to losing money.

As for Dann, after NOAH Limits 2 he would continue to run the Colchester Hippodrome by himself for a short time, before starting up his own all-female wrestling promotion called ChickFight. Its name was later changed to Pro-Wrestling:EVE and today, Dann and his lovely wife Emily run regular women's wrestling shows in Sudbury using the best female grapplers from all over the world.

Aside from giving a platform to talented female warriors who previously were buried on shows dominated by males, the worldwide popularity of Pro-Wrestling:EVE DVDs has enabled Dann to finally make a steady income from the wrestling business. Not only that, but in 2012, Pro-Wrestling:EVE became the first grapple company in Europe to beam a show live on internet pay-per-view.

I couldn't be more pleased for my old mate that his hard work and passion for the business over a decade has been rewarded not only financially, but with his place in history as a true champion and pioneer of women's wrestling.

Incidentally, in an interesting NOAH Limits 2 footnote, the show also saw Leroy Kincaide squash a pair of youngsters called Matt Vaughn and Ricky Hype. The well-built Hype, real name Richard Martin, would later prove his business acumen and become a household name as winner of the 2012 series of hit BBC show The Apprentice.

Meanwhile back in spring 2006, Richard Price was really making a positive impression on us. Our dedicated new Midlands promoter drove all the way to Essex just to watch the show and also turned up at our next Morecambe event two weeks later. Mark Kay and I hung out with Rich afterwards and were impressed with his plans for a summer programme of FWA shows in Halesowen, Daventry, Stroud, Chippenham, Rugby and Worcester. Rich told us to sit back, relax and leave everything to him . . . he guaranteed these were proven successful venues, where the shows would sell out and make us money. Price definitely seemed to know his stuff, although we did remark, half-jokingly, that our new colleague was a little too good to be true.

FWA's return to Morecambe on May 13 2006 was another runaway success. Brookside had debuted at The Dome two months earlier, costing Stevie Knight certain victory in the Goldrush, then delivered another pro-All-Star, anti-FWA diatribe. This set the scene for an FWA versus All-Star inter-promotional card, which would determine if Brookside was right . . . and if Brian Dixon's group was indeed superior.

I'd had the idea for an FWA v All-Star show from Ricky Knight, who had devised a brilliant concept called the British Inter-Federation Cup. In May 2005, I'd travelled down to Bournemouth to manage an FWA squad against Paddy's team of WAW wrestlers on their home patch. There were five bouts that night—four singles, then a four-on-four elimination main event. Whoever won the most matches, would take the cup. FWA triumphed 3-2 and the WAW fans were enraged. The packed house and partisan atmosphere made me realise a similar promotion v promotion clash for the Inter-Fed trophy would work a treat in front of Morecambe's devoted FWA loyalists.

There was also definite real-life needle between the FWA and All-Star contingents that I felt would translate well into the live wrestling environment. Some of the ill-feeling still exists today, especially on the All-Star side. I've noticed some of Brian Dixon's regulars like to have a pop at Alex Shane and other 'part-timers' on social media.

"I like all the All-Star guys equally, but a lot of them are very bitter because they've been working full-time for years, but that doesn't mean s__t," said James Curtin.

"If you've been working full-time for years and never got a job with WWE, then you need to take a look at yourself . . . especially when they had Drew McDonald right next to them for years, it's not like they couldn't have asked him what they needed to do differently. A lot of them spend hours in the car travelling to shows, bored s__tless, and they end up going on the internet and bitching about the part-time wrestlers.

"I see every wrestler in the UK as like my brother or sister. As far as I'm concerned, they're bitching about their own family. And some of them bitch about wrestling itself. How can they say this is s__t? I would never have had the confidence I've got, never have met the women I have, but for wrestling.

"I've got a full-time job and I wrestle at weekends. I don't take wrestling any less seriously than them even though I work less, because I *love* wrestling. Wrestling is the only girlfriend I've ever wanted to be with. But I don't see it as a way to make money, like a lot of the full-time lads do. And I don't think you *can* make a proper full-time living out of it over here. What happens at Christmas? It's not a dependable wage unless you're with WWE or TNA."

I've had nothing but positive experiences when dealing with Brian Dixon though. I have untold respect for what Mr Dixon has accomplished as a promoter, and after my dealings with him in the run-up to May 13, my respect increased tenfold. Brian could not do enough to help and gave his unconditional backing to my show. The great man sent a strong team to Morecambe that night of his son-in-law Dean Allmark, Robbie Dynamite and Brookside as captain.

"It was great to have Dean Allmark there," said Curtin.

"Now he's a wonderful bloke, his positivity is second to none for someone who's been doing this for 10 years, and he absolutely loved working on a non-All-Star show because he didn't usually get the chance to do it when he was younger."

I then added Mark Belton to their squad. Although Five Star was not an All-Star regular, he was sympathetic to the ASW cause. In real-life, Mark and I often engaged in friendly debates about which promotion was better, and the single-minded Belton would always side with All-Star, even though he worked for FWA!

FWA v All-Star could not have gone any better. I was particularly delighted with how the Brookside-Storm story unfolded that night. Robbie is another of my favourite people in wrestling, mainly because of our shared passion for Merseyside football . . . even though he is a rival Evertonian. I particularly enjoyed our banter on May 13 2006, because the mighty Reds of Liverpool won the FA Cup that afternoon. I loved good-naturedly rubbing Robbie's nose in our win!

But who would leave The Dome that night with the British Inter-Federation Cup? I picked the strongest possible team for the FWA, selecting Spud, Jonny Storm, captain Stevie Knight and Hade Vansen, who according to storyline, had put his differences with the FWA's fan favourites aside for one night to wear our colours. After four matches, the scores were locked at 2-2 and the sold-out Dome was at fever pitch.

The deciding elimination match had come down to Storm and Vansen v Brookside and Belton. But then Hade showed his true feelings, laying out his own team-mate with the South City Driller DDT, before deliberately getting counted out. The Morecambe fans showered the unrepentant Vansen with boos and even Nikita was disgusted by the champion's treachery.

Sadly for us, this would mark a premature end of the all-too-brief Hade-Kat double act. The lovely Miss Waters had signed a WWE contract and was about to join Paul Burchill on the other side of the pond . . . another significant loss to the FWA. Nikita went on to compete for WWE as Katie Lea (where she was initially billed as Burchill's sister) and later moved on to TNA under the name of Winter.

Kat credits her success Stateside to her grounding in the Frontier Wrestling Alliance. "If it wasn't for them, I wouldn't be where I am today," she told me in a Power Slam interview in 2010.

As the decider built to a crescendo, Brookside then got himself intentionally disqualified by dropping Jonny on his head with a piledriver, an illegal move in the FWA. The Wildcat had sacrificed himself hoping Storm would be easy pickings for his sidekick Belton.

But Jonny fought back against all the odds. When Harlow's finest nailed Five Star with the match-ending Wonderwhirl for the one . . . two . . . . THREE, I swear the crowd's joyous eruption made The Dome shake to its foundations!

I was Master of Ceremonies that night, and within seconds of announcing FWA as the winners, I was engulfed in a rugby scrum of celebrating fans. The happy hordes mobbed me and then pushed past me on their way to the ring. Such was their delight at seeing the FWA beat the hated All-Star invaders, nothing was going to stop our supporters from personally congratulating the hero of the hour. Soon The Wonderkid was submerged under a human pile of back-slaps and hugs, then found himself lifted shoulder high as he paraded the cup around the ring.

For my beloved hometown fans, wrestling is as real as real can be; they truly believed what they had just seen. It was a perfect snapshot of why Morecambe, and particularly the Morecambe Dome, was such a special place for wrestling.

In 2009, Stevie Knight explained the magic of Morecambe.

"The crowd at Morecambe is always fantastic. I do enjoy doing Morecambe. It's a good atmosphere.

"I think the town is a doss-hole though. The first night the FWA wrestlers went out in Morecambe we got into about 18 fights. We went to a nightclub called Crystal T's and we were only in there for half-an-hour before it all kicked off. There was me and Doug and Colt Cabana. Colt had only just arrived in the UK, and he told these guys in the club: 'Yeah, we're all wrestlers!' And I thought, oh no, don't say that.

"Steve Corino was there too. I remember he wasn't very impressed with his hotel accommodation in Morecambe, with the blood on the wall . . .

"But I think Morecambe is the best crowd. Even when the All-Star guys were there—and they do 1,000-seater places for Dixon—I think they really enjoyed themselves as well."

"The magic of Morecambe was a combination of Greg's writing, the talent and that crowd," said James Curtin in 2012.

"They were so engaged by the characters. It was like watching EastEnders for them. They cared so much about the wrestlers, whether they hated or loved them. I remember the Morecambe fans used to buy loads of Jonny Storm's merchandise; he was always earning good money.

"The wrestling was part of Morecambe. The Dome was just this big theatre, with a great stage, bright lights, big characters, Stevie Knight, The Morecambe Raffle . . . it was great. A special town."

The party atmosphere at the end of the FWA v All-Star show was certainly one of my all-time favourite memories as a wrestling promoter. And it was moments like this which erased all the arguments, problems and financial losses of the past 18 months, and made my entire involvement in professional wrestling seem entirely worthwhile.

Of course, in British Wrestling the exultant highs don't last forever. The FWA's promising comeback was about to come crashing down.

CHAPTER 16

ANNUS HORRIBILUS

Exactly a week after FWA v All-Star, I was in Asda car park having just done the shopping, when I had a telephone conversation with Hade Vansen.

"Hey pal, did you pick up the FWA Title belt last week?"

I thought Hade was pulling my leg at first. As champion, it was his responsibility to look after the belt.

"No of course I don't have it. You took it home with you last week, didn't you?" I replied.

"Er . . . no I didn't. I left it on your table at ringside during the main event. That's the last time I saw it."

My stomach immediately turned a somersault as I racked my brain to recall the sequence of events of seven days earlier. Then I remembered the celebrating mob of fans surrounding the ring at the end of the show.

Oh no.

I immediately phoned The Dome manager Simon Armstrong. Had the championship belt been handed in? Did you have it safe? Maybe someone took it backstage to the dressing room . . . was it there?

No, no and thrice no.

The FWA Title belt had been stolen, taken from the ringside table during the melee, and whisked away into the Morecambe night.

I called the police, but it was already seven days after the theft, and there was little they could do. We offered a reward. We even placed a photo of the belt in The Visitor, pleading for the culprit to return it. All to no avail. The original FWA Title was gone, never to return, and we had to fork out for a new one.

Our new guardian angel, Richard Price, arranged for an exact replica to be made at a reasonable cost. This made us respect and trust Richard all the more.

But this embarrassing and costly mishap made FWA a laughing stock. Fancy not being able to look after your own title belt? I was deeply ashamed and although upset with Hade for not taking care of the championship, more angry at myself for not assigning someone else to keep an eye on it. I felt totally gutted and stressed out.

I'd also had a phone call from Alex following the All-Star show which riled me a little. We'd presented Nikita with a bouquet of flowers in the ring after the main event, to thank her for her services and wish her well on her new adventure in the States. My heart was in the right place here, but Alex gave me a right ticking off, saying Kat had been embarrassed by the gesture—that I should have checked with him first and he could have warned me how much she hated flowers. I felt Alex over-reacted, but I was still beginning to feel that I couldn't do anything right.

Within a week, came another major headache. A flustered Richard Price called me to say the Halesowen show, the first of his Midlands tour, would have to be cancelled. Apparently the local council had decided they didn't want wrestling at their venue because it was too violent (I wondered if they'd consulted with the Broxbourne Civic Hall). Richard said he'd tried everything to change the council's mind, telling them that FWA was now family-friendly, but they were adamant. Although we'd begun promoting the event, only a handful of tickets had been sold. I reluctantly agreed to announce the Halesowen show had been called off due to matters beyond our control and issued refunds.

Within minutes of our website announcing the cancellation, I was phoned by Mark Sloan. I'd never heard him so irate. He laid into me for cancelling the show, demanding to know why I hadn't asked him to call the council and talk them round.

As a local journalist, I deal with councils every day of my working life. I know only too well that once they make a decision, they can't be dissuaded. But Sloan's cutting words made me feel clueless and irresponsible for daring to announce the cancellation. In fact, his dressing down made me feel about two-feet tall. He absolutely tore into me.

I put the phone down and immediately burst into tears.

It was the first and only time wrestling has ever made me cry for real. I couldn't understand why I'd let Mark get to me. But my sensitive nature got the better of me on that occasion, and the constant pressure was just making things worse.

I'd taken on too much. I was working in a full-time job, while trying to be a father and a husband to a disapproving wife, and simultaneously dealing with the impossible expectations and over-sized egos of FWA fans, wrestlers and staff, who all constantly shoved in their two penn'orth about how things should be done and harkened after a glory era of expensive events which simply wasn't feasible any more. And I was becoming sick of the constant hassle.

I kind of understand why the principled Sloan lashed out though. The Founding Father was just frustrated with the way things were going in the FWA at the time. He said as much in an interview with Fighting Spirit Magazine in 2007.

The reason Sloan gave for his irritation completely baffled me, though. In that interview, he said his lowest point was "sitting at home" while I was using wrestlers who weren't in his league (I'd love to know who he was referring to). Yet Mark actually wrestled on 10 out of the FWA's 14 cards in 2006, performing that year on more events than anyone else apart from his tag partner Ollie Burns. Sloan was usually at the shows anyway selling his merchandise, so it made sense to let him wrestle. He was rarely "sat on the sidelines" like he claims.

Anyhow, I pulled myself together, took a few weeks off, and then on June 29 we travelled east for an event at The Winter Gardens in Cleethorpes with renewed optimism. Stevie Knight always worked hard at advertising. So this event was *bound* to be a success.

The show drew a crowd of 70.

It was a schoolboy error to schedule a show for a hot Thursday night during the football World Cup. Stevie had been convinced the event would draw. But despite his best efforts, the curse of the Carnage Tour continued. And the fact that some of the wrestlers cracked jokes and laughed about the pitifully tiny turnout made me feel even more embarrassed and depressed.

I met Steven Gauntley that night for the first time. He'd come to watch the show. Nice guy, I liked him. But he must have gone away thinking that the FWA was no longer any kind of competition for his fast-rising 1PW, which had by then firmly taken our place as Europe's most talked-about wrestling company.

Sadly for Gauntley, mega-spending on overseas talent turned out to be an unsustainable business model for him too. 1PW shone brightly for a couple of years but then burned out, crippled by debts and amateurish behind-the-scenes organisation that made the FWA look like a North Korean military parade in comparison. After passing between several different owners, by 2011, 1PW was history.

After Cleethorpes, the FWA was deep in crisis too but thankfully my Morecambe fans never, ever let me down, and they turned up in their usual droves to our next hometown event on July 15 2006. This ended with Robbie Brookside capturing the FWA Title, and the brand new championship belt, in a three-way against Vansen and Storm.

This was also Hade's Morecambe swansong. The handsome son-of-a-gun would soon join the British exodus to WWE, signing up in summer 2007.

"I don't credit the FWA with getting me a shot with WWE, I credit Kat with getting me a try-out and then I credit *myself*," said the ever-modest Hade, reflecting on the experience.

"At the time there were talks going on about WWE setting up offices in the UK and they wanted to sign a bunch of British guys. Sheamus, Drew McIntyre and Wade Barrett were all at the same try-out as me. But I'm the only Brit who got signed the first time they saw me . . ."

Hade went to WWE's training ground in Florida and at first, had the time of his life in The Sunshine State.

"I was 26 and being British definitely helped with the ladies, if you know what I mean. I was out all the time . . . it was like being back at university!"

Then in 2008, Hollywood movie star turned WWE scriptwriter Freddie Prinze Jnr sat the former FWA and All-England Champion down at a Smackdown TV taping, and gave him some life-changing news.

"They were going to put me in a big storyline with The Undertaker.

"I was going to lead a gang of X-Men style mutants. Every week, I would send one of these guys after The Undertaker. After he had beaten them all, he would eventually face me at WrestleMania 25.

"It was f___ing incredible. Freddie was really excited about the idea, he'd cleared it with (Vince's daughter and head scriptwriter) Stephanie McMahon and she loved it."

On December 13 2008, Hade made his debut on Smackdown, cutting a shadowy, sinister and cerebral speech. It was supposedly the first of many to set up his mega-money feud with the legendary Dead Man, one of the biggest superstars in American Wrestling of the past 20 years.

As far as I was concerned, my old buddy performed extremely well for a debutant, showing all the verbal confidence and charisma I'd always known he possessed in abundance.

But then?

"Then they told me they were putting the storyline on hold.

"I went home for Christmas, and within a week I had been let go. They fired me."

Hade's is the most frustrating story, and a perfect example of the fickle and unforgiving nature of the wrestling business and especially its market leader, the global beast that is World Wrestling Entertainment. He left British Wrestling and seemed to have it made in American Wrestling. But in the end, American Wrestling chewed him up and spat him out.

Vansen was always a survivor though, with a 'que sera sera' attitude to life which served him well after this heartbreaking rejection.

"Nobody ever gave me a reason why I'd been released, but there is one story that keeps doing the rounds, and I don't know if this is true or not, and that is Vince McMahon saw me backstage and thought I was way too small to be hanging with The Undertaker.

"But I wasn't devastated. When Freddie first told me about The Undertaker feud, although half of me had fireworks going off inside, the other half thought: 'Hang on a minute, this is too good to be true, you're not at WrestleMania yet, boy!'

"So when they said they had nothing for me, I decided to shrug my shoulders, have a cup of tea, and move on."

Shawn Michaels ended up taking Hade's spot as Taker's 'Mania opponent, not a bad substitute all in all. Meanwhile The South City Thriller quit wrestling altogether and went to seek his fortune in sunny Los Angeles, the ideal home for his Hollywood looks. The real-life Hadrian Howard still lives in LA and has no intention of coming home, or returning to the squared circle, any time soon.

"I'd been wrestling for 10 years and kind of gone as far as I wanted to go.

"I didn't want to work on the American independent circuit and wait for WWE to come along, pat me on the head and give me another go. So I thought I would be my own boss.

"I've done some acting in commercials, small film roles and appeared on (US soap) Days of Our Lives, and I run a head-shot photography business as a sideline.

"I have my own flat in LA, I'm 20 minutes from the beach, the sun is always shining and you can't beat the women in California. I'm living the American Dream!"

Yes, life could certainly be worse for our Hade. Remember, getting out of the wrestling business can seriously . . . well, you know the rest.

But back in the *slightly* colder climate of Morecambe on July 15 2006, Robbie Brookside's FWA Title win was the perfect storyline development because the man who hated everything FWA stood for, now wore the company's championship. The Scouse interloper milked his victory on enemy turf for all he was worth, taking great delight in rubbing the outraged Dome fans' noses in his triumph.

The cackling Brookside even punched me, the hometown promoter, in the face afterwards, to rub salt further into Morecambe wounds. For reasons I've never quite understood, as Master of Ceremonies and authority figure for the FWA at Morecambe shows, I'd become quite a popular 'good guy'. My home town fans respected me and so they voiced their disgust at Robbie's awesome heel antics.

Morecambe had been great . . . but then again, Morecambe is *always* great. But then eight days later, our UK tour arrived at Rugby. That's when the FWA hit rock bottom.

We drew a crowd of 23.

I'll repeat that number, in case it didn't sink in the first time.

We drew a crowd of 23.

Last time FWA came to the Midlands was British Uprising 3 at Coventry Skydome, when 1,500 fans turned out. Now, 20 months later, not even two dozen people had paid to see the FWA.

What on earth had happened to Richard Price's promises of sold-out shows?

Mark and I were so busy that summer, running one event after another all over the country, while both simultaneously working 9 to 5 in our office jobs, with so little time to breathe, and had put so much faith in Richard, that we hadn't been monitoring him closely enough. He'd told us he'd handle the local advertising. He'd told us not to worry. He told us he'd make sure there were bums on seats. He'd been so confident and convincing. But what exactly *had* he been doing?

Price himself was bemused by the pathetic attendance. He swore blind he'd put in the donkey work to make people aware the show was happening. But Dann Read went out that afternoon, looked around Rugby town centre, and saw little evidence of any kind of effective promotional campaign. The FWA's hardcore fan base had already deserted us and without effective advertising in and around the town, casual wrestling fans in Rugby had no reason to come either.

Rich Price was indeed too good to be true.

Once again, the wrestlers just took the mick in the near-deserted Rugby Leisure Centre. Jonny Storm and Hade Vansen clowned around during the main event, barely bothering to put in any effort in front of the rows upon rows of empty seats. And I sat backstage, my head in my hands, utterly devastated, and massively out of pocket.

Then Mark Sloan told us he wanted reimbursing for his stolen FWA title belt. This deflated us all the more.

When news of the Rugby disaster leaked out, the UK Fan Forum had a field day. The smart marks revelled in how the mighty FWA had fallen.

Rugby cleaned us out completely. I cancelled the planned Daventry and Stroud events. Damage limitation, tickets weren't shifting, and not even Sloan could argue after the Rugby episode. We did go ahead with Chippenham in August and Worcester in November. Yes, we'd realised by then that Rich Price couldn't walk the walk as well as he talked the talk. But he was such a well-meaning fella and we really liked him, so we wanted to give him another chance. We advertised more heavily, and both drew slightly better, but well short of Richard's over-optimistic promises. Dann's second Sudbury show of the year on August 5 lost money too. My Suffolk pal had warned me that wrestling never drew well in his hometown in the summer holidays . . . but I hadn't listened.

I can't possibly describe just how soul-destroying it was for Mark Kay and I to climb into the Corsa every couple of weeks in mid-to-late 2006, and drive hundreds of miles to a show in a strange town, knowing even before we got there that advance ticket sales had been appalling, and we were inevitably going to lose hundreds of pounds.

I am one of the most positive people you'll ever meet. But that period of my life, of travelling up and down the country losing money at every turn, was the closest I've ever been to suffering from depression. It also made me respect Brian Dixon all the more for somehow managing to remain a full-time nationwide British Wrestling promoter, with all its pitfalls, for over 40 years.

When Windsor Castle burned down and Prince Charles and Princess Diana were divorced within a 12-month period, the Queen described that year as her 'annus horribilus'. That's how Mark and I felt about 2006. We couldn't wait for the year to end. It had begun with such hope, but things had gone horribly wrong.

Sure, I'd made mistakes. But I honestly feel that even if 2006 had been a 100% successful year, the FWA name would always have been an albatross around my neck. Whatever I did, fans and wrestlers were always going to compare my FWA to Alex Shane's FWA.

And you know what? There was always going to be no comparison. I couldn't do what Alex did. I didn't have the cult of personality, the ruthlessness or the sheer force of will to catapult FWA to the heights Alex Shane had achieved. Nor did I have the time. I was just an ordinary lad from Morecambe, who'd suddenly come to realise that running Britain's most famous wrestling company was a full-time job. But I already had one of those, and had no intention of giving it up for the unstable world of British Wrestling.

Mark and I were fed up. We'd lost so much money and we couldn't afford to lose any more. We'd tried our best, but the FWA was clearly finished. And we wanted to put it out of its misery.

CHAPTER 17

FINAL FRONTIERS

One of the main reasons why FWA attendances declined dramatically in 2005/6 was because since 2002, there had been a growth spurt in the number of British Wrestling promotions. A considerable amount of these new companies came about because of the influence of the FWA.

Some of these new promoters were originally fans who watched the Frontier shows, just as I did, and thought: "I can do that." Then they went out and did it. They included Dan Edler of IPW:UK, Sanjay Bagga as you know, and Dave Pownall (Dave Rayne) of FutureShock Wrestling in Stockport—an excellent promotion formed out of a training school set up by Alex in Manchester in 2004.

The irony is that by inspiring so many, the FWA actually accelerated its own decline. By 2007, British Wrestling's die-hard fans didn't need to travel to Broxbourne to watch 'new school' shows featuring the cream of the UK talent and maybe even a foreign import or two. They could see them in high school gyms, leisure centres and small halls, put on by any number of British promotions all over the country, and usually for a much cheaper ticket price than the FWA charged. This is a major reason why the army of smart marks deserted the FWA in 2005 and 2006.

But this rapid increase in new British Wrestling companies is also a significant part of the FWA's legacy. The FWA singlehandedly made British Wrestling *cool* and inspired so many people to want to be part of it.

"We are always 10 years behind America," explained James Curtin.

"Before the FWA there was Stevie Knight's generation, whose ring attire wasn't that good. Then along came the FWA and suddenly wrestlers are starting to get proper ring gear; we were catching up to the Yanks. Ten years later, everybody's got a good body and a tan, and a gimmick. Now unlike 10 years ago, everybody's saying you can't just promote shows using the UKFF . . . and suddenly all the good promoters in Britain are starting to draw crowds. Going to see a British Wrestling show is becoming a really entertaining night out."

The FWA also influenced an improvement in the standard of wrestling in Britain and kick-started a rise in the number of talented wrestlers on these shores. And the North Americans began to sit up and take notice.

"I only have good things to say about England and its wrestling scene," said Joe Legend.

"You can't have a bad match with Doug Williams. He's awesome. And then there's Alex. I hear a lot of negative things said about Alex. But for a supposed ego guy, when I wrestled him he always had the intention to put on the best match possible. I always liked wrestling Alex Shane.

"For All-Star, Mikey Whiplash is probably the best kept secret on the UK scene. He's phenomenal. And James Mason is the most respected. Everybody in All-Star wants to wrestle him and they rush to the booking sheet hoping they've been put against him."

It wasn't long before WWE and then TNA recognised there was a talent pool over here and began a major recruitment drive on UK shores. They gave our wrestlers more regular try-outs (auditions) which led to an increasing number of grapplers making the transition from our small-time circuit to the bright and well-paid lights of American Wrestling's weekly TV shows or monthly pay-per-views. The British scene became a productive training ground where homegrown wrestlers could learn and hone their craft before moving on to earn big money overseas.

"All the Brits take it more seriously because they can see there is something to aim for, because WWE, TNA and the big Japanese promotions come over here for regular tours," explained Doug Williams.

"There are guys like Spud, Marty Scurll, Zack Sabre Jnr, Noam Dar from Scotland is fantastic for his age . . . I love Johnny Moss too, and think he's fantastic. With the amount of talent around, I think I'd struggle to be a top guy in Britain today."

The Brits to sign for WWE or TNA in recent years have included Drew McIntyre, Stu 'Wade Barrett' Bennett, Doug Williams, Paul Burchill, Kat Waters, Nick 'Magnus' Aldis, Nigel 'Desmond Wolfe' McGuinness, Saraya-Jade Bevis, Hade Vansen, Joel 'Redman' Pettyfer, Martin Stone, Pac, Barrie 'Mason Ryan' Griffiths, Tom Latimer (Kenneth Cameron from WWE NXT), Steve Lewington, Stevie Starr . . . the list goes on and on. And then there's Ireland's Sheamus, who was also a regular on the British circuit before he joined Vince McMahon's global roadshow. Granted, some of the names mentioned have been more successful in America than others. But at least they're all getting a shot at the big-time.

"British Wrestling is starting to get really good . . . there aren't all that many really rotten wrestlers anymore," continued Curtin.

"We're in a small pond here and because of that, British wrestlers will get noticed quicker by WWE and TNA than wrestlers in a country as big as America."

The major wrestling companies of the world are snapping up UK talent left, right and centre, and I guarantee there will be more of our homegrown warriors making waves abroad in the near future.

"There are a lot of reasons why this has happened," said Dann Read.

"Some of it is down to the WWE agents and scouts, and who they like. For example, Martin Stone told me that Arn Anderson was a big supporter of his and he wouldn't have got the chance but for Arn shouting up for him.

"But I also think it's because now, the British Wrestling business is more open and accessible. The 'old guard' of promoters has all but gone.

"Look at what I had to go through just to get my Dawn of a New Era show off the ground in 2002. Had that been a couple of years later, I wouldn't have had any of the same problems. I was probably the last new young promoter to have to deal with that. After that, Scott Conway left the scene. A lot more promoters came in, which meant more shows, and more opportunities for British wrestlers. Before that, there were lots of wrestling shows going on around the country but run by the same nucleus of promoters, using many of the same wrestlers.

"Also, British wrestlers' physiques have improved. A lot more of our guys now have 'the look' the American companies want. This isn't necessarily down to steroids. Steroids *are* available over here, but remember WWE has a Wellness Policy so any British wrestler who gets in there has to adhere to that. It's more because over the past 20 years, British wrestlers have become more exposed to American Wrestling through TV and video tape trading and so now they know what they have to look like in order to get signed by WWE.

"Look at Rollerball Rocco and Tony St Clair, two of the best British wrestlers of the '80s and early '90s. They were huge stars in Europe and Japan. But they didn't have the physique for WWE. William Regal and Fit Finlay were the same. They are exceptionally talented, but would they have been signed had they not already been in America working for WCW?

"But today, you could put Wade Barrett in a line-up with all the other American WWE guys, and he wouldn't look out of place.

"The resurgence of British Wrestling over the past decade has also been tied in to the popularity of American Wrestling over here. For the most part, if American Wrestling is doing well on TV, then wrestling fans will go out and watch British Wrestling because it's the only live wrestling they can see."

And that's exactly what they are doing in their droves, according to Ricky Knight.

"Today, British Wrestling is the healthiest it's been for a long time," said the 27-year veteran.

"There are always peaks and troughs but we seem to be having a few good years. There are so many promoters putting on a good product."

While nobody has yet managed to recapture the kind of buzz that surrounded the FWA in its heyday, there are dozens of promotions around today which are a credit to the British Wrestling scene. To name just a few: GPW, FutureShock, Liverpool's Infinite Promotions and Preston City Wrestling on a thriving North West scene; New Generation Wrestling in Hull; Fight Club:Pro in Wolverhampton; PROGRESS Wrestling and Lucha Britannia in London; Revolution Pro Wrestling in Kent; WAW and its female wrestling off-shoot WAWW; the ever-present All-Star Wrestling; Pro Wrestling Elite, Insane Championship Wrestling, Source Wrestling, Fierce Females and Premier British Wrestling in the wrestling hotbed of Scotland; 4 Front Wrestling in Swindon; House of Pain Wrestling in Nottingham; Premier Promotions (which marks its 25th anniversary in 2012); Southside Wrestling Entertainment in the Midlands; Dann Read's Pro-Wrestling:EVE; 3CW in the North East; Welsh Wrestling; Chris Curtis is still running Stoke with his renamed British Wrestling Alliance . . . . the list goes on and on.

Today, there is good wrestling to be found in every nook and cranny of the nation. The era of fat men in trunks is indeed well and truly over, because now British Wrestling is an exciting spectacle for smart fans, casual fans, *all types* of fans to enjoy.

The quality of live shows is better than 10 years ago. The *quantity* of good shows is much higher than 10 years ago. There are definitely better wrestlers coming out of Britain than there were 10 years ago. It's certainly fair to say that British Wrestling has become relevant again over the past decade and we are moving in the right direction.

But if British wrestlers are ever to achieve the levels of national celebrity enjoyed by Big Daddy and Giant Haystacks, there is still a long, long way to go.

One of our biggest problems is that today, we don't have a British grappler who is as recognisable to the average man on the street as Daddy and Haystacks were in the '80s or even The British Bulldog was in the '90s. I don't believe there is a single British-based wrestler capable of drawing game-changing crowds on name value alone. Until this situation changes, until we have our very own Hogan, Rock or Steve Austin, even the decent houses will remain in the hundreds, and the thousands will continue to be a rarity.

But without TV, you can't create superstars, remember?

British wrestling personalities have made cameos on mainstream telly over the years, like the Knights on Channel 4. But episodic weekly televised British Wrestling on a channel watched by millions remains very much a pipe dream. And the biggest reason why this is the case, is because we simply don't have the cash.

"Unless somebody comes along with about £10million, who is willing to lose money, British Wrestling is never going to have what Vince McMahon and TNA have got," said Steve Lynskey.

"I'm about to go out to work for a promotion in the Middle East, and they're putting one million dollars into their *first show*. That's the kind of money I'm talking about. It's what the fans want. They don't want to watch wrestling in a working men's club, they want John Cena, Randy Orton, The Undertaker and all the high levels of production that comes with them.

"You look at who is in the British Wrestling business now. The Knight family has all the knowledge in the world. But they don't have the money to get the TV rights. Maybe if Len Davies had come along today instead of five years ago, with his money, he might have done it . . . who knows?

"One thing's for sure, someone needs to come along with a huge wallet that is *always* open."

So Mr or Mrs Multi-Millionaire Investor, if you're out there, *please* make yourself known. This is your chance to get behind the underdog and go down in history as the person who financed the revival of British Wrestling.

But until then . . . ?

"British Wrestling only does as well as WWE and TNA allow us to do," said Dann Read.

"We are still being carried on their shoulders and until we can stand on our own two feet, until British Wrestling becomes capable of carrying the entire industry if WWE or TNA wasn't there any more, you can't say there has been a proper revival of British Wrestling."

So perhaps the true story of British Wrestling's revival is that there hasn't really been a *true* revival after all. At least, not yet.

But let's go back to 2006, when the new wave of British Wrestling promotions was being led by a company called International Pro Wrestling:UK.

At that point, the FWA was yesterday's news as far as most dedicated British Wrestling fans were concerned . . . outside of Morecambe, at least. Instead, they were embracing IPW:UK as the south's new flagship promotion.

Dan Edler, the longtime FWA fan I mentioned earlier, set up IPW:UK in September 2004. By 2006, Britain's online wrestling community was raving about Edler's regular events in his hometown of Orpington in Kent, on the other side of London from Broxbourne. At first, I thought IPW would be a flash in the pan, but here we were, two years later, and they were still going strong. While FWA was viewed as a spluttering old-timer, IPW was the rising new kid on the block. And from all accounts, these upstarts were getting the formula right.

Backed by the help and finance of his supportive parents, young Edler ran monthly shows in the same locality, featuring a roster of cult overseas newcomers like Super Dragon and Stevie Douglas, hungry young Brits like Ashley Reed and Paul Robinson, and established FWA stars like Jonny Storm and Andy Simmonz. And a young student from Portsmouth, FWA referee (and Theo Walcott lookalike) Andy Quildan, was proving to be a surprise revelation as booker.

IPW appealed to both smart and casual fans, specialising in exactly the kind of athletic wrestling and edgy product the young adults loved, but with interesting plotlines to keep the kids and families coming back to find out what happened next.

I hadn't seen IPW in person, but they were making a big noise, and were very much on my radar.

Alex Shane took notice of IPW's growing reputation too. During Ring of Honor's debut UK tour of August 2006, Alex ran a sequel to Frontiers of Honor, only this time he included IPW:UK alongside the FWA and ROH.

This three-way inter-promotional show was called Frontiers of Honor 2, and took place on August 18 2006 on IPW turf, at a leisure centre in Swanley, Kent. The main event was a three-way between ROH champ Bryan Danielson, FWA main man Robbie Brookside and IPW title holder Martin Stone. I was too drained from my 'annus horribilus' to attend, so I sent Dann Read along as FWA's management representative. I was intrigued to find out if IPW was all it was cracked up to be.

My trusted lieutenant reported back. He said the show had been a colossal mess, a pale shadow of the original FOH. Only a couple of hundred fans turned up (seems I wasn't the only promoter struggling to draw that summer) despite the presence of the cream of ROH like Danielson, Austin Aries, British star Steven 'Nigel McGuinness' Haworth, Roderick Strong and The Briscoe Brothers. Dann also said the IPW wrestlers had performed disappointingly and weren't in the same league as the Americans or FWA's squad of Jody, Jonny, Doug, Tighe and Burridge.

The fact that Martin Stone was in the main event really surprised me. I'd never really understood why Edler and Quildan had picked Stone as IPW:UK's figurehead anyway. The burly Londoner was a rugged brawler, a tough guy with a chiselled jawline and barrel chest, and an intimidating presence for sure. But in FWA, Stone had been nothing more than a lackey as security guard for Alex Shane, then a tag team champion with Stixx. I'd never seen anything special in him, certainly not to warrant being a heavyweight singles champion.

I also had question marks about Martin's attitude. Stone had pulled out of a couple of FWA events that summer and I'd also heard that he'd been badmouthing the company behind my back, saying FWA was past its best and not worth bothering about.

I was forced to eventually strip Stixx and Stone of the FWA Tag Team Titles, although this wasn't solely due to Martin's disinterest, but mainly because the belts belonged to Barry

Charalambous and he wanted them back. Another example of FWA's tin-pot organisation . . . it seemed *everybody* owned a piece of the company.

Aside from the FOH2 flop, Alex's Ring of Honor tour was a resounding success. Mark Kay, Dann and I had attended the packed ROH event at Liverpool Olympia on August 12, headlined by a ferocious war of attrition between Danielson and the super-talented McGuinness, who is another really nice bloke. I was also glad to see Robbie Brookside successfully defend the FWA belt against American Chad Collyer. Shame our champ was the hometown favourite though, and couldn't use the microphone to spew his usual anti-internet venom. There were certainly a fair few 'keyboard warriors' there that night who deserved taking down a peg or two!

At the time, Alex Shane was going through a drastic personality change. No longer an active wrestler, he'd had plenty of time on his hands. He'd spent it wisely by starting to read widely, particularly on the subjects of philosophy, economics and political conspiracy theories. He'd become influenced by Nietzche and Gandhi, turned peace-loving vegetarian, and planned to become a life coach. The self-possessed wide-boy from a rough housing estate in London who'd known nothing but the wrestling business since the age of 13 had suddenly matured, and become a deep-thinking intellectual who cared about much more than just himself and the all-consuming quest for The Holy Grail.

The change in Alex was dramatic, bewildering, but very welcome. When I phoned him that month, the usually manic and distracted Showstealer was much more chilled out, at ease with life, and eager to share his beliefs and offer useful advice, not on wrestling booking, but on my present emotional turmoil. Alex was very supportive and understanding, and helped me put things in perspective. I almost couldn't believe it was the same guy!

"It's because I'd had a break from wrestling," Alex told me recently.

"I guess it was like coming home from war. I had time to think about it, the pressure I'd put my body and mind through, the enemies I'd made, the steroids and alcohol I'd consumed. I was a performer, a promoter, a trainer . . . I was doing the job of three people in the wrestling business and it burned me out.

"For years I'd been constantly either wrestling, on the road or out clubbing. Dino always used to instil in me that I was The Showstealer, I was the 'main event'. So if I was out until five in the morning then that was fine, that's what The Showstealer was supposed to do. But I'd still be in the ring later that night, putting myself under pressure to deliver a main event calibre performance.

"When I took a step away from wrestling, I reflected and realised that I'd been hard for other people to deal with. For someone with quite a questioning brain, I never questioned myself enough. I got a level of perspective, then regret and then frustration which led to motivation to do something about my character flaws. It led to a big change in me, an evolution of my personality which is still going on today. It's called growing up."

During our conversation in the summer of 2006, I told Alex I wanted to put out a press release announcing the FWA name was dead. I then intended to set up my own wrestling promotion under a different name, solely to run shows in my comfort zone of Morecambe. Alex listened (and Alex had rarely listened in the past . . . he usually just talked, and talked, and talked . . .) and said he understood my reasons. But he also suggested this would be a waste of an opportunity.

"Why don't we do one final farewell FWA show first? We could call it Final Frontiers. And what about, if we kill off FWA . . . but only after a big feud between FWA and IPW:UK where the losing company goes out of business?"

I loved the idea. Once again, we could turn reality into a wrestling storyline. If the FWA had to go down, why not go down in an inter-promotional feud? The phenomenal crowd reaction to FWA v All-Star in Morecambe was fresh in my memory. FWA v IPW:UK had the potential to be even bigger. And by beating the FWA and finishing us for good, Dan Edler's group could officially take our mantle as Europe's most talked-about wrestling promotion. It would be a poetic passing of the torch from the old guard to the young upstarts.

After listening to Dann Read's reports from FOH2, I knew exactly what Greg 'The Truth' Lambert would think of IPW:UK. He'd think they were over-rated. He'd think they weren't in the FWA's league. He'd think they'd ripped off the FWA, stolen all our fans and most of our wrestlers, and gorged on the fruits of our legacy. And such was his ego, he'd want revenge.

I immediately realised I had the perfect storyline motivation for declaring all-out war, and I was completely re-energised. FWA v IPW:UK was something I could really get my teeth into.

We'd scheduled one final Broxbourne date in case we wanted it but we decided it made perfect sense to hand the date over to IPW:UK. So instead of FWA Hotwired at Broxbourne Civic Hall, October 16 2006 would see *IPW:UK* Hotwired in the FWA's southern spiritual home, where the first shot would be fired in British Wrestling's brand new Civil War!

Results from IPW:UK Hotwired were:

Darren Burridge pinned Aviv Maayan, Jonny Storm beat Paul Robinson, Exodus defeated Lucian, El Generico pinned Pac, Jody Fleisch beat Jorge Castano, IPW:UK Champion Martin Stone downed Colt Cabana, and Dragon Phoenix and Spud defeated Dave Moralez and Jack Storm in a Tables, Ladders and Chairs Match.

IPW's Broxbourne debut was an exciting show, and following the thrills and spills of the main event TLC Match, the Broxbourne fans who used to chant "FWA! FWA!" were happily yelling "IP-DUB! IP-DUB!" at the top of their lungs. The turncoats!

Dan Edler came to the ring and thanked the Civic Hall for accepting IPW with open arms. "THANK YOU EDLER!" was the traitor fans' response, as if they'd forgotten FWA ever existed. At this, yours Truth-fully came striding out to interrupt, a look of incredulous disdain etched across my twisted face.

My promo that night was so nearly one of my best ever, but I screwed up a couple of lines towards the end so I don't remember it fondly. But for 95% of my speech, I was on top verbal form as I ripped into Edler for copying the FWA, stealing our venue then putting on a show with Jonny, Burridge, Pac, Aviv, Spud and others who made their name with us. The audience was gripped as I reminded everyone that Broxbourne was the house FWA built, informed Edler that this town wasn't big enough for the both of us, then challenged him to a Winner Takes All, Losing Company Must Fold Match where we would both handpick a wrestler to fight each other with everything at stake!

"All right Greg, you're on!" retorted Edler, who was excellent on the mic. "But you're absolutely right. We've taken all your wrestlers. There's no-one left to fight for the FWA. Who exactly have you got?"

I looked smug. Then the Civic Hall was pitched into darkness.

When the lights came back on, Alex Shane was standing in the ring behind the unsuspecting Edler, holding a metal folding chair! Broxbourne duly went berserk. And as the portly IPW promoter turned around, the fired-up Showstealer cracked him full in the skull with one of the hardest chair shots I have ever seen!

Maximum respect to Daniel Edler, a non-wrestler, for absorbing this heavy blow. I'm not sure I would have been quite so keen.

Martin Stone and Pac—still the FWA Flyweight Champion but firmly behind IPW—led the charge of the dressing room as IPW wrestlers stormed the ring, trying to get their hands on The Truth and The Showstealer. But we were gone, like thieves into the night, out of the Civic Hall front door. Our dirty work was done and our statement had been made, in the most physical way imaginable.

Afterwards, the internet was buzzing like it hadn't been since FWA's heyday. What was going to happen next? So many wrestlers worked for both companies—whose side would they pick? And which company was going under? My juices were really flowing now. It was just like the old days.

The feud also reignited Alex Shane's passion for wrestling, as he'd agreed to come back at Final Frontiers to defend FWA's honour against his old protégé Martin Stone, Edler's choice to fight for the very existence of IPW. But there were four months and several IPW shows between Hotwired and the original Final Frontiers date of February 3 2007, back at Broxbourne. We had to keep the feud heated up and maintain the fans' interest.

So Alex invaded Orpington Halls, gatecrashing IPW Extreme Measures six days after he'd battered Edler and delivered a vicious beating to Martin Stone on the night he lost the IPW Heavyweight Title to Andy Simmonz. Then on November 19 at IPW Brawl at the Hall, Shane was awarded 10 minutes of microphone time to explain his actions.

The master launched into an inspired, venomous, reality-based rant about how he was solely responsible for launching the careers of most of the IPW wrestlers (which was true), interspersed with spitting some of the vilest insults at the partisan Orpington crowd I personally have ever heard. The morally questionable world of wrestling is about the only place where a performer can get away with calling paying customers "losers", "geeks" and worst of all . . ."retards". But this wasn't Crunch '06. The punters weren't offended to the point they started walking out in disgust. Instead, they responded with the right kind of heat, by booing and insulting Alex right back, creating an atmosphere of tension and genuine emotion.

Shane pointed out that Martin Stone was just a wrestling trainee at British Uprising 1, who (like me) had attended as a fan, predominantly to support his idol, former FWA Champion Phil 'Flash' Barker. Afterwards, Alex gave him an opportunity to live his dreams by following in the 'Quadruple Hard' Flash Man's footsteps.

Shane went on: "And there was a time when Andy Simmonz couldn't even look me in the eye and shake my hand without pissing his pants until I made him into a butler, and now he's the IPW Heavyweight Champion!" Oh, The Showstealer was really enjoying himself that night!

On a roll, The Showstealer then turned his attention to MC John Atkins, accusing him of being a turncoat from the FWA cause. Suddenly, an old face from FWA's distant past ran to the ring and grabbed the startled Hardcore John. To help him do his dirty work, Shane had brought back a former All-England Champion named Scottie Rock, who hadn't wrestled for the promotion since 2002. Rock placed a black bag over the trembling ring announcer's head, forced him to his knees, and threatened him with an enormous monkey wrench, holding him hostage as Alex Shane demanded Dan Edler come out to kiss his feet!

Edler was left with no choice but to comply . . . until The Wonderkid Jonny Storm ran out to confront Shane and Rock, seemingly to defend IPW. But of course, Dan Edler should have realised that Jonny Storm bleeds the colours of the FWA! Storm turned around and kicked the IPW promoter full in the face, knocking him spark out, then joined Alex and Scottie in fleeing the ring as the angry IPW roster led a charge of the light brigade to save their fallen colleagues further punishment.

Alex had one final warning before he left.

"FWA is coming back and is taking over. You'll all be finished and there's no going back, and there's no-one in IPW who can stop me!"

What an angle! The Orpington Halls was in uproar!

Interestingly enough, in amongst the defiant hometown chants for "I-P-DUB!" there were an audible smattering of chants for "F-W-A!" Whether it was due to nostalgia or excitement over FWA's flawless involvement in this compelling storyline, some of our old fans were slowly returning to the fold.

At that point, FWA was dominating IPW. The Brawl at the Hall angle definitely had Alex's fingerprints all over it, but huge credit must also go to booker Andy Quildan. Andy knew that building up FWA as the biggest threat IPW had ever faced was the right thing to do for business. The stronger the FWA appeared, the better IPW would look when they finally sent us packing.

So the FWA's domination continued. And to continue the feeling that absolutely anything could happen in this Civil War, Dann Read invited IPW:UK to hold their own mini-event on the afternoon of his own show on December 10 2006 at Colchester Hippodrome. Yet again IPW was encroaching on FWA's old turf, the swines! But Dann's benevolent gesture turned out to have an ulterior motive . . .

Later in the evening, Pac was exhausted after winning a gruelling seven-man 'Five Minute Warning' match. Out of nowhere, FWA loyalist Ross 'RJ Singh' Jordan gatecrashed the ring, grabbed the microphone and informed Pac that as promoter Dann Read was also an FWA management team member, he'd sanctioned an FWA Flyweight Title defence right there and then. The Man Gravity Forgot was severely weakened and had no chance against Ross, who quickly pinned him and then scarpered, having brought one of our championships back into the loving bosom of the FWA in the most deliciously dastardly manner!

Reigning All-England Champion Leroy Kincaide had also sided with IPW and Edler was by then calling our title the IPW All-England belt, the ingrate! So the FWA sent Iceman to challenge Leroy at Orpington on January 28 2007. Sure enough The Insane Icon pinned Kincaide to bring that championship back to the FWA too. The fans were frothing at the mouth at all this unpredictable spontaneity and couldn't wait for Final Frontiers.

Unfortunately by then, the original show date had been postponed. Sanjay Bagga had booked an LDN show at a nearby Cheshunt venue, owned by the same council as Broxbourne Civic Hall. The local authority was reluctant to allow two wrestling events in such close proximity and Bagga the businessman was more than happy to encourage them to cancel Final Frontiers.

"I can't remember exact details but knowing me, I am the type of person who would tell a venue that you can't have two wrestling shows in the same area at around the same time," admitted Bagga when I asked him about the incident.

"There was a similar instance in another town not too long ago. There was an LDN show booked at a venue, and they were going to allow another wrestling show in the same week. I went *mental* at them. You've got to protect your business interests.

"I run a lot of Brian Dixon's old venues, and I know some of the All-Star guys aren't happy about it. They say a lot of nasty, small-minded things about me on line. But I don't listen to what other people say, so I tend to just ignore it. If I'm getting under people's skin to that degree, then I must be doing something right."

So the date was put back first to March 16, then switched away from Broxbourne altogether. The new date for the final showdown in British Wrestling's Civil War would be March 25 2007, on enemy territory at Orpington Halls.

This worked out better for both promotions, because it gave IPW:UK time to squeeze in extra build-up events in Kent. Meanwhile we held one final show under the FWA banner at The Morecambe Dome—FWA Goldrush '07.

Results from the last ever FWA show in Morecambe on February 3 2007 were:

Johnny Phere pinned El Ligero, The Manchester Massive defeated Andy Simmonz and Ross Jordan, FWA Champion Robbie Brookside beat Darren Burridge in a World of Sport Rules match, Johnny Angel beat Stevie Knight in an 'I Quit' match, Jonny Storm won the 15-man Goldrush to become number one contender to the FWA Title.

Most of our fans up north were unaware of events down south—hey, not everyone reads the internet!—so we deliberately kept IPW away from Goldrush '07 and instead tied up Morecambe storyline loose ends on another stupendous, completely sold out night at The Dome.

By then, Johnny Phere was a Morecambe regular—yes!—and The Psychotic Warrior was repaying my faith in him and then some. Phere was outstanding in beating Yorkshire's favourite 'masked Mexican', the supremely talented young high-flyer El Ligero. It was the start of a winning streak that would end up with Phere taking Stevie Knight's place as Morecambe's biggest wrestling star.

"Johnny Phere is such a developed character and his talent, combined with Greg's writing, made something of him in Morecambe that no other promotion has been able to duplicate," said James 'Spud' Curtin.

"Phere is so underrated, but promoters have to invest time in him so he can get over. You can't just stick Johnny Phere on a show and expect it to happen straightaway. He needs to evolve, like Triple H evolved in the WWE, for the people to understand what he's about."

The show also saw The Manchester Massive, who had lost every single prior FWA match they'd ever had, bring the house down by finally scoring a victory. Their defeated adversaries were Jordan and Simmonz, who—yes!—turned out to be a brilliant heel as he wound up the seaside crowd with obnoxious aplomb.

Knight and Johnny Angel beat the holy hell out of each other in a brutal 'I Quit' match which ended with 'The Shining Light' pulling one of the most convincing 'sell jobs' (pretending to be badly hurt) I've ever seen. Knight lay in the ring, acting as if he'd been knocked out cold from an Angel piledriver, for well over 10 minutes as a hush of concern fell over The Dome. I actually thought my old pal was hurt for real. But as soon as the stricken Stevie was helped backstage, he stood bolt upright, right as rain, exclaimed: "Good show so far, Gregor!" and lit up a fag. Bless him!

But the main development at Goldrush came when Jonny Storm, despite all Robbie Brookside's attempts to stop him, eliminated Five Star to win his second Goldrush rumble. Finally, this meant Storm would challenge his mortal enemy for the FWA Title, scheduled for War on the Shore on Easter Saturday, April 7.

Would the FWA still be in existence by then? It didn't matter. We already knew that long-awaited, meticulously built-up and highly-anticipated title match was definitely going to happen on April 7, only we would deliver it under our new name of the XWA.

Why XWA? What does the 'X' stand for? Answer—nothing. We chose XWA for the same reason we called our website WrestlingX . . . because the business-orientated Mark Kay said 'X' was a marketable letter of the alphabet, believe it or not. Also we didn't want to change the name too much out of respect for our Morecambe fans. Unlike their southern counterparts, they had never fallen out of love with the FWA. We wanted the transfer to the new company name to be as seamless, and easy to chant, for them as possible.

"I always thought the FWA was more of a *concept* when Alex Shane ran it," said Mark.

"It was like when you build a concept car, it's done to show what it's possible to do, but it's not something you'll make into a working model. The FWA was like that. It was like, this is what it's possible to do with British Wrestling talent, this is how good you can make it, but it isn't a business yet.

"The idea for XWA was to move it towards being a more practical business, but have a wrestling product still containing the best bits from the FWA."

And that's exactly what we eventually did. Over time, I definitely learned from my painful business mistakes. In Morecambe, we *always* nailed it.

But northern and southern fans alike remained blissfully unaware of plans for the launch of the XWA. Instead, they were rabid for the next instalment in the Civil War. IPW Battle 2 on February 18 2007 would see Greg 'The Truth' Lambert enter the lions' den of the Orpington Halls for the first time. But the night before, I paid a visit to a familiar stomping ground, a place I hadn't set foot in since I'd watched Paul Travell nearly burn alive in front of my eyes.

Three years after the events of British Uprising 2, Alex Shane proved he had fingers in more pies than Desperate Dan. The irrepressible Showstealer had managed to get his foot back in the door of the York Hall in Bethnal Green by assisting a newcomer to the British Wrestling scene, a veteran musician, actor, sound engineering whiz and wrestling fan called Len Davies. Len was pumping money into a new promotion called Real Quality Wrestling, running monthly shows in the York Hall, airing on The Wrestling Channel. And Alex wanted me as part of the roster, to manage Hade Vansen and a renowned hard man and submission expert called Jon Ryan.

I worked on three RQW shows in early 2007, but it wasn't the York Hall I remembered. Production quality was top-notch, as this was Len's area of expertise. But crowd numbers were poor and the atmosphere was dead. Still, I enjoyed myself managing Hade and Ryan, and working for Len, who is a lovely guy, has the best sideburns in wrestling and always paid me. I also got to share a dressing room with three hot-shot newcomers to the UK scene called Drew Galloway, Stu Sanders and Alex's old friend Seamus O'Shaughnessy, who are today better known as WWE's Drew McIntyre, Wade Barrett and Sheamus.

Incidentally, one of those RQW events in early 2007 saw Martin Stone, the man I'd claimed was over-rated, wrestle Japanese legend The Great Muta. Although Stone held his own against the face-painted icon, I still wasn't all that impressed with the self-styled 'Guvnor of London Town'.

While in London for one of the RQW shows, I stayed with Alex in his beautiful Rotherhithe flat overlooking the River Thames. The boy from the violent Finsbury Park council estate had certainly done well for himself. While I was there, the new and improved Alex Shane shared with me his theories on how 9/11 was an inside job, how there was a secret society called the Illuminati running the world, and how this unseen authority used subliminal messaging through global corporations like McDonalds and Coca-Cola to control our minds. I was fascinated by most of Alex's teachings and a lot of what he told me made perfect sense, although some of his more complex ideologies went completely over my head. Still, I definitely preferred the new Alex to the old one.

After everything we'd been through together over the years, my uneasy business relationship with Alex had actually evolved into a strong and hopefully enduring friendship. And today, it's a friendship of equals. Conversations between us these days are 50-50 exchanges of views, and not always solely about wrestling.

During the past five years, Alex Shane has continued to reinvent himself as a human being, while adding to his already impressive wrestling CV. In 2007, he and Doug Williams organised a ground-breaking two-night tournament in Liverpool called the King of Europe Cup, featuring representatives of 16 different worldwide wrestling promotions. In 2008, he promoted TNA Wrestling's first ever UK tour. In 2009, he achieved a long-time goal by introducing a standardised syllabus for budding wrestlers at training schools all over the country.

Then in 2010, Alex began to produce a television version of his old radio show. Wrestle Talk TV was initially a chat show put out on YouTube, hosted by former Radio 1 disc jockey Joel Ross (of JK and Joel fame) and Patrick Lennon, featuring exclusive interviews with monster names of the industry like Hulk Hogan, Mick Foley and Chris Jericho, and discussion about the hot grapple topics of the day. It also showcased the cream of established British Wrestling talent like RJ Singh, El Ligero, 'Rock Star' Spud and Leroy Kincaide through taped matches filmed, in a first for televised British Wrestling, on high-definition TV cameras which gave the footage a similar quality to that produced by WWE and TNA.

The production of the programme wasn't perfect, but still much slicker than FWA TV and the format was digestible to all wrestling fans. In other words, it wasn't solely about the Brits. It earned such a following with 350,000 views on YouTube, that Alex was eventually able to sell it to leading satellite channel Challenge TV.

At time of writing, a 12-part series of WrestleTalk TV has just debuted on Challenge. Prospects are positive. The show has attracted major advertisers and sponsors like TNA Euroshop (TNA's European merchandising arm) and Fighting Spirit Magazine, so has much more of a fighting chance of becoming financially self-sufficient than FWA TV ever did.

Not only that, but WrestleTalk TV is airing in a prime slot to capture the attention of grapple enthusiasts—immediately after the weekly showing of TNA Impact. Over the past few years, TNA's popularity in the UK has skyrocketed. At time of writing, due to its availability on Freeview as well as to satellite subscribers, Impact on Challenge is regularly attracting more British viewers than either WWE Raw or Smackdown on Sky Sports. Alex hopes this captive audience will all stay tuned after Impact and watch WrestleTalk TV as well, and therefore be exposed to an exciting new generation of British wrestlers including Mark Haskins, Kris Travis, Marty Scurll, Zack Sabre Jnr and Nathan Cruz.

The initial one-hour episode of WrestleTalk TV aired on August 26 2012—just over 10 years after Revival and just shy of a decade since the demise of Talk Wrestling radio. There's a certain poetic symmetry to that, and Alex certainly hopes WrestleTalk TV will really take off and validate his continuing efforts to put British Wrestling back on the map.

The debut episode of this 'Soccer AM for wrestling fans' was watched by 105,000 viewers, a more than respectable result for a new niche programme in a late-night time slot on a digital channel . . . especially considering WWE Smackdown was averaging less than 100,000 viewers in September 2012. At time of writing, Challenge TV was delighted with its new baby and talks were under way for a second series.

WrestleTalk TV may not be quite The Holy Grail. But it is another positive step forward for my friend Alex and the mission to which he has devoted his life—to give exposure to the considerable talents of British wrestlers.

Yet still, there remains a minority on the forums and on social media who try to denigrate Alex and his achievements. The UKFF, and now even some British wrestlers and promoters on Facebook and Twitter, have stuck the knife in at every opportunity to give Talk Wrestling a vicious slating. They don't like the presenters . . . they don't like the set . . . they don't like the content . . . Alex only gets his mates in as guests . . . there's not enough talk about wrestling and too much larking about . . .

Some of it is constructive criticism and that's fine. But quite a lot is the online nastiness that never goes away.

The more things change, the more things stay the same.

"In British Wrestling, so few of us want to drive the bus . . . the majority would rather sit at the back of the bus and shout: 'Are we there yet?'" Alex told me in 2012.

"I still, to this day, think I have more belief in British Wrestling than anybody else in it. I will really, really put myself out there to push things forward and not just keep the status quo. But there needs to be more of this way of thinking collectively amongst British Wrestling people."

Alex isn't satisfied that British Wrestling has revived to the point that it's now a production line of talent for America. And his crusade won't end until the Brits can make big money from wrestling in this country without needing to cross The Pond.

"Why should all the money go to America? I want the money to stay here, to go back into our own economy,

"I want wrestling to be accepted by the general British public. I want parents to be proud of their kids for doing it. Instead of saying: 'I'm taking my son or daughter to football or to dance class' I want them to be saying at the school gates 'I'm taking my kids to wrestling school'.

"But not enough British wrestlers are helping. They're not proud of who they are.

"With WrestleTalk TV, British Wrestling finally has a TV platform. It's drawn more viewers than WWE Smackdown. So let's embrace it. But instead of offering to help, I see British wrestlers on Facebook slagging it off or complaining that they're not on it. And the Americans are looking and laughing at us.

"I've always cared too much about people's opinions on the internet and do you know what? I don't think I do any more. All I care about is getting the contract with Challenge TV renewed for another series of WrestleTalk TV which means I can do more things to promote British Wrestling in future. And if getting more viewers to stop flicking through the channels on a Sunday night and watch WrestleTalk TV means having Marty Scurll play a dating game because it's more appealing to casual viewers, rather than have him sit down on a sofa to talk about wrestling, then that's what I'll do.

"My mindset has completely changed. I guess I've turned into Tommy Boyd . . ."

The last 10 years has been quite a journey for British Wrestling and a personal journey of self-discovery for me. And, it seems, things have come full circle for Alexander Spilling too. I really hope one day this polarising character will finally get the credit from both peers and fans that he fully deserves.

Like Alex, I learned my lesson about The Internet. Smart wrestling fans certainly have their place and as paying customers, they have every right to voice a constructive opinion. But if you allow their critiques to get under your skin, they will drive you round the twist. And if you let this minority group dictate how you run your wrestling company, you are doomed to failure.

Young wrestlers and promoters, *please* take heed.

Back to my stay with Alex in Rotherhithe in 2007, when he told me a benign but troublesome growth had appeared in his dodgy neck. Shane said he needed surgery to remove it, a procedure he'd scheduled for the same week as Final Frontiers. This meant he wouldn't be able to wrestle Martin Stone. Bollocks!

One of the biggest criticisms levelled at Alex that he leaps from project to project, never quite able to finish what he starts. But he's just leaving trails where there is no path. Your biggest strength is also your biggest weakness, remember?

Now he would be unable to see the IPW:UK feud through to its bitter end. Suddenly, the irrepressible momentum of the Civil War was in danger of being curtailed by the loss of our general.

It was down to me to rescue the situation, by cutting the best heel promo of my life in Kent. And I did just that. The IPW fans were baying for blood as I swaggered into "that poxy air raid shelter" the Orpington Halls to boast about FWA's superiority and run down IPW's plagiarism. I also uttered a chilling promise that although Alex Shane wouldn't be fit to finish the job, I would "stop at nothing" to find the best replacement possible to bring IPW down for good and send all their wrestlers to the dole queue.

It was a powerful piece of oratory where I vented all the real-life emotions and frustrations of the previous two years. And how did the Kent faithful respond? Like this:

"F___ YOU, LAMBERT!"

(clap, clap, clap-clap-clap)

"F___ YOU, LAMBERT!"

(clap, clap, clap-clap-clap)

It was New Frontiers 2003 all over again. And then moments later, it was *Crunch* 2003 all over again as my old Family colleague 'The Messiah' Brandon Thomas made a stunning appearance, blasting IPW's Ashley Reed with the much-missed Crucifixion Chair Shot!

It was a resurrection! The Second Coming! Like Scottie Rock, a member of the old guard had come out of the woodwork to join the FWA cause!

Later in the evening, I managed FWA stalwart James Tighe against Martin Stone but became increasingly frustrated as Tighe failed to put The Guvnor away. In the end, Stone got the win and I gave James a verbal roasting for letting the FWA down. At this, Tighe switched sides. One of FWA's favourite sons played Brutus to my Julius Caesar as he grabbed me and handed me over to a mob of delighted IPW wrestlers. The likes of Jack Storm and The Kartel took great delight as they lifted me roughly onto their shoulders, carried me across the Orpington Halls in front of the fans like some human trophy, then dumped me into the cold night air out of the fire exit!

The IPW fans were in ecstasy. Job done . . . we still had that unstoppable momentum. I then enjoyed the marvellous hospitality at the Edlers' home in suburban Orpington. There, Dan and myself, two wrestling promoters who had put egos aside to work together for our mutual benefit, toasted the impending climax of our wrestling storytelling masterpiece over Chinese food and a beer.

And so we came to the events of Sunday, March 25 2007.

I'd travelled down to Kent that weekend with Dirk Feelgood, Declan O'Connor, Joey Hayes and Johnny Phere. Being with my fellow North West brothers, it turned out to be one of my most memorable wrestling road trips. I recall Dirk was in an uncharacteristically rotten mood because he had to take the wheel for the entire 500 miles himself, because none of the rest of us knew how to drive.

Meanwhile young Declan, a master wind-up merchant with insatiable energy, spent the entire journey trying to get a rise out of Johnny Phere by singing Arctic Monkeys and Tenacious D songs at the top of his voice while bouncing on the passenger seat like some demented Mancunian kangaroo.

As for Johnny, he did what he spent every single wrestling road trip doing. He moaned constantly about his injuries.

"Look, I've had some injuries that have been extremely painful," said Phere in 2012.

"I once tore my lat, the biggest muscle in my back, doing some big elaborate move with Five Star in training. It actually paralysed me in the ring. I couldn't actually get out of the ring for minutes. It was the only time in wrestling that I was scared. A few weeks later we had a show and it hadn't healed. So I just taped myself up and went out and wrestled

"I've broken my ribs three times, twice on the right side and once on the left. I've broken my toe and broken my heel bone. I've had multiple muscle tears and multiple concussions. I'd love to have a brain scan to see what damage has been done to my head over the years.

"This is why I tell all wrestling trainees, you have to respect the business. If you don't, you will end up getting hurt or hurting someone else. You will damage yourself physically and psychologically, and get very little out of it unless you get that one big break every wrestler is waiting for, somewhere down the line."

Once we finally got to the Orpington Halls that Sunday, we couldn't believe our eyes. They were hanging from the rafters that night . . . the place was absolutely rammed. And there wasn't an overseas import in sight. This was British Wrestling at its very, very best.

The raw emotion I felt from the fans was like nothing I've experienced before or since. From the moment JP and his opponent Dave Moralez came out for the opening match, the crowd never stopped making noise.

And most pleasingly of all, they were split 50-50. The FWA's fans had come back, just when we needed them most.

Half the crowd were in those iconic black FWA T-Shirts they'd probably stuffed at the back of a wardrobe after British Uprising 3. The other half were Orpington regulars in their "I-P F'N-W" tees. For four solid hours, they screamed at the top of their lungs trying to outshout each other.

"I-P-DUB!"

"F-W-A!"

"I-P-DUB!"

"F-W-A!"

It was magical.

I had begun a storyline in Morecambe where Phere had vowed to go the entire calendar year of 2007 undefeated, calling his quest 'The Year of Phere'. I was humbled when Andy Quildan and Dan Edler offered to enhance my plotline by allowing Johnny to beat the tank-like Moralez, who British Wrestling followers will know today as Dave Mastiff. Andy and Dan didn't have to do that. This was their show and Dave was being groomed as a future IPW Heavyweight Champion. They could have had their guy steamroll my guy and wreck Phere's growing reputation.

Instead, The Psychotic Warrior pinned 'The Human Hate Machine' with his new finishing move, an impressive-looking spinning spinebuster he called the Ram Slam. Half the crowd cheered. The other half booed. It was like John Cena had come to Kent. And JP, ever the entertainer, stood on the middle rope, conducting the FWA fans with one hand and giving the IPW fans the finger with the other. I was so proud of him!

"It was one of the best feelings I've ever had," said Johnny.

"It was such a split audience, I was getting cheered through one ear and booed through the other, and it was clashing in my head.

"To have the fans you want to love you cheering you, and the ones you want to hate you booing you, that just summed up what the Johnny Phere character was all about for me. I was never a good guy or a bad guy, I was an inbetweener. I don't care if you hate me or love me, I just want a reaction."

By the way, for those of you who don't know what Johnny Phere is doing now, well, his life is more settled than it has ever been. Originally from Warrington, he now lives near me in Morecambe and has become something of a local celebrity thanks to his status as reigning XWA Champion and head trainer of my wrestling school.

JP also holds down a steady job as assistant to a television and film stuntman called Martin Shenton, whose biggest claim to fame is he was the stunt double for Ken Barlow on the infamous Coronation Street tram crash episode at Christmas 2010. I actually introduced Johnny and Martin to each other, and unsurprisingly the two intrepid action heroes hit it off.

Shenton employed Johnny to run his extreme sports training centre in Morecambe, and then in 2011, they worked together to convert a former snooker hall into a unique horror-themed paintballing game. The game was featured on the BBC TV programme Dragons' Den in 2012 and has proven incredibly popular, mainly thanks to JP's hands-on approach. His job is to dress up as horror characters like Freddy Krueger and Jason Vorhees and chase terrified gameplayers around a mock laboratory.

Yes, you read that right.

You didn't actually think Johnny Phere would have a normal profession, did you?

Today, The Psychotic Warrior also has a new fan. This unlikely Johnny Phere supporter is someone who gradually became impressed by how much he'd improved over the years, who slowly changed his mind about him and eventually admitted I'd been right about Phere all along.

Someone called, believe it or not . . . Alex Shane!

As Final Frontiers developed, every single character was over like crazy and fed off the crowd's electricity to perform better than they'd ever done before. The precocious Declan O'Connor cut the promo of his life, delivering a series of side-splitting taunts to the hometown fans as he and Joey Hayes came out to sell knock-off IPW merchandise for knock-down prices. James Tighe and Doug Williams put on a scientific wrestling clinic superior to their Uprising 2 main event of 2003.

And speaking of Clinic, Dr Dirk Feelgood laid the ghosts of Enfield '05 to rest in a riotously funny angle where he reunited with his old buddy JC Thunder, now IPW's leading cult babyface, only for the former Young Doctors to fall out over their split promotional allegiances and their nurse. No, it wasn't Stephanie Scope, but a tall, bearded male wrestler called Blok Busta, who was clad in a preposterously ill-fitting nurse uniform!

215

Watching from backstage, I marvelled at just how much the IPW crowd despised the previously beloved Andy Simmonz. Now known as 'The Hated Hero', Simmonz spat foul insults at the Kent throng as he and Robbie Brookside wrestled badly on purpose, turning their match into one interminable 15-minute chinlock. The IPW Champion who loathed the IPW fans versus the FWA Champion who couldn't stand the FWA fans was only going to end one way, with both men walking out in disgust for a deliberate double countout at the crowd's chants of "BORING!" which both men had deliberately encouraged in order to help bring our story to its thrilling conclusion.

We even had duelling Masters of Ceremonies at Final Frontiers: John Atkins (IPW) and Dean Ayass (FWA). Just before the climactic main event, 'Hardcore' John became sick of The Twisted Genius and rugby tackled him to the canvas. "CATFIGHT! CATFIGHT!" bellowed the fans as the two non-athletes rolled around, and this was The Truth's cue to come stomping to the ring.

The World's Number One Wrestling Journalist demanded that Ayass get on his feet, and suddenly I was face-to-face with my old sparring partner. It was like the Uprising 3 build-up all over again. There, standing in the ring tearing verbal strips off each other, were the two greatest wrestling managers ever to emerge from the British Isles.

By the way, that isn't necessarily *my* opinion. But it *is* the view of The Wrestling Press fanzine, who ranked Dean Ayass and Greg Lambert in their Top 25 wrestling managers *worldwide* of *all time* in 2011 . . . yes, right up there with our heroes Bobby Heenan and Jimmy Hart. Now I'm not sure if I'm quite in their league, but I'll gladly accept the accolade.

"How many World Champions did you ever manage?" asked Ayass. "Well, who's now the owner of the FWA, and who's the poxy ring announcer?" I retorted. At this, I fired Ayass as FWA's mouthpiece and took great delight in informing him I would personally introduce the main event. Deano responded by removing his FWA shirt . . . to reveal an IPW garment underneath. Orpington exploded as Ayass flipped me the double bird and disappeared through the 50% of the audience who thoroughly appreciated his treachery!

I then cut my final promo as owner of the Frontier Wrestling Alliance. I dedicated the upcoming match to three men. Mark Sloan was sitting at the merchandise table, so despite our differences, I made sure to acknowledge his role as the FWA's originator. I also name-checked FWA's most loyal fan Ben Corrigan (who seemed much more pleased at the mention) and most of all, I thanked the man who couldn't be there, but the man who deserved to be there the most, 'The Showstealer' Alex Shane.

"This match is for you, my friend," I said, almost welling up for real as I threw my arms into the air in the Alex Shane 'SHOW!' gesture I'd first seen at Revival over five years before. And I meant every single word.

Working with Alex Shane had at times been frustrating, stressful and costly, but I wouldn't have changed it for the world. Looking back, Alex was the main reason why I got to live out my dreams and I appreciate every single thing he ever did for me. I also recognise his status as unquestionably the single biggest reason for the resurgence of British Wrestling in the 21st century. This was my own small way of thanking him.

Martin Stone then emerged, wielding his trademark cricket bat. I watched IPW's great hope pace around the ring as the IPW fans screamed his name in fervent support. Stone had developed such a phenomenally intense aura . . . he oozed main event presence. I was definitely warming to him as a performer.

Stone, like everyone in Orpington Halls, wanted to know who I had found to replace The Showstealer . . . who we would trust to fight for the FWA's survival . . . who we believed capable of beating the double-tough Guvnor of London Town. Was it Jody Fleisch? Jonny Storm? Maybe even the return of Ulf Herman?

I milked it for all I was worth on the microphone, building the anticipation before delivering the shock announcement.

Nobody expected Flash Barker.

Phil Barker had been retired for over three years. He hadn't been training, was considerably out of shape and had to wear an FWA T-Shirt to hide his fleshy torso. But when the call came for somebody to step into the breach and wrestle for the very existence of the Frontier Wrestling Alliance, it made perfect sense to bring back the former Commissioner, the former FWA Champion, one of the most beloved personalities in FWA history.

Most importantly for a desperate wrestling promotion needing a psychological edge over its bitter rivals in a duel to the death, Flash Barker was Martin Stone's *idol*.

And boy, did Flash Barker ever roll back the years that night. The match was epic, simply epic.

I watched at ringside, cheering Phil on, as these representatives of two rival British companies, representatives of two different generations of British Wrestling's hard men, took each other to the limit in a fight so believable, so engrossing, so dramatic and so, so *beautiful* that it not only convinced me (and Dann Read) once and for all that we had been dead wrong about Martin Stone, but was without a shadow of a doubt my favourite match *ever*, and that includes my entire 25 years of watching professional wrestling on television and in person.

Stone and Barker battered each other senseless during this high stakes encounter. They cracked each other with a bamboo kendo stick, which made the sound of gunshots when it ricocheted off their bodies. I still have that kendo stick, by the way. Flash gave it me afterwards, and it's my prized souvenir of that incredible night.

Barker power bombed Martin through a table, then later the IPW kingpin returned the favour, throwing The Flash Man back and neck-first through another table which was propped in the turnbuckles. The enthralled crowd went mental for that one. Patrolling ringside, I could barely hear myself think.

The finishing sequence was a roller coaster of such peaks and troughs that I wish Dino Scarlo himself had been there to see it.

First referee Andy Quildan took a heavy fall when he found himself in the way of a meaty Stone clothesline. Andy Simmonz took advantage to run to the ring, paused to survey the situation, then smacked his IPW rival Stone in the face with his title belt. But Simmonz had no love for FWA either anymore, so he belted Barker with the championship too! I watched, open-mouthed with feigned disbelief, as the beloved butler-turned egotistical heat machine smirked at me upon leaving the ring. How I wish I'd seen his potential as a villain two years before!

Stone then planted Barker with his lethal London Bridge DDT as a new referee, Chris Hatch, came down to administer the count. I covered my eyes, moaning in despair as Martin moved in for the cover to surely defeat the valiant veteran and end the FWA's eight-year odyssey . . . but then Flash, dear Flash, in his first wrestling match for over three years, summoned up the energy and determination to kick out from Stone's finisher. I hugged the FWA fans in the front row with relief.

The pure emotion in the building that night was off-the-charts. I'd never experienced anything like it.

Next to make an unscheduled appearance was Hade Vansen, FWA to the core. The South City Thriller drilled Stone with his patented DDT, I leaped onto the apron and high-fived Hade in delight, then waved Flash over to finish the job.

But the honourable Barker didn't want to win through outside interference. And he also remembered Hade's part in his career-shortening knee injury three years before.

So instead of thanking his fellow former FWA Champion, Barker took the startled Vansen down and wrapped him up in a Sharpshooter. From ringside, I gestured with wide-eyed desperation for Flash to leave Hade alone because Stone was gaining valuable recovery time . . . but to no avail. As soon as Barker released Vansen, Stone was on him like a predator. The Guvnor nailed his hero once again with the London Bridge DDT, then crawled over to make the cover.

One!

Two!

Before Hatch could count three, I grabbed the diminutive ref by the leg and pulled him out of the ring. Then I smashed him across the face with the most realistic-looking knockout forearm I'd ever thrown. I put everything I had into that smash (although I pulled the punch perfectly so Chris never felt a thing) wishing I'd had the guts all those years ago to deliver that kind of defiant blow to the bullies who'd made my life hell. If only they could see me now!

Now two referees were down and both combatants were reeling around the ring from the titanic struggle. So who should come out to rescue the match but everybody's favourite corrupt FWA official, Steve Lynskey.

As on-the-take Steve slid into the ring, Barker nailed Stone with his Flash in the Pan finisher, and it looked like all the stars were aligning in the FWA's favour. But as Barker moved in for the cover and Lynskey made the count, the hero of IPW kicked out at the last possible second to keep the match alive.

The Guvnor simply would not be denied, the man was superhuman, and he came back swinging, flattening Barker with a pulverising clothesline. Stone moved in for another cover . . . surely this time to finish off the FWA once and for all . . . but that marvellous heel referee Lynskey managed only a one count before being struck down by a mysterious stiffening of the shoulder.

At this point I was struck by a flying shoe, thrown from the crowd by an angry IPW fan. The passionate spectators were so caught up in the drama, they really believed it was real. It was just like being back home in Morecambe. This was professional wrestling at its very, very best.

Lynskey clutched his 'injured shoulder' and winced in mock pain, but Martin Stone is not exactly the sympathetic type. IPW's last hope shaped to crack Steve across the face, only for Flash Barker to intervene and usher Martin to one side . . . not to save the FWA's biased official, oh no . . . but so he could deck the slimy Lynskey himself!

So that was three referees unconscious and the watching fans were going absolutely mental with excitement. What on earth was going to happen next? Who was going to win? FWA or IPW:UK? IPW:UK or FWA?

The final twist in this monumental tale was left to the legend that is Robbie Brookside. As Flash hooked Stone for one final Flash in the Pan, which would surely have ended the bout in FWA's favour and put IPW six feet under, the snarling Scouser who hated everything the FWA stood for rushed in and smashed Flash with the FWA Title belt. Cackling in triumph, this wonderful performer fled the scene after pie-facing me down to the floor, then chucked a pile of sound cables on top of me and put the boots to my head. And I've never been so happy to be beaten up in my life.

Then with the IPW fans clapping their hands and stamping their feet in ear-splitting anticipation, and with the FWA supporters covering their eyes in horror, Martin Stone fired up like he'd never fired up before, hooked the head of the man he respected like no-one else in professional wrestling, and drove the valiant Barker into the canvas with a third London Bridge.

Flash Barker was finally done. And it was Andy Quildan, poetically, who crawled over to count the final dagger into the FWA's storied, tumultuous, era-defining heart.

One.

Two.

I dragged myself upright, scrambled under the bottom rope and dived in desperation towards Quildan, in a last-ditch attempt to prevent the . . .

THREE!

Too late.

It is a wrestling cliché, but never has it been more appropriate to use. As Martin Stone pinned Flash Barker, the roof came off the Orpington Halls.

And as the IPW dressing room emptied and Stone's colleagues swamped him in celebration, I collapsed into Dann Read's arms, weeping sweaty tears of defeat on my good friend's shoulder, just over five years since we'd first met and shared such lofty goals at Revival.

It was over. The FWA died right there in Kent, on Sunday, March 25 2007.

But bloody hell, we didn't half go out on a high.

Results from FWA v IPW:UK Final Frontiers were:

Johnny Phere beat Dave Moralez, Zebra Kid, Ross Jordan and Paul Travell beat Paul Robinson, Luke Phoenix and Max Voltage, Sam Slam beat Iceman to win the All-England Title, James Tighe pinned Doug Williams, Hade Vansen beat Spud, Andy

Simmonz battled Robbie Brookside to a double countout, Martin Stone pinned Flash Barker in a Losing promotion must fold match to put FWA out of business.

Afterwards, the backstage camaraderie was like a being back in a Broxbourne or York Hall dressing room in 2003/4. The low morale and motivation, bad feeling and poor performances of 2005/6 were nowhere to be found. Everyone hugged and slapped each other on the back, realising they'd just been part of an event that would be remembered forever by everyone who was privileged to see it.

I was delighted to have Dann and Johnny Phere there with me, it was just a shame Mark Kay, Dino Scarlo and Alex Shane couldn't be there too. But it was a treat to see other members of the FWA's Golden Generation—Doug Williams, Hade Vansen, Flash Barker, James Tighe, Ross Jordan, Roy Bevis, Spud, Andy Simmonz, Steve Lynskey, John Atkins, Dirk Feelgood, The Manchester Massive, Martin Stone, Dean Ayass, Paul Travell and 'Solid Gold' Scott Parker, all back together again. Longtime British Wrestling photographer Sarah Barraclough even took a photo of the IPW and FWA rosters, all standing together in solidarity.

Granted, there were probably only 300 paying customers in the Orpington Halls that night. There were no TV cameras, no radio or newspaper coverage and only a small mention in Power Slam. Fame and fortune didn't come calling afterwards and British Wrestling remained very much off the radar of mainstream culture.

But Final Frontiers was still as close to perfection as I'd ever witnessed on *any* live wrestling event.

For me, British Wrestling showed that night exactly how far it had come over the previous five years. Maybe it wasn't quite far enough to gain that terrestrial TV deal. Maybe not quite far enough for our fascinating cast of characters to become the household names they deserve to be.

And maybe it wasn't quite far enough to get our hands on that elusive Holy Grail.

But at Final Frontiers, the underground stars of British Wrestling showed exactly the kind of gripping, emotional, high quality entertainment they are capable of providing when the UK scene stands on its own two feet . . . with no Tommy Boyd, no Danny Williams, no expensive American superstars, no Wrestling Channels nor Skydome Supershows, and most of all, with no bleedin' celebrities ripping off Gladiators on prime time Saturday night TV.

Myself and my wonderful, hard-working, talented friends and colleagues proved at Final Frontiers just how great modern-day British Wrestling can be when we believe only in *ourselves*.

And do you know what? If the mainstream doesn't want us, then that's their loss.

CHAPTER 18

EPILOGUE

Two weeks after Final Frontiers, on April 7 2007, Jonny Storm pinned Robbie Brookside at a sold-out Morecambe Dome to become the first ever XWA British Heavyweight Champion.

So Brookside finally got his come-uppance and Storm finally won the big one.

The fans then invaded the ring in joyous celebration to deafening chants of "*X*-W-A!" . . . because it's Real in Morecambe.

And XWA pretty much continued where the FWA left off in Morecambe for the next few years with big characters, great reviews and sold-out shows.

Until the local council demolished The Morecambe Dome. A bulldozer moved in and razed it to the ground in 2011 due to cutbacks. There's nothing there now but flat land.

They might as well have put that wrecking ball right through me too.

I never quite had the same passion for wrestling after that.

About the Author

Greg Lambert is from the English seaside town of Morecambe. Greg is a local newspaper reporter and also writes for Power Slam, Europe's top independent wrestling magazine. As a promoter and matchmaker, he was involved with some of the biggest UK wrestling events of the past decade and is widely regarded as one of the best wrestling managers and commentators in Britain today.

Acknowledgements

Front cover design—Owen Lambert; Front cover photographs of (clockwise from top left) Bret Hart, Mick Foley, Alex Shane and Doug Williams all by kind permission of Tony Knox

Photographs by kind permission of Tony Knox, Sarah Barraclough, Paul Travell and Phil Jones

Interviews were conducted by the author with Jonny Storm, Steve Lynskey, Paul Travell, Hade Vansen, Dann Read, Johnny Phere, Doug Williams, Joe Legend, Ricky Knight, Sanjay Bagga, Mark Kay, Dean Ayass, 'Rock Star Spud' James Curtin and Alex Shane (all 2012); Steve Knight (2009); Robbie Brookside (2003 & 2011), Jon Farrer (2003), Simon Rothstein (2004), Tommy Boyd (2002) and Alex Shane (2002).

Other sources: talkSPORT website interview with Tommy Boyd (2006). talkSPORT website interview with Simon Rothstein (2002), Sean Herbert statement on the UKFF (2009); Mark Sloan interview with Fighting Spirit Magazine (2007); Shiny Pants fanzine (2003); issues of Power Slam magazine (1999, 2000, 2002, 2004, 2005); The Wrestling Press: Top 25 wrestling managers of all-time (2011); TWA review by Greg Lambert from WrestlingX.com (2002); FWA British Uprising 1 review by Greg Lambert from WrestlingX.com (2002); Alex Shane statements on the FWA website (2004 & 2005); Jon Farrer statement on The Smart Marks forum (2005).

Lightning Source UK Ltd.
Milton Keynes UK
UKOW040310011212

203022UK00002B/79/P